C0-ARS-002

Trust and the Health of Organizations

CLINICAL SOCIOLOGY
Research and Practice

SERIES EDITOR:

John G. Bruhn, *New Mexico State University*
Las Cruces, New Mexico

CLINICAL SOCIOLOGY: An Agenda for Action
John G. Bruhn and Howard M. Rebach

HANDBOOK OF CLINICAL SOCIOLOGY (Second Edition)
Edited by Howard M. Rebach and John G. Bruhn

THE LIMITS OF IDEALISM: When Good Intentions Go Bad
Melvyn L. Fein

THE PARTNERSHIP MODEL IN HUMAN SERVICES: Sociological Foundations and Practices
Rosalyn Benjamin Darling

RACE AND MORALITY: How Good Intentions Undermine Social Justice and Perpetuate Inequality
Melvyn L. Fein

TRUST AND THE HEALTH OF ORGANIZATIONS
John G. Bruhn

A Continuation Order Plan is available for this series. A continuation order will bring delivery of each new volume immediately upon publication. Volumes are billed only upon actual shipment. For further information please contact the publisher.

Trust and the Health of Organizations

John G. Bruhn

New Mexico State University
Las Cruces, New Mexico

Kluwer Academic / Plenum Publishers
New York, Boston, Dordrecht, London, Moscow

Library of Congress Cataloging-in-Publication Data

ISBN 0-306-47265-1

233 Spring Street, New York, New York 10013

http://www.wkap.nl

10 9 8 7 6 5 4 3 2 1

A C.I.P. record for this book is available from the Library of Congress

Printed in the United States of America

To my parents,
who showed me how to trust

Preface

During my thirty-five years in higher education, as a student, teacher, researcher, and administrator, I worked in several universities and colleges and observed and experienced a wide range of trust and distrust. Usually the focus was on the leader, who as the literature in leadership tells us, sets the stage for trust or distrust. It struck me that effective leaders can usually not change the culture of a deeply entrenched distrusting organization, but ineffective leaders often flourish in such cultures. On the other hand, when trustful leaders and trustful organizations meet, the resulting healthy synergy creates high morale, exceptional pride and productivity, which are reflected in the organization's low turnover, low absentee rate, and loyalty at all levels.

Organizations are not permanently trustful or distrustful; they have life cycles and are influenced by external events that alter the degree of trust or distrust over time. When trust exists at most levels of an organization, its healthiness is evident to all. By the same token, when distrust is practiced by organizational leaders, and reinforced by the organization's culture, the organization's unhealthiness is apparent. Too often, when problems arise organizations replace leaders rather than examine and rectify the organizational culture.

Most leaders would say that they work to instill trust in their organizations and that they see their actions as trustful. When leaders fail, they often blame the organization. When organizations fail, they change leaders.

I thought what I was observing and experiencing was unique to academic organizations until I began to talk with people at different levels in profit and nonprofit and public and private organizations. The ingredients of trust and distrust, healthiness and unhealthiness seemed to be universal in organizations. The people I talked with were preoccupied with, and made comparisons between, different leadership styles and personalities in their attempt to explain the current state of trust and health in organizations. Few people took a global and historical view of their organization in order to put leaders and their actions in context.

This led me to undertake this project. I wanted to see if I could determine some common characteristics of trust and better understand how leaders and cultures become distrustful. Ideally, we all want to work in organizations that are trustful, that help us to develop personally and professionally, that we can be proud to work for, especially since we spend the majority of our time each day at work. By interviewing current CEO's, and former CEO's in a variety of organizations I hoped to learn how trust works and how it can be used, as well as abused. This book is an the result of that effort.

Acknowledgments

I am grateful for the editing skills of Paula Levine, long-time assistant and friend. Many of the ideas and perspectives in this book grew out of shared experiences with many colleagues from different organizations over the past decade including Alan P. Chesney, Charles J. Fey, William B. Sanders, Ray Lewis, Jr., Billy U. Philips, Gary Zajac, Loren D. Prescott, Jr., Charles Fensch, Anthony Herbst, Garland O'Quinn, Beverley Cuthbertson-Johnson, and Roberto Villarreal. Special thanks to Eliot Werner, my editor at Kluwer/Plenum for his advice and encouragement. I could not have completed this study without the CEO's and former CEO's who so generously gave of their time to talk to me about their organizations. I gave them my promise of anonymity so I have retained the essence of their contributions while altering some facts to respect their confidentiality and protect their identity.

Contents

Trust and the Health of Organizations

Chapter 1

The Decline of Trust

> *The genie released by our encouragement of naked self-interest has eroded our sense of belonging to a community. Every individual pursues the ethos of 'looking out for number one'.*[1]

INTRODUCTION

Trust, unhappily, is not a part of the American, or global, political way of life. In fact, our present national culture—social, economic, even artistic, as well as political, is inhospitable to trust.[2] The Pew Charitable Trusts, created and funded a National Commission on Civic Renewal in 1996 to obtain an accurate and balanced portrait of our civic condition and suggest practical steps citizens can take to improve our civic life. The Commission created an Index of National Civic Health (INCH) which measures and combines trends over the past twenty five years in five categories: political participation, political and social trust, associational membership, family integrity and stability, and crime (The National Commission on Civic Renewal, 1998). The Index as a whole showed the overall civic condition of the U.S. has declined markedly since 1974. While the newest measurement announced in 1997 showed an upward movement in civic health, there is still need for significant improvement (Figure 1.1). Two of the components of INCH, trust in the federal government and trust in others, have showed massive declines since 1960 (Figure 1.2).

Professionalism, along with trust, integrity and commitment, is a virtue that seems to be declining in importance in the United States. In his book, *Integrity*, Stephen Carter (1996) states that the people of the United States have a serious problem, they neither mean what they say or say what they mean. Moreover, they do not expect anybody else to mean what they say. Carter says that integrity is like

Figure 1.1. The Index of National Civic Health.

Source: The National Commission on Civic Renewal, The Index of National Civic Health, University of Maryland, College Park, M.D., 1998, p. 5. Reproduced with permission.

the weather: everybody talks about it but nobody knows what to do about it. Integrity is that stuff we always say we want more of. We want more integrity in our elected representatives, schools, churches, workplaces, healthcare system, in our spouses, children, and friends. Integrity is like good weather; everyone needs the same amount (Carter, 1996).

We read about integrity, or the lack of it, every day in the newspapers. It used to be that the spouses who attended the Congressional Club's annual First Lady's Luncheon came away with their arms full. Every luncher, married to a member or former member of Congress, used to receive a tote bag filled with goodies, such as perfume, earrings, umbrellas, and cosmetics. Then, in the year that followed the change in the ethics laws, according to *Washingtonian Magazine* (Milk, 1994), each of the spouses received a $25 Thomas Jefferson dessert plate. Since the cost of the luncheon was $35, this was considered a legitimate party favor. Organizer Lois Breaux said she thought the change was welcome because there had been too many goodies in the bag in previous years, but not all the attendees were as happy. "What am I going to do with one plate?" one wife asked. Breaux said that several attendees solved this problem by lifting additional plates from the tables. Virtue has acquired a bad name, it is the opposite of having fun (Wilson, 1993).

Integrity is the basis of trust (Bennis, 1989). A national survey, conducted in 1995 by the Washington Post, Harvard University, and the Kaiser Family

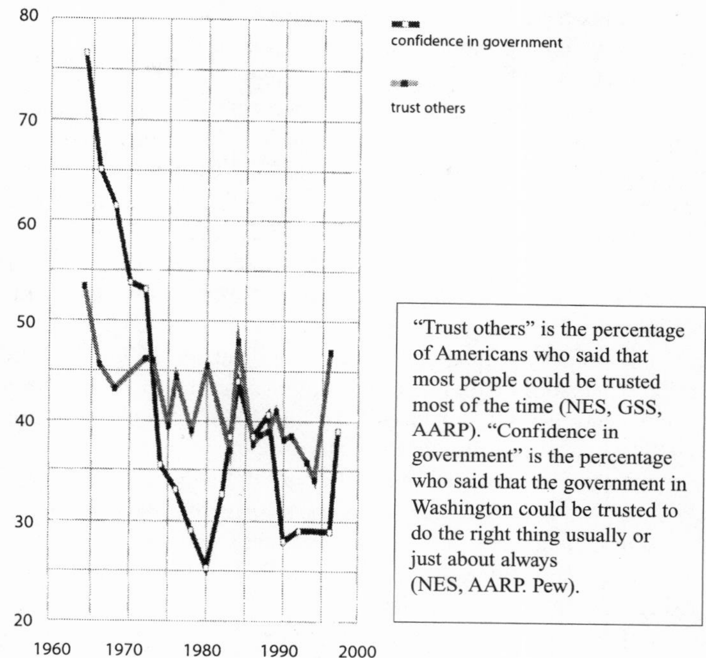

Figure 1.2. INCH Trust Components.

Source: The National Commission on Civic Renewal, The Index of National Civic Health, University of Maryland, College Park, M.D., 1998, p. 5. Reproduced with permission.

Foundation, found that America is becoming a nation of suspicious strangers, and it is this mistrust of each other that is a major reason Americans have lost confidence in the federal government and virtually every other major institution (Brossard, 1996).[3] Each succeeding generation that has come of age since the 1950's has been more distrusting of human nature. Today, nearly two in three Americans believe that most people can't be trusted; half say most people would cheat others if they had a chance, and half say that most people are looking out for themselves (also referred to as the "ethic of personal advantage").[4] The survey found that those who distrusted other people were significantly less likely than others to be registered to vote or to have voted in the last two national elections. Many Americans are out of touch with who their political leaders are, they don't know their names, and are uninformed, misinformed, or disinterested in national affairs. A third of all Americans think Congress has passed healthcare reform legislation already, or aren't sure (Brossard, 1996). The most recent General Social Survey, conducted periodically since 1972 by the National Opinion Research Center at the University of Chicago (Davis & Smith, 2000), found that most differences in attitudes between the younger generation, aged 18 to 24, and older people have narrowed over the past 30 years, but the younger generation is becoming more distrustful of society than were their counterparts in previous decades. Among the current younger generation, only 20.5 percent read a daily newspaper, compared with 47 percent in 1973; 14 percent attend church weekly, compared with 21.2 percent in 1973; 77.4 percent report a religious affiliation, compared with 86.9 percent in 1973; 27.1 percent report having voted for president, compared with 46.9 percent in 1973; and 48.2 percent report identifying with a political party, compared with 57.3 percent in 1973.

A study of the decline of social capital in American youth from 1976 to 1995 showed that mistrust among today's youth is highly correlated with value change, specifically a greater preoccupation with material things and an erosion of the values of traditional institutions (Rahn & Transue, 1998). The authors point out that preoccupation with material things erodes trust in other people.

Drawing upon recent data from the Roper Social and Political Trends and DDB Needham Life Style surveys that report in detail on Americans' changing behavior over the past 25 years, Robert Putnam (2000), in his book *Bowling Alone,*[5] shows how Americans have become increasingly disconnected from family, friends, neighbors, and social structures. Putnam found that our shrinking access to social capital, that is, the reward of communal activity and community sharing, is a threat to our civic and personal health. Social capital is a strong predictor of the quality of life and life satisfaction in a society and, according to Putnam, we have become a nation of users rather than builders of social capital.[6]

Raoul Naroll (1983), a cultural anthropologist, has studied the family and community connections, or "moralnets", that tie people together in different cultures. According to Naroll, strong moralnets are built by deep social ties, emotional warmth between members of the community, social and economic support for those who have difficult times, and various cultural symbols and traditions that make a society cohesive. When moralnets are weak, there is more crime, drug and alcohol abuse, suicide, domestic violence and mental illness. Moralnets are similar to the term social capital used by Putnam to describe a trend toward decreased social trust in America. Singer (1995) fears that in the United States today, the social fabric of society has decayed to the extent that it has passed the point of no return. He says that obsession with the self has been the characteristic psychological error of the generations of the seventies and eighties. The error consists in seeking answers to problems by focusing on the self. He suggests that unless there is a significant movement toward reducing the dominance of materialistic self-interest and reinstating the idea of living an ethical life, the world will remain a tough place in which to live. Charles Handy (1994) sees decreased trust as an unintended consequence of our organization society.

> "One unintended consequence of the organization society was to remove from many of us the need to belong to anywhere other than our workplace. As a result, when we leave

> it we have nothing. We also substituted the homogeneous communities, which our work provided, for the mixed communities of the old neighborhoods. We replaced the community of place with the community of common interest. When you do that, there is no longer any need to think of sacrificing anything for your new neighbor because you neighbor is in the same position."[7]

When trust begins to erode in a society, fear, alienation, loneliness and hostility take its place (Gibb, 1978). And it appears that we have become a society that no longer values caring. Certainly, the exodus of women into the workforce have made traditional caretakers less available, but our focus on individualism has fostered a climate of independent, freely choosing individuals who don't care about others individually or collectively (Glenn, 2000).

Fukuyama (1995) examines a wide range of national cultures (Japan, China, Korea, Germany, France, and the United States) in order to find the hidden principles that make a good and prosperous society. Economic life is pervaded by culture and depends on moral bonds of social trust. This is the unspoken, unwritten bond between fellow citizens that facilitates transactions, empowers individual creativity, and justifies collective action. In the global struggle for economic dominance, cultural differences will be a key determinant of national success. The social capital represented by trust will be as important as physical capital. Like Tocqueville, Fukuyama believes a state can only be powerful if it is in a relationship of trust with its citizens (Hall, 1992).

Fukuyama states, "It is no accident that the United States, Japan, and Germany were the first countries to develop large, modern, rationally organized, professionally managed corporations. Each of these cultures had certain characteristics that allowed business organizations to move beyond the family rather rapidly and to create a variety of new, voluntary social groups that were not based on kinship. They were able to do so because in each of these societies there was a high degree of trust between individuals who were not related to one another, and hence a solid basis for social capital."[8]

The causes of the growth of American individualism at the expense of community are numerous, but not new.[9] Rights-based individualism is deeply embedded in American political theory and constitutional law. The consequences of the restructuring of the American economy—mergers, downsizing, loss of low-skilled jobs, the expansion of the welfare state, electronic technology, and the evolution of a culture of "rights"—have all contributed to a climate of low trust. Howard (2001) says that there was a massive redefinition of freedom in the 1960's as a rejection of all authority. The rhetoric of modern justice is individual rights, but its foundation is avoidance of authority. Avoiding authority provides opportunities for reducing personal bias and prejudice, but carries a high risk. "The spirit of distrust of authority ... can be used against the trustworthy too. An equal opportunity weapon, it can be invoked by the misguided, the mendacious, and the malevolent, as well as the mistreated" (Kagan, 1991, p. 375). What matters is not what's moral, but what anyone can argue is legal. Therefore, people distrust others, behave defensively, and walk on eggshells fearing their own honesty (Howard, 2001; Fein, 1999). We have lost the art of drawing the line (Howard, 2001) and follow what Wolfe (1998) has called the eleventh commandment, "Thou shalt not judge." America is drowning in law, legality, bureaucratic process. Abandoning our common sense and individual sense of responsibility, we fear the law, have become obsessed with procedures and rules, and are at war with one another (Howard, 1994). In a recent study of what Americans think of morality in eight different communities, Wolfe (2001) discovered that the virtues of honesty, loyalty, self-restraint and forgiveness are still alive, but people no longer are willing to follow the old rules of previous generations; Americans want the moral freedom to decide as individuals what a good life means.

According to Robert Bellah and his colleagues in their book *Habits of the Heart* (1985), some of our deepest problems, both as individuals and as a society are linked to our individualism. One of their interviewees expressed this issue succinctly: "American society has become very self-oriented, or very individual-oriented: what's in it for me, how much do I get out of it, am I getting everything I'm entitled to in my life?" People don't look at the repercussions, outside themselves, of their individual actions. A strong commitment to individualism can result in one's failure to perceive the importance of getting involved in the responsibilities of citizenship and participating in social institutions concerned with citizenship, marriage and family, religion, and public affairs. Over concern with doing one's own thing can lead to the attitude that one doesn't need others, or at the least, can't count on them.[10] This attitude, along with withdrawal from others, perpetuates a reciprocal pattern of "You don't trust me—I don't trust you."

Bellah and his associates call for a new paradigm, a new pattern of cultivation. Our institutions, they say, are functioning badly and are in need of repair or drastic reform. Symptoms of this disrepair are evident in the speed with which individuals threaten "to see my lawyer" when something does not go their way. Threats have replaced efforts to understand, dialogue or compromise. Because litigation in America has increased, fewer disputes are capable of being resolved informally, through negotiation or third-party arbitration. The rise in litigation reflects a decreased willingness to accept the authority of existing social structures and to work things out under the environment they provide. The decline in trust has indirect social costs, in addition to the direct cost of lawyers. Many employers have stopped writing substantive letters of recommendation because they fear legal repercussions if they are too honest when they express their opinions.[11] Similarly references contacted by phone may give only general and positive opinions because they are eager to pass on an employee who may have been a problem. As job interviews have become more question-sensitive, interviewers have become more grievance-protective.

Trust varies from society to society. Contrary to assumptions, the United States, historically has been quite similar to Japan in levels of social trust, and both countries differ from low-trust Confucian China or Latin Catholic countries like France or Italy. Fukuyama argues that only those societies with a high degree of social trust will be able to create the kind of flexible, large-scale business organizations that are needed for success in the global economy. The greatness of the United States was not built on the ethos of individualism, but on the cohesiveness of its civil associations and the strength of its communities. Fukuyama warns that our country's drift into more extreme rights-centered individualism, a departure from our past communitarian tradition, will hold more peril for the future of America than any competition from abroad.

Accompanying the trend toward greater individualism is an increasing irony and cynicism. Purdy (1999) decries the contemporary attitude of any detachment that avoids taking anything or anyone seriously and easily merges into sarcasm. He points out that as a result of this attitude, we hold ourselves apart from the real things around us and avoid facing the world as it confronts us. While he points out that no one is ironic all the time, the increased prevalence of irony does not improve us as a society. Cynicism is common (Kanter & Mirvis, 1989). In 1964, 75 percent of Americans said they trusted the federal government to do the right thing most of the time; today, only 25 percent of Americans admit to such trust (Nye, 1997). Over the past three decades, public confidence has dropped in half for many major institutions—from 61 percent to 30 percent for universities, 55% to 21 percent for major companies, 73% to 29 percent for medicine, and 29% to 14 percent for journalism (Nye,1997). Similar declines are present in other countries, for example, Canada, Asia and Europe (Kouzes & Posner, 1993). Neustadt (1997) discussed the many causes of the politics of distrust, including the Vietnam War, Watergate, stagnation in the real incomes of families, and downsizing.

Cynicism among employees in organizations is common as they take lightly new initiatives for improving employee and customer relations, especially teamwork and quality improvement (Dean et al., 1998; Morris & Moberg, 1994; Reina & Reina, 1999; Lynn, 1999). High levels of executive compensation, poor performance in some organizations, and announcements of harsh and immediate layoffs all have contributed to employee cynicism (Anderson & Bateman, 1997). Public cynicism also has been reinforced by the media's dissemination of information on violations of public trust or what has been called, "the bad news bias".[12]

Integrity is closely associated with professional life. Professionals typically are portrayed as examples of dedication who strengthen the larger fabric of society (Sullivan, 1995). Yet, there is evidence that professional integrity is breaking down and the models of professional behavior that were held out to be emulated have been greatly tarnished. Trust in the major social institutions, has declined as they have become unstable due to instances of unethical or questionable behavior of members, a lack of consistency in actions, and the number of disillusioned people, who leave their profession early. According to Bok (1978), "Trust in some degree of veracity functions as a *foundation* of relations among human beings; when this trust shatters or wears away, institutions collapse."[13] We will examine some evidence of the decline of trust in a few institutions, namely the health professions, government, corporate business, education, churches, and Wall Street.

THE HEALTH PROFESSIONS

The general societal trends previously noted, along with the increasing cost of health care, its unequal distribution and coverage, and the complexities of accessing care, have all contributed to an erosion of public trust in the health professions. Profound changes in the configuration of health care institutions, and organizational and professional boundaries, have created a business of health care (Scott et al., 2000). The health care sector is now managed increasingly by for-profit corporations, which present medicine as a marketplace and view patients as clients or consumers (Mechanic, 1996). New arrangements for financing and managing care that affect how physicians work increasingly place the interests of patients and physicians, and physicians and insurance providers, in direct conflict (Rodwin, 1993). These arrangements have had a profound effect on the limits of autonomy in the physician-patient relationship and trust between the partners (Bruhn, 2001a).

Physicians have blamed managed care for preempting their professional judgment. Other authors, too, argue that health reforms have threatened and downgraded professionalism by integrating commercial and professional tradition (Southon & Braithwaite (1998); McArthur & Moore (1997); and Friedson (1990). But, Engelhardt and Rie (1988) suggest that, historically, there has been a profit motive in health care and that now, we need to develop canons for behavior that will help to retain traditional health care's commitment to altruistic goals while channeling the natural human drive associated with the profit motive. This assumes, however, that corporations can mass market professionalism and mass produce individualized care successfully.

Most health professionals blame the government, for-profit corporations, and politicians for making their careers in health care less rewarding and more frustrating, and for making it more difficult to be professional. In other words, the incentives for being good and doing good in the health professions have all but disappeared (Bruhn, 2001b). Mahoney (2000) says that medicine has lost its soul because physicians are not taking a stand and speaking up on issues related to managed care. Professions have become jobs. Careers last only as long as the next job offer. Some health professionals have left for employment outside the field of health. Others stay and try to subvert the existing system of care. A recent survey of internists in eight cities found that 45 percent of the physicians considered it ethical to deceive insurance companies and health maintenance organizations in order to secure payment for treatment when patients cannot get it another way (Freeman et al.,1999). Most of the physicians (76%) believed their primary professional responsibility was to practice as their patients' advocate. The more potentially lifesaving the coverage, the stronger the support for lying.

One might argue that deception or lying to third-party payers is for the patient's good and that the physician is not lying to or deceiving the patient. One could make an analogy to Robin Hood who, when he stole from the rich to give to the poor, was a hero. But one might ask how truthful is the physician who is willing to lie or deceive third-party payers, and how far is the physician willing to go, in the name of serving a particular patient, to get back at a system he resents?[14]

There also is a public disillusionment about medicine's broader involvement in community, national, and international health. Our best hope for a healthy life is not medical or curative care, but self-care (Beasley, 1991). The primary causes of chronic disease, in addition to genetics, are lifestyle, environment, diet, and our behaviors and attitudes. Medicine has been slow to assume leadership in education and prevention. Despite the superb technological and pharmacological achievements in medicine, we will, as a society, make little progress in reducing the social and emotional costs of illness and the financial costs of care, unless people change. Medicine has focused on diagnosing and curing disease to the exclusion of preventing disease and enhancing total health.

There is a public expectation—a trust—that medicine and government will be partners in ensuring good health for all citizens. In a recent, carefully researched book on the successes and challenges of global public health, Laurie Garrett (2000) states:

> "Public health is a bond—a trust—between a government and its people. The society at large entrusts its government to oversee and protect the collective good health. And in return individuals agree to cooperate by providing tax monies, accepting vaccines, and abiding by the rules and guidelines laid out by government public health leaders. If either side betrays that trust the system collapses like a house of cards."[15]

She says that many factors have contributed to the diminution of trust in public health, worldwide, at the close of the 20th century: some are related to the erosion of old systems of protection; others signaled a failure to address new paradigms of health for the globalized 21st century.

> "To build trust, she continues, "there must be a sense of community. And the community must collectively believe in its own future. At the millennium much of humanity hungered for connectedness and community but lived isolated, even hostile, existences... trust evaporated... the new globalization pushed communities against one another, opening old wounds and historic hatreds, often with genocidal results. Public

health needs to find ways to bridge the hatreds, bringing the world toward a sense of singular community in which the health of each member rises or falls with the health of all others."[16]

GOVERNMENT

Weisberg (1996) contends that while we do not fully understand why the American public has lost faith in its government, we know when it happened. Polls since the mid-1960's have shown consistent dislike of government at all levels. The beginning of the decline, according to Weisberg, corresponds to 1960 radicalism at Berkeley, urban unrest in the Watts riot, and protests against the Vietnam War, all of which took place between 1965 and 1972.

Judis (2000) enumerates many telling signs that something is wrong with America's political system: the lowest voter turnout in a presidential election (1996) since 1924; the lowest voter turnout in Congressional races (1998) since 1942; a noticeable lack of popular political activity, except for the Christian right in the South and the environmental movement in the West; the disbanding of many grassroots organizations; and the loss of labor movement's hold over the working class. The political system is ruled by large contributors; Congress appears incapable of passing significant reform legislation; the president and executive branch seem paralyzed; and foreign policy decisions lack acceptance and rationale. Judis also notes that corrosive public cynicism and skepticism have hardened over the last two decades of the 20th century.[17] These forces, together with a massive withdrawal from public activity, have made Americans like holiday travelers, prepared for the next stop but ill prepared to handle even small crises.

According to Gallup polls, Americans' faith in their country's future has been at a low ebb for the most of last two decades. In July, 1995, Gallup polls indicated that two-thirds of respondents said they were dissatisfied with the way things were going in the United States. In April, 1995, Gallup reported that 60 percent of Americans believed the future would be worse than the present. Many people believe that government makes things worse when it tries to make them better (Golay & Rollyson, 1996).

Almost all of the professions received higher ratings of confidence than did congressmen. Only car salesmen edged out politicians as having the lowest ethical standards. And, 42 percent of the respondents said that they had little or no confidence in the criminal justice system. The military continued to receive the most favorable rating (64 percent) of the professional groups.

Bok (1978) points out that decreased trust in government is not limited to the citizens of the United States; the sense of being manipulated is stronger, and the trust in one's own government or that of others is shrinking. Citizens the world over have lost confidence in their ability to influence what their governments do.

CORPORATE BUSINESS

A Louis Harris poll which measured public confidence in corporate executives, showed that only 18 percent placed "great confidence" in American executives in 1983; it was 29 percent in 1973 and 55 percent in the mid-1950's. The Opinion Research Corporation found, in 1983, that only 29 percent of respondents rated corporate executives "excellent or good" in ethical practices; the percentages were 33 percent in 1981 and 36 percent in 1975. Other polls and panels have documented a laxity in business ethics; what is most striking is that respondents said they felt pressure to behave unethically and admitted they had engaged in an unethical act (Calhoun et al., 1999).

Courses in business ethics have become popular in colleges and universities, but as one college professor said, "ethics need to be lived. We live in a society that is more inclined to use economic justifications to override ethical conduct. Our culture says money is what matters most." "Virtue," Mark Twain said, "has never been as respectable as money."[18]

Following are a few stories relating to ethical conduct in business during 2000:

- On August 9, 2000 Bridgestone/Firestone Corporation recalled and replaced 6.5 million defective tires, tied to over 200 deaths, after failing to act for three years on complaints.
- Ford Motor Co., which put the recalled tires on the popular Ford Explorer, recommended a lower tire pressure than Firestone because a test showed that an Explorer with fully inflated tires was more prone to roll over.
- On June 1, 2001, Bridgestone/Firestone Corporation expanded its recall to include 13 million Wilderness AT tires and asked the U.S. Government to investigate the safety of the Ford Explorer.
- Mitsubishi Motors admitted that it illegally concealed complaints about tens of thousands of defective cars. A cover-up was carried out to avoid expensive recalls, but the company is now recalling more than 600,000 vehicles.
- Publisher's Clearinghouse agreed to pay $18 million to 24 states to settle claims that it used deceptive practices. The company also agreed to stop the misleading tactics it used to persuade people to buy magazines.
- The United States Chamber of Commerce called the legal fees of $246 billion in the tobacco settlement outrageous. The fees would bring $11 billion to the lawyers, in some cases amounting to $110,000 an hour. The Association of Trial Lawyers of America said that only a handful of the group's 60,000 members had been involved.[19]
- The United Way of America has established new fiscal controls following the ouster of President William Aramony, who had an annual salary and benefits

> package of $463,000. Tens of thousands of dollars in consulting contracts passed from United Way of America to friends and associates of Mr. Aramony, who also established seven spin-off organizations not controlled by United Way; $1 million annually passed through United Way of America to the spinoffs. Mr. Aramony also charged more than $92,000 in limousine expenses to the charity over five years.[20]

The list could go on and on. The overriding problem is that hypocrisy is not readily observed. Leaders of organizations can talk about standards and expectations in their companies, but appear surprised when ethical lapses are uncovered in their organizations (Calhoun et al., 1999). The bottom line is that more instances of the loss of credibility are making news, which leaves one wondering what the real extent of the problem is (Kouzes & Posner, 1993).

EDUCATION

Schools often have been convenient lightning rods for problems in other institutions in our society, especially the family. Some countries appear to do a better job of educating their children than the United States, for example, Japan and China.[21] Kearns and Harvey (2000) outline current problems in education in America, among them misplaced smugness and complacency about the quality of suburban schools, problems with rural schools, and state that urban education is a disgrace—nothing seems to work. These authors emphasize that our standards are not clear enough or high enough. As a result, we have cookie cutter schools that fine-tune failure. We need to develop common expectations for what students should know and be able to do. While the authors enumerate nine keys to systemic reform, they stress that these will be difficult to achieve because of inherited attitudes, emphasis on process, sheer inertia, and warring camps inside and outside schools. Cynicism regarding education is common and teachers seem to be expected to perform many of the traditional functions of parents. Delattre (1988) argues that not only educational reform is needed; if parents want the education of their children to be fertile, they will have to plow the ground at home.

Although public criticism of American higher education is not new, it has reached a fever pitch in the last decade (Berube, 1996). Academia is undergoing intense scrutiny by legislators and the public with respect to its accountability. Corporate America finds troublesome, a professional ethic and sense of independence that makes professionals resistant to "the bottom line." Other segments of society are concerned about the rising cost of higher education and the accountability of professors with respect to teaching loads and availability to students. The same cultural climate in society that breeds distrust of other professionals, breeds distrust of tenured faculty.[22]

Colleges and universities also have not been as effective as they could be in self-policing the conduct of individual faculty members (Bruhn et al., 2002). Tenure often is a reason not to take action against a faculty member for misconduct; hence, there are gross differences in how unprofessional behavior is viewed and sanctioned among institutions. Inconsistencies in dealing with faculty members who do not conduct themselves professionally creates cynicism and fear among the faculty and hostility and distrust between them and administrators.[23]

CHURCHES

Traditionally, religion and family have been the arenas of American social institutions where covenants have prevailed. This is changing; the pastor is becoming less of a spiritual leader and more of a professional service delivery agent, and the parishioner, more of a client and consumer. This shift has led to the erosion of the covenant and emergence of the contract as the primary definition of the bond between pastor and member (Shupe et al., 2001).

The prevalence of misconduct among clergy is unknown, but the violation of a contract elicits a greater public outcry than does the violation of a covenant, where the victim's pain often remains private. Misbehaving clergy, who break a contract through sexual activity, fraud, and psychological abuse of those who turn to them for help, appear to be receiving greater attention. In 1999, for example, more than 200 cases were reported of pastoral sexual misconduct in the United States (Veenker, 1999). The general counsel of Church Mutual Insurance Company, one of the nation's leading insurers of religious organizations, has said that every week he learns of about five incidents of clergy sexual misconduct from among the 70,000 churches his company covers. Not all incidents lead to lawsuits and insurers now offer counseling for victims as a means of heading off lawsuits (Hudson, 1998).

Ministers placed in a position of trust can use that authority to take advantage of vulnerable members of their flock or church employees. Even in a completely consensual situation, there is an issue of credibility. The manager of the judicial process for the Presbyterian Church (U.S.A.) said, "If the adultery is a onetime violation of trust and the pastor's wife is the only person who knows and is willing to forgive, it's one thing. It's very different, though, if it's semi-common knowledge and the pastor is standing in the pulpit talking about faithfulness. That brings the ministry into disrepute" (Hudson, 1998).[24] In 1998 the Roman Catholic diocese of Dallas was ordered to pay $110 million for negligence in dealing with a priest who allegedly abused eleven children. Most major religious denominations in America have formed committees to educate clergy about sexual misconduct. Church insurance, after some scandals, has increased as much as 300 percent, effectively making it very difficult for some churches to stay solvent financially (Veenker, 1999).

WALL STREET

The Buttonwood Agreement of May 17, 1792 formulated at a meeting under a buttonwood tree at 68 Wall Street, established a formal exchange for the buying and selling of shares and loans (Geisst, 1997; Carosso & Sobel, 1975). Wall Street's approval to finance and invest was a matter of powerful, moneyed, and politically connected interests speculating on the basis of inside information and creating financial speculations of which the average person could seldom take advantage. Exchange members were an exclusive group tending toward monopoly by pledging "ourselves to each other," solemnly promising to charge outsiders established commissions and give each other preference in negotiations (Elias, 1971).

Clews described trust in Wall Street in 1887:

> "There is no place in the world where people are trusted so much on faith as they are in Wall Street; not even in the Church. The men of Wall Street have become world-renowned for straight forward dealing, and have thus obtained the first position as leading spirits in the speculative affairs not only of their own country, but the entire world" (Clews, 1887, p. 33).

In 1955, trust was still a valued way of doing business:

> "The words on the telephone, which express that judgment (about tomorrow's market, or at the next year's market) represent a binding contract, at least as good as anything signed and sealed and notarized in the presence of lawyers. It is the shibboleth of Wall Street that in finance 'a man's word is as good as his bond;' and this is quite true, because there is an unwritten bond behind the word. All of the business of the Street is done on the basis of verbal contracts, and if a man cannot be trusted to keep his verbal contracts nobody will deal with him" (Mayer, 1955, p. 18).

But things have changed considerably on Wall Street, especially in the last two decades. In July, 1986, Robert Wilkes, a first vice president of E.F. Hutton, and Ira Sokolow, a former vice president of Shearson Lehman Brothers, were accused in a civil complaint drawn up by the Securities and Exchange Commission, of conspiring with Dennis Levine, a former managing director of Drexel Burnham Lambert, as part of an insider-trading ring. They allegedly enriched themselves by using or selling important advance information about companies and profiting on the movement of those firms' stocks. Levine pleaded guilty to criminal charges of income tax evasion, securities fraud and perjury; Sokolow and Willis signed consent decrees to settle SEC's civil charges against them (DeMott, 1986).

A prominent Los Angeles stock trader, Boyd Jefferies, pleaded guilty to two felony counts. Jefferies built a reputation for going to extraordinary lengths for his clients. In one charge, the Government accused Jefferies of purporting to own $56 million worth of stocks that had actually been bought by a client, Ivan Boesky. In this illegal practice, called parking, Jefferies was allegedly holding the stock to hide the identity of Boesky who was the real owner. The scheme enabled Boesky to control more stock than was permissible under Government regulations. The more alarming charge is that Jefferies helped a customer manipulate the price of a public stock offering. Jefferies is accused of briefly boosting the market price—and thus illegally rigging the price of new shares—by buying blocks of Fireman's Fund stock right before a public offering (Koepp, 1987). Forty of the partners who invested in Ivan Boesky's arbitrage firm filed a first lawsuit to seek damages from both the arbitrager and his investment firm, Drexel Burnham Lambert, because of its links to Boesky's ventures (Koepp, 1987).

Investors are now suing investment banks and brokers for alleged poor investment advice. Former AT&T manager, Jim Luzzi, invested his life savings of $295,000 in the $10.6 billion initial public offering of AT&T's wireless unit. From the prospectus, he understood that along with AT&T itself, the unit was racking up revenues. But five days later after the IPO, AT&T's disappointing first quarter results sent the stock below its $29.50 offering price. Luzzi lost roughly a third of his savings. Luzzi and other investors filed a class action suit alleging that lead underwriters—Goldman Sachs, Merrill Lynch, and Salomon Smith Barney—were negligent because they failed to disclose problems such as the loss of major long distance service contracts. Some legal precedents have already gone against Wall Street. Investors are keen to seek revenge against Wall Street wizards (Thornton & Timmons, 2001).

IS THE TREND REAL?

Some people dismiss the persistent trends in mistrust in our social institutions and in our behavior as merely the consequences of rapid social change and generational differences. They point out that public opinion polls are subject to sampling errors, that respondents' opinions are shaped by their circumstances at the time they were interviewed, and that the fluidity and impact of life events can have dramatic effects on polling results, hence, they have limited generalizability and prognostic usability.

Putnam[25] addresses these criticisms, emphasizing that no single source of data is flawless, and that is why he used many diverse sources covering different periods of time to capture change. It is also important to note that observations, experiences and data of many researchers came to the same conclusion; the exact beginning of the decline of social trust is not firm (although most date it to the 1960's), but the *trends* toward lessened social trust, are consistent and persistent over several decades, and the symptoms of disconnectedness are observable in our society, and in the world, in the increase in all kinds of violence toward each other.[26]

The decline of trust is a phenomena which does not have an easily defined starting point or limited effects. Tao has expressed it as follows: "every cause is an effect and every effect is a cause. There is no absolute way to figure out why anything happens."[27]

Trust is important enough that people talk about it, according to Robert Wuthnow (1999), but trust is far more complicated than surveys have determined. Trust is culturally constructed so people draw upon their cultural repertoires to frame their ways of thinking about trust. One approach to learning how people think about trust, how it works and is used, and the consequences of mistrust, is to study trust in organizations. We spend the majority of our time, by choice or obligation, in organizations. Organizations, public and private, profit and non-profit, have different cultures, but trust and distrust are common to all. Therefore, a good way to understand how trust works in our society is to study it in organizations.

OUR FOCUS: TRUST IN ORGANIZATIONS

The basic assumption of this book is that a relationship exists between trust and the health of an organization. The idea of a completely trusting and healthy organization is idealistic. Organizations are never fully stable, they never maximize their potential, and they never achieve complete homeostasis. Organizations are living systems with their own needs and lifecycles. Like other living things, they experience change as they grow and develop. On the basis of published literature, an organization with a trusting culture and environment, trusting leaders, and trusting members would be expected to be more healthy than an organization that lacks trust (Bruhn & Chesney, 1994). The purpose of this book is to examine the parameters of trust and health and their interrelationships in various types of organizations. Understanding how trust and distrust affect organizational health should help in creating healthier places to work, and result in more satisfied and productive workers.

During 2000–2001, the author interviewed 60 CEO's and former CEO's (or their equivalents) of private and public, for profit, and non-profit organizations of different sizes in different geographic areas of the country. These included bankers, stock brokers and investment managers, hospital presidents and CEO's, university presidents and deans, mayors and city managers, religious leaders, school superintendents, small business owners, directors of chambers of commerce, and development officers and fund raisers. Respondents were diverse with respect to age, gender, ethnicity and geographic location (Appendix A). Interviews were conducted using a semi-structured interview schedule (Appendix B), lasted approximately 30 minutes, and were conducted by the author. While most were face-to-face, some had to be conducted by phone due to logistical and time constraints. The information collected in these interviews, along with the published literature, and the author's experiences provide the data for this book.

SUMMARY

It is well documented in the results of various polls conducted by creditable polling agencies and the recorded observations of social scientists, historians, and political analysts that trust and its allies, honesty, integrity, and commitment, have been declining in the United States. The onset of this decline has been noted to have begun in the early 1960's. The reasons for the decline are numerous; they include Watergate, the Berkeley and Watts riots, and the Vietnam War. Social change, including the advent of more women in the workforce, technology, and new configurations of the traditional family, has been pointed out, along with generational differences, to account for the loosened social fabric in our society that is resulting in less caring, decreased social support and connectedness, decreased participation as citizens, and therefore, less social capital and trust. Some critics say that polls are not accurate barometers of true change and dismiss the decline of trust to some peoples' wish to return to the good old days of the late 1950's and early 1960's.

But there are increasing symptoms in our country, and in the world, of less connectedness. Wars over differences in beliefs and values still erupt, violence, especially among youth, is more common, terrorism is a worldwide threat, and the extent of human abuse and brutality in many forms (and even animal abuse) is a growing concern. The anger and intolerance titer in the United States has risen as evidenced by road rage, drive-by shootings, and the incivilities of people who are in a hurry and impatient about getting their own needs met.

Some people have asked why these conditions exist in a country that espouses the importance of virtues and values. While virtues and values continue to be espoused, their weights and rankings have changed. We have personalized them to the extent that we feel, as individuals that we own them, deserve them, and therefore demand them. We have lost the idea that our country's virtues and values are part of our shared culture not individual possessions.

As we seek to protect "my rights," "my space," "my choice," "my time," we become frustrated, impatient, angry, and even violent towards anyone who seems to be intruding on "my values." If we perceive other people to be potential predators we can't trust them, work effectively with them, or possibly co-exist with them. That is why "Let's fight" is the increasingly common response to "It's my right" (Howard, 1994).

There are positive stories of how some leaders and organizations have transcended the broader societal climate to be productive, innovative, rewarding, and trusting. We need to learn, from these stories, how trust is established and built upon in some organizations and how trust has failed in others. Trust is a personal value that cannot be inherited or transported; however we can learn about the conditions for creating trust, how it is learned and modeled, how it works, and what situations can cause it to turn into mistrust. Hopefully, we can work to create healthier organizations, even in a society of distrust. Maybe we can learn from the leaders and organizations in our society who are creators, not just users, of social capital. As Arthur M. Schlesinger, Jr. said:

> "The problems are indeed complex. The answers are not in the back of anyone's books ...; It is common sense to take a method and try it, FDR said. If it fails, admit it frankly and try another. But above all, try something."[28]

Chapter 2

Trust in Persons

"Trust is a matter of choice and therefore a kind of behavior rather than a state of mind."[1]

INTRODUCTION

What is Trust?

This question has been receiving increasing attention by scholars in organizational science and related fields. Agreement on the importance of trust in human conduct appears to be widespread; disagreement on a suitable definition of the construct also appears widespread. For example, trust has been viewed as a personality characteristic, an attitude, a rational decision, a preconscious expectation, and a willingness to be vulnerable. Bigley and Pearce (1998) propose a problem-centered framework for viewing trust that makes use of elements of many definitions and viewpoints. Whatever its theoretical and conceptual framework there is agreement that trust exists in various forms and that these forms are observable and measurable in their effects on human behavior both at the individual level and at more complex levels of social interaction.

Gabarro (1978) has provided an excellent definition of trust to focus our discussion in this book. "The level of openness that exists between two people, the degree to which one person feels assured that another will not take malevolent or arbitrary actions, and the extent to which one person can expect predictability in others' behavior in terms of what is normally expected of a person acting in good faith."[2] Whenever instinct, knowledge or both give us a sense of being able to be ourselves with others, that provides a basis for trust (Gibb, 1978).

Seligman (2000) says that a distinction critical to any preliminary understanding of trust is the distinction between trust and confidence (or control). Control or confidence is what you have when you know what to expect in a situation; trust is what you need to maintain interaction if you do not have control. Confidence is predicted on the knowledge of what will be. Trust is what you need when you do not and cannot have confidence or predict behavior and outcomes. Trust is what you need when you interact with strangers.

CREATING TRUST

Trust is created. It is a dynamic aspect of human relationships that must be initiated, maintained, sometimes restored, and continuously authenticated (Flores & Solomon, 1998). Trust is created through dialogue and conversation and through gestures, looks, smiles, handshakes and touches. According to Flores and Solomon, trust is a set of social practices defined by our choices to trust or not to trust. They suggest that there are different forms of trust, specifically, simple trust, blind trust, and authentic trust. Simple trust is naive, unquestioned, and unchallenged, e.g., the faith of a child. Blind trust is trust taken for granted; it can be foolish and sometimes tragic. Authentic or basic trust is that in which the risks and vulnerabilities are understood and distrust is held in balance. Authentic trust, as opposed to simple trust, does not exclude distrust, but accepts it and overcomes it. Authentic trust can be betrayed, but there is no denial or self-deception as in blind trust, or naivete, as in simple trust.

Trust and distrust are not exclusive or opposites or the absence of one another. Both are processes that are created. Trust or distrust should not be taken for granted, but are part of the dynamics of a relationship that takes place in a cultural context. Therefore, trust and distrust are influenced by the context in which the relationship occurs (Flores & Solomon, 1998).

THE BEGINNING OF TRUST

Trust is learned. The underlying assumptions are laid down in infancy and tied to the early socialization experiences of the individual (Seligman, 1997, Luhmann, 1979). The first of Erikson's (1963) eight ages of man is the development of basic trust. He notes that trust implies not only that a person has learned to rely on the sameness and continuity of outer providers—an extension of an infant's relation to its parent, especially its mother—but also that a person learns to trust himself (Hardin, 1991). During the first year of life the individual develops an "attitude" toward oneself and "toward the outer world " which can be called the "trusting attitude" (Kinsella, 1973). The word "trust" is closely related to the word "truth." The trusting attitude, then, is one in which we take social life and specific aspects of it for granted (Holzner, 1973). Infant trust does not need to be won, but is there unless and until it is destroyed. Trust is much easier to maintain than it is to get started and is never hard to destroy (Baier, 1986).

Trust and distrust are based on experience (Hertzberg, 1988). While degrees of trust vary among individuals, trust is clearly a personality characteristic or attitude that is modified in the course of social relationships (Godwin, 1976; Scott, 1980). Trust is not an all or nothing phenomenon. There are degrees of trust which vary with every contact (Govier, 1997). The readiness to trust another person varies from individual to individual and from situation to situation. Some people enter a new situation with an almost naive trust, others may evidence an almost pathological distrust in the same situation. However, most people distinguish between situations of safety and risk (Worchel & Austin, 1986). Henslin (1972) says that the specific variables that lead to trust and distrust change with each situation, but the fundamental principles of evaluating others are the same. He describes how a cab driver must evaluate the trustworthiness of each new rider. He points out that each new rider presents him or herself differently but the driver evaluates the rider on the basis of his perception of the fit or misfit among the parts he has learned to associate with previous trustworthy or untrustworthy riders. The cabbie's evaluation leads to a reaction of trust or distrust. Trust, according to Rogers (1961), is a process which should increase as individuals find themselves, free themselves from defensiveness, and become more open to a wider range of environmental and social demands, and their own needs.

The development of a propensity to trust involves extensive investment, especially by others, such as parents (Barber, 1983). If there has been little investment during the early years, far greater investment may be required in later years to compensate (Hardin, 1993). We may, therefore, have different capacities for trust. Some researchers say that a high or low capacity for trust is a by-product of our experiences (Hardin, 1993), while others (Coleman, 1988, Luhmann, 1979) speak of trust or the capacity for trust as a form of human capital or regard it as a commodity (Dasgupta, 1988). The capacity for trust comes about through the deliberate investment by key persons in the development of the child. The extent of the family's social capital or the nature of the relationships between the child and its parents, and the child's ability to use the social capital of its parents, influences the development of trust.

Worchel (1979) points out that the process of learning how to trust is evident in psychotherapy. In the first few sessions, a client—unsure of how much he or she can trust the therapist—usually reveals little more than the presenting complaint. Each subsequent visit is followed by the disclosure of more intimate details, as the client experiences uncritical acceptance by the therapist. Self-disclosure needs to be reciprocal: it indicates a basic trust in the other person, which, in turn, obligates the other to reciprocate. It has been shown in laboratory experiments that people disclose more to another person who discloses more about himself (Worchel, 1979; Worchel & Austin, 1986).

The Dynamics of Trust

Trust is the result of mutual expectations and influence between two people. Hardin (1991) points to three aspects that are key to how trust works: (1) the persons involved need to have some degree of openness about tasks, problems or related issues; (2) the persons need to have expectations of each other that involve some degree of obligation; and (3) the persons have to feel that there is a safe comfort zone regarding risk. The key to understanding trust is that it is reciprocal, predictable, and its risks are, for the most part, known and controllable (Carnevale, 1995). Trust is, in part, inherently a rational or intentional commitment or judgment that one person's expectations are grounded in his belief in the other person's fairness or self-interest (Hardin, 1991).

Mutual trust is most likely to occur when people are positively oriented toward each other's welfare. However, mutual trust can occur, even under circumstances when the people involved are overly concerned with each other's welfare, if the characteristics of the situation are such to lead them to expect their trust will be fulfilled (Deutsch, 1964).

Trust seems to evolve in several steps or phases (Gabarro, 1978). First there is the stage of *impression-making or sizing up*. This requires a degree of openness and frankness. Second, there is the *tacit testing* stage, a sharing of past experiences and "what ifs" regarding the present. Third, after a degree of comfort about mutual expectations is achieved, an *interpersonal contract* can be agreed upon. This can range from a verbal agreement with a handshake to a formal written agreement. Gabarro points out that the *way* the persons involved work through these stages is what determines an effective relationship. Indeed, as contact and experience with the two people evolves, trust has a circular self-heightening quality, that is, different levels of trust (low vs. high) also evolve. The level of trust is additive, the more successful and frequent their working relationship, the less likely will two people need to reexperience all of the stages (or at least their intensity). How trust evolves and the level experienced is also time-bound. There may be time pressures that do not permit a sufficient degree of trust to emerge, or one or both parties may perceive or feel something about the interaction that they want to "check out", and feel a need to get together again. Time pressures can make one or both of the persons uneasy about power and control when there is insufficient time or information to assess the degree of risk. As Riker (1974) notes, power and trust are alternatives, but not exclusive alternatives. How persons go about assessing risk will provide some insight as to how they will go about the process of trusting.

Trust, and its development, is multidimensional and includes interpersonal, cultural, emotional, and cognitive dimensions (Lewis & Weigert, 1985; Sztompka, 1999; Corazzini, 1977). The practice of trust is contextual (Rousseau et al., 1998) or as Earle and Cvetkovich (1995) have put it, trust is a matter of the culture of shared worlds, we trust persons who share our cultural values.[3]

Learning to Distrust

While we learn to trust, we also learn to distrust. Trust and distrust coexist in most relationships. Managing any relationship requires that we both create trust and manage distrust (Lewicki & Wiethoff, 2000). Distrust is taught often at the same time as trust. A friend of mine relates the following story about her father's attempts to teach her sister to swim:

My sister would stand on the edge of the pool looking at my father in the water with his hands outstretched calling, "Jump, I'll catch you." My sister jumped several times and was caught and my father supported her while she kicked and stroked. But my father, who had a devilish side to him, occasionally did not catch my sister. Upon hitting the water, my sister panicked and cried. It was not long afterward that my sister refused to go into the pool. She never learned to swim.

A man attending a pet grief self-help group was especially heartbroken after he had had to put his 11 year old cat to sleep. He recalled that as a young boy he had several cats as pets but every winter they would disappear. He always wondered why until one day while reminiscing with his father he brought up the mystery. The father said, "Well, you are 40 now so I guess I can tell you that I took the cats and released them in the countryside. It was too much trouble and expense to have cats in the house during the winter." At age 48 the man was still angry at his now deceased father for his betrayal of trust.

Other lessons of distrust are more subtle. My sister and I were told that the Tooth Fairy would leave a dollar under our pillow the evening we lost one of our baby teeth. This occurred as promised until one night there was no dollar bill for a lost tooth because my parents discovered they did not have a dollar bill. My sister and I were certain that there was no longer a Tooth Fairy or at least one who was reliable.

Every one has similar stories about how trust and distrust are taught and learned simultaneously. We learn that you cannot always count on trust. Sometimes, we expect trust and encounter distrust and vice versa. We learn to change situations and people that give us mixed expectations. Our experiences with ambiguity about trust teach us to be suspicious about trusting.[4] Sometimes these lessons are dramatic, cruel, and destructive. A child might be told he is loved and when in the presence of others be treated positively, only to be abused when the parent and child are alone. People go to great lengths to maintain an image of trust in everyday life until an event, crisis, or misstep reveals the facade. This is because trust carries a perception of power. I think that the unknown of how another person might react if he were a victim of mistrust helps to foster a game-like aspect to trust behavior, e.g. the threat, or actual withholding of a trustful action by a person as a punishment to another. Trusted people can open doors and create opportunities, so trust is an important attribute in negotiating everyday life. Similarly, people with power can create distrust and dependency. Indeed, the concept of the key jingler illustrates how mental patients can become further debilitated in a distrusting institutional setting (Hartman, 1969). The key jingler is a derogatory term for the non-helpful staff person in any institution or organization who sets up fronts to maintain the impression he hopes to convey. It is calculated to serve the needs of the person doing the key jingling and it creates mistrust and fear in those who report to or who depend on him. Key jingling can involve a certain amount of dishonesty such as withholding information, placing obstacles in the path of someone who has the power to make a decision, or delays in paperwork that cause deadlines to be missed. The key jingler can then blame the system. The key jingler enjoys the many bureaucratic features of an organization, such as extensive record-keeping and paperwork from which he can gain power and keep others in their roles. The key jingler can be found in hospitals and doctor's offices keeping patients in their place by insisting on the completion of certain procedures before other activities can occur. For example, a doctor's nurse refused to call in a refill for a long-standing prescription until the patient had an office appointment to obtain the doctor's order for blood tests. Only when the blood tests were completed would the patient be able to obtain another six month renewal of his prescription for cholesterol medication. The key jingler not only asserts his control but disrupts the bond of trust between doctor and patient. In some instances, an entire institution or organization is part of the key jingling process of creating and maintaining dysfunctional and distrustful aspects of bureaucracy. As Saul Alinsky said, "Power is not only what you have, but what the enemy thinks you have."[5]

We all know people who live lives distrusting others. They usually have been victims of distrust in their early lives and perhaps have never experienced trust. Many do not know how to go about trusting and therefore, become adept at gambling with the risk-taking of others. Those people who are rescuers, or who naively believe that all people are good-intentioned, become easy victims of those who have become skilled at distrust.

Intimidation is a way of teaching distrust. Some administrators use it as their management style to remind employees who holds the power in the organization. Intimidation discourages dissent, openness, innovation, change, risk-taking, and trust. It fosters a work climate of "covering oneself," carefulness, guardedness, and fear, in which doing only what is known to be accepted by the leader and obedience to the leader are the only ways to earn rewards.

Periodic intimidation keeps employees subservient. The underlying message conveyed by the intimidating leader is, "Don't challenge me or you may be dispensable." Intimidating leaders usually see to it that no one occupies a position of authority or responsibility in the organization long enough to establish a competing power base. Competent employees are cooled out in subtle ways such as not giving them salary raises or promotions despite their productivity, and fault is found to discredit the work they do.

Intimidators practice verbal and psychological abuse and often get away with it because their public behavior is that of strong, aggressive, positive persons. Outsiders do not know what goes on inside an organization. For example community leaders in one community thought that the high turnover in personnel at the university was due to the university's lack of competitiveness in retaining good employees, while in actuality the president of the university was an intimidator who discouraged people from staying. Intimidators tend to select close associates who also practice intimidation. As a result, employees avoid contact with managers, and managers avoid contact with each other. The result is a fragmented pattern of leadership. Fragmented contact and communication help to perpetuate a noncohesive, distrustful, and suspicious staff who compete to stay in favor with the leader (Bruhn, 1996a).

RISK AND TRUSTING

Our views about trust are constantly being modified by our experiences. One aspect of trust that we constantly modify is our accuracy in assessing the risks associated with trusting. Risk reminds us of our ignorance or uncertainty about other people's behavior (Gambetta, 1988). To trust someone is to be able to make an accurate prediction that his behavior will be cooperative (Held, 1968). We perceive a situation as bearing risk if entering this situation might lead to negative consequences and if we are not able to control the occurrence of these consequences. The degree of risk is perceived to be higher the more negative the consequences are and the less we can control them (Koller, 1988).

Trust allows us to engage in risk-taking. The assessment of risk is a process by which we keep ourselves open to evidence, acting as if the other person can be trusted (Gambetta, 1988). Risk-taking is highly dependent upon a person's sense of his own worth (Morgan, 1973). The deeper one's doubts about oneself, the greater the fear of rejection, and the less likely one is to take risks that he cannot control. A person brings his past to each situation, which is also key in assessing risk. Gratton (1973) points out that the intensity of risk varies in accordance with what one person trusts another *with*: image, litigation, or one's "whole life." The level of intensity of the risk involved determines the level of trust that will be experienced. When risks are shared and perceived to be equal, the likelihood of trust is greater. In this respect, Conviser (1973) has tested, and found support for, his theory that people are more likely to trust one another if they have a shared goal they can both realize, and if their beliefs about control, relative to the goal, are dependent upon the possession of resources, abilities, or status to achieve the goal (Deutsch, 1964). In other words, when we believe that the results of somebody's intended action will be appropriate, from our point of view, we are likely to take risks in trusting (Misztal, 1996).

Ring (1996) has suggested that risk assessment is related to two types of trust, fragile trust and resilient trust. Fragile trust permits persons, particularly in business situations, to deal with each other in guarded ways. Fragile trust also is known as "situational trust" because reliance on trust in these kinds of circumstances depends more on the ways the parties characterize their deal than on the ways in which they characterize each other (Noorderhaven, 1994). This is a calculated, rational way of approaching trust. At the other extreme, resilient trust is a noncalculative reliance on the moral integrity or good will of others when they deal with unpredictable issues. Resilient trust survives transactions, is based on loyalty, interpersonal competence, and often is on prior relationships between the parties. This does not mean that there is no risk involved in resilient trust, but many of the risks are already known, may have been encountered in prior dealings with the other person, and may involve expectations of a continuing bond. This is what Hardin (1993) has called "thick trust"—that is, one may know a small number of persons that one deals with regularly to know the limits of their trustworthiness. Among these people, you know who you can trust for what purposes. Resilient or thick trust is not a resource depleted through use. Risk assessment is a delicate process because, according to Gambetta (1988), asking too little of trust is just as ill-advised as asking too much.

A TRUSTED PERSON

There have been several studies to ascertain what characterizes and differentiates high trusting persons from low trusting persons. High trusters read cues as well or as poorly as low trusters. They differ, however, in their willingness to trust the stranger where there is no clear-cut information. The high truster says, "I will trust the person until I have clear evidence that he or she can not be trusted" (Rotter, 1980).

People who trust more are less likely to lie and possibly are less likely to cheat or steal. They are more likely to give others a second chance and to respect the rights of others. The high truster is less likely to be unhappy, conflicted, or maladjusted; he or she is liked more and sought out as a friend more often, both by high-trusting and low-trusting others. In novel situations, the high truster is more likely to trust others than the low truster, but neither is above being fooled by crooks or honest people (Rotter, 1980).

A trusted person also has been found to be one who is highly influential, is less influenced by external or situational factors, has a low need to control others, has high self-esteem, and is open to being influenced by others (Frost et al., 1978).

Trusting persons are open to mutual learning and communication, and creativity (Covey, 1990). Most people tend to think in terms of dichotomies, which are based on power and position. Not all relationships, agreements or interactions will be win/win. But win/win solutions build trust because it's a frame of mind that seeks mutual benefits for all parties.

Becker (1998) points out that trusted persons have integrity. A person of integrity understands that acting on principles of rationality and honesty leads to greater self-esteem and to his or her long-term survival and well-being. Therefore, such employees do not steal organizational resources, treat others unfairly, or deceive themselves or others. These employees are trustworthy and are excellent candidates for leadership and followership positions. Employees with higher integrity are better workers than those with lower integrity. Therefore, organizations with more employees with high integrity are more likely to survive and thrive than are organizations with few such employees (Becker, 1998).

How does one become a trusted person? In a study by Into (1969), both direct reinforcement and modeling were found to be influential in the development of trust. Into investigated a wide range of child-rearing practices by obtaining statements from college students describing their parents' behavior when the students were children. He found that the parents of high trusting children were reported to be more trusting of their children, more trustworthy, trusted others more, and directly taught trust and trustworthiness. Low trusters tended to report that their parents made no threats or did not keep threats when they made them.[6] High trusters were more likely to relate that their parents both made and kept their threats. Other evidence confirming the effects of modeling has been reported by Katz and Rotter (1969). They compared the responses of college students on the trust scale with those of their parents. They found that fathers of high trusting sons scored higher on trust than fathers of low trusting sons. Fathers' trust scores were not related to those of their daughters. Mothers' trust scores showed equal influence on both sons and daughters.

WHEN TRUST FAILS

New situations are particularly vulnerable to the failure of trust.[7] In new situations, the person has to be able to decide how much to trust and how much to mistrust. The process of establishing a relationship of trust involves a sequence of steps involving an increasing risk of self-disclosure and reinforcement (Rotter, 1971). Whether the reinforcement following each self-disclosure is sufficient for the process to continue depends on perceptions of the other person's response (Weber & Carter, 1998). The failure to establish trust can occur at any point in this series of mutual testing. Indeed, some individuals at first contact, in person, by phone or letter, may be sufficiently "turned off" by what they consider cues or indications of untrustworthiness that they may not even attempt to establish a trust relationship. For example, an aggressive telemarketer may phone offering a product and persists in asking for a credit card number. Because the receiving party is "turned off" by the telemarketer's telephone personality he/she abruptly terminates the conversation.

It takes a series of positive experiences to establish a relationship of trust; sometimes, only one betrayal establishes distrust. Sztompka (1999) says that distrust refers to a neutral situation, when both trust and distrust are suspended because of a lack of clear expectations and therefore, hesitation about committing oneself. It is a temporary phase in the sequence of trust-building. Once established, distrust is resistant to change (Webb & Worchel, 1986). Even when the betrayer tries to correct the wrongdoing, a fear persists on the part of the betrayed person that he or she may be hurt again in the future. Distrust produces the perception that the other person is a threat, leading to greater distrust, and the cycle continues. The person who has been betrayed will either avoid the other person or retaliate (Webb & Worchel, 1986). Persons protect themselves with all kinds of rationalizations when they do not want to attempt to establish a trust relationship or have been hurt or harmed by another person in a prior relationship and do not want another contact with them (Goffman, 1952).

The greater the harm experienced by the betrayed, the greater the distrust, and even though trust might be learned anew, scars can be lasting. Psychiatric investigators from Freud onward have recognized that early parental loss is directly related to a wide variety of childhood, adolescent, and adult psychological problems. Extensive physical, emotional, and intellectual damage can result when a child is separated from its parents for extended periods of time, particularly if this separation occurs in the first few years of life (Bowlby, 1953). Dr. René Spitz (1950) described the physical wasting away of infants who suddenly lost their mothers. Some infants would refuse to eat, lost weight, despite good food and meticulous medical care, and died.

These observations led to changes in the way orphanages and hospitals care for children. Children who "failed to thrive" while in the hospital were provided interpersonal support from nurses and improved. Pediatricians noticed that infants deprived of maternal love failed to develop strong attachments to people (Ordway et al., 1969).

Most infants and children are not raised in total social isolation. However, new living patterns continue to chip away at the traditional American family. According to the U.S. Census for 2000, women's single parenting increased by twenty-five percent, nearly double the percentage of the growth of the nation's population. The number of women heading a household without a husband grew to 12.9 million, and six of ten had children under 18. More than six million children are living with heads of households who are not their mother or father, an increase of thirty percent since 1990. In many cases the householder is a grandparent, aunt or uncle.

With the increase in single parent households, and the fact that an ever-growing number of mothers are forced to hold jobs outside the home, many single mothers and single fathers, have no choice but to leave their child(ren) with a caretaker. A new form of loneliness is associated with the growing number of "latchkey" children. Lynch (2000) notes that hundreds of studies have shown that the lack of parental contact or the early loss of parents can seriously undermine the emotional stability of children, resulting in depression, suicide, various neuroses and psychoses, sociopathy, delinquency, school drop-out, and physical illnesses. When trust fails, the repercussions can be life long.

Attempts are being made to reestablish trust among abused and neglected children. A newly established nonprofit organization in Phoenix, called Gabriel's Angels, takes certified pet therapy teams to visit children in local shelters. Pam Gaber, Executive Director, says, "If we can weave in unconditional love, trust, empathy, we can teach humane education. These kids learn to trust the dogs because we keep coming back. Because their mom or dad and other human beings keep saying they're going to be back and they aren't. The children also learn how to be caring in return."[8] Gaber said that studies indicate that in homes with pets where domestic abuse is occurring, there is an 88 percent chance the pet is being abused as well. "Children learn to mimic that," she said.

When a trust relationship fails, the parties usually quickly engage in posturing, blaming, face-saving activities and mobilizing support from others for their position. These efforts are important so that the failed relationship does not undermine their existing reputation regarding trustworthiness. Depending upon the personalities involved and the extent of betrayal, litigation or other forms of revenge may be pursued (Bies & Tripp, 1996).

Karen (2001) says that the more we blame, the further away we get from ourselves. Forgiving ourselves involves owning up to our feelings. There has to be a limit to how long we make ourselves suffer. We need to ferret out the good and let go. Karen concludes that we will have a better chance to stay connected, to expand our zone of connection, and to dissolve the residuals from hurt and conflict, if we move on.

Forgiveness and Reconstructing Trust

Although serious violations of trust may bring a relationship to an end, Weber and Carter (1997, 1998) found that even serious violations may result in the reconstruction of trust and the reconstruction of the relationship. When the involved parties deemed the relationship worth salvaging, they participated in a negotiation process that included the passage of time, an assessment of the seriousness of the violation and the intent of the violator, and the offering of an apology with the rendering of forgiveness.

The act of forgiveness, even though it may not be accepted by the other party, always makes a difference to the forgiving individual and creates a permanent difference in the relationship, which, over time, can lead to a full conflict resolution and restoration of the relationship. Schneiderman (1999) points out that healing begins with forgiveness. The characteristics of authentic forgiveness are: (1) it is unconditional; it is offered to the other person regardless of the response; (2) it is self-regarding as well as altruistic; forgiveness is offered for the well-being of the relationship and requires that the persons break free of old habits and feelings; (3) it does not take place instantaneously; and (4), it is not symmetrical; one party usually instigates the process and becomes the prime mover in restoring the relationship. Schneiderman notes that if forgiveness is to be an effective intervention, a full conflict resolution is necessary.

When managers forgive their employees they communicate that they are not being judged or defined solely by their negative behavior or wrongful action. Forgiving an employee for past indiscretion can provide a foundation for trust and respect. Forgiveness is a transforming process that empowers the forgiver and forgivee (Kurzynski, 1998).

The reconstruction of trust is more complicated when it involves a family. Divorce creates a crisis in the family lifecycle—a state of disequilibrium experienced by all members throughout the nuclear and extended family system. The process continues through a series of stages. As a result, marriage, divorce, a single-parent household, and/or remarriage are simply points along a continuum (Peck & Brown, 1991). The loss of trust (if, indeed it was ever established) and the process of repairing the effects of distrust is a long-term process. One of the tasks of a therapist, if help is sought, is to prevent the individual from reliving old patterns that led to the problems in the previous marriage. The issues of loyalty or trust for the children or step-children are also key. Peck and Brown (1991) say the re-weaving of the family fabric, in whatever form works for it, takes from three to five years.

The effects of divorce are most dramatic and lasting among children. A flawed experience of trust with parents affects the development of trust in themselves. The lack of trust from family members can help children and adolescents to turn to peer groups and gangs to win esteem. Saunders (1994) has found, gangs provide a variety of identities so that members can show that they have loyalty, integrity, courage, and are trustworthy. Gang violence, dealing in drugs, and other anti-social activities are only a part of the reason gangs exist. Gangs offer members the opportunity to develop virtues such as loyalty and trust when they can't be found elsewhere.

NETWORKS OF TRUST

Our daily lives involve many complex relationships that interface and involve others, from family members to government agents. Any person's attitudes and experiences regarding trust are colored by all of these relationships which involve varying degrees of trust and distrust (Baier, 1986). Loomis and Loomis (1973) talk about our society's "two-story culture" in which most trust relationships concern small, intimate groups such as the family, neighborhood, church, school, work team, voluntary organizations, and friendship groups. Boundaries exist between this level and a larger level in which we do not usually participate intimately on a daily basis and in which we usually have little power and influence. The larger level impacts the smaller, more intimate level, and we make assumptions about trust at the larger level based on our and other's experiences and perceptions. For example, although we might not, personally, have had an audit encounter with the IRS, we may make assumptions about how trustful the Internal Revenue Service considers taxpayers based on what we hear and perceive to be the behavior of government officials.

Our personal networks of trust are tied to other trust networks involving other individuals, families, social institutions, and societies. With the effects of social change our trust networks cross geographical and cultural boundaries and continually expand and retract. As we interact in these various networks we tend to apply what we learned in our early childhood about trust and distrust and our personal comfort with taking risks to trust. As we encounter new networks and attempt to transact trust with representatives of these networks, we may find instances where it is impossible to "get to first base" regarding the establishment of trust. This often is due to our lack of knowledge about the meaning and rules of trust in another culture (Zucker, 1986).

Nee and Sanders (2001) point out, while ethnic ties constitute the basis of trust in immigrant communities, they also can be a source of apprehension. Ethnic ties meet the immediate practical needs of immigrants, especially in the early period of their accommodation to work lives in the United States. Yet reliance on ethnic ties does not come without cost. Immigrants become obligated to the trusted party who provides assistance. This feeling of obligation binds immigrant workers to jobs in ethnic firms that provide lower returns to investments in human capital than comparable jobs in the open economy. Immigrant workers employed in the ethnic economy generally have few social relationships outside their kinship and ethnic groups. Social life is confined primarily to the family household and the community of fellow immigrants. The immigrant community may provide a feeling of security and an ease of communication that helps to compensate for the lower wage structure of the ethnic economy. However, many immigrant workers are discontented with their jobs in the ethnic economy. Being locked into low-skilled, low-paid jobs in the ethnic economy is likely to foster distrust, as well as trust, in ethnic ties.

Each of us functions in a network of trust. Fukuyama (1995) describes three broad paths of trust in societies: the first is based on family and kinship; the second on voluntary associations outside kinship, such as schools, clubs, and professional organizations, and the third on different levels of government. There are different expectations about trust in these paths. Fukuyama points out that the United States is heir to two distinct traditions; the first highly individualistic, and the second much more group and community oriented. The balance between individualism and community has shifted dramatically in the United States over the past fifty years. As pointed out in Chapter 1, there has been a noticeable deterioration in community life, including family life since the 1960's. The importance of the family increases with the deterioration of other forms of sociability because it provides the only remaining opportunity for moral community. Examples of the growth of American individualism at the expense of community are numerous. The "rights culture," a focus on "I" instead of "we," and an obsession with immediate rewards, have affected trust, what we learn about it, how we practice it, and what kind of expectations we have of others regarding trust.

Our institutions and networks have become porous, which make it harder to trust (Wuthnow, 1998). As people adapt to a porous society, they also invent their own ways to decide who they can trust and under what conditions. While Wuthnow says that a certain level of mistrust is simply a way of adapting to complex social realities, there is no question that the meanings of trust have changed. Self-help groups are an example of how people find alternative ways to trust. Community is what people say they are seeking in small groups. Members of self-help groups rate them high on trust. The groups provide intimate interpersonal support in a setting of structured informality (Wuthnow, 1994). Four out of ten Americans belong to a small group that meets regularly and provides caring and support for its members, e.g. youth groups, singles groups, discussion groups, sports and hobbies groups, political and civic groups, church groups, groups focused on specific problems such as drugs and abuse. The self-help and small group movement seems to provide a new way to trust in a fluid, mobile society where lost personal ties need to be replaced (Wuthnow, 1994, 1998).

The Companion Animal Association of Arizona, Inc., offers a monthly self-help group for persons grieving the loss of a pet. The group is led by a certified grief counselor. Individuals can return to the group as they feel the need. The only element that bonds the group is the experience of losing a pet. The feeling of trust is sufficient to permit group members to discuss personal and family problems and openly share their emotions. The purpose of the group is powerful enough to erase differences, at least for the duration of the group, that might otherwise separate them, such as age, gender, social status, and sexual orientation.

There also is a related service of the Association, the Pet Grief Helpline, which is available daily where the caller can be counseled by a trained volunteer. Callers can remain anonymous unless they wish to receive grief-related materials by mail. All callers are referred to the self-help group. Many times, a pet's death or decision to "put down" a pet, seems incidental to other personal or family issues the caller brings up. Some callers respond to the word "Helpline" and do not hear the word grief. The opportunity to discuss and express personal feelings with an anonymous person provides a critical link for callers who are alone, without transportation, with minimal financial resources, or who do not know how to connect with available services.

SUMMARY

Learning the meaning of trust and distrust occurs during the first year of life and is continually modified by life's experiences. The readiness to trust or distrust varies from person to person and from situation to situation. Our previous experiences with trusting and distrusting persons, cues we sense and feel in each new situation and our own willingness to risk, help to shape our degree or extent of trust or distrust in another person, group or organization.

Distrust is not the opposite of trust. Once distrust develops, trust is difficult to re-establish. Distrust can develop outright, when another person does not make any attempt to explore trust, or it can develop as a result of failure in a dialogue exploring trust. When trust fails, there is a need for face-saving behavior to protect the reputations of the involved parties.

While we often focus on two party trust relationships, we are all part of networks of trust involving other groups and organizations at local, regional, national, and international levels. As a result of our highly mobile, fragmented society we have lost many opportunities to form close personal relationships that develop trust. We have substituted, instead, self-help groups and other small groups, which we can join and leave easily, to fill our needs for intimate personal support and trust.

Distrust is not always unhealthy. But when trust or social capital is spent, it may take years to replenish, if it can be replenished at all. At the individual level, a person who follows a life of distrust will find that his world is constantly narrowing; usually chronically distrustful persons become cynical and depressed, and their behavior alienates them from others, leading to further social isolation.

Chapter 3

Trust in Organizations

"There is little truth in organizations without trust."[1]

INTRODUCTION

Changes in the U.S. Work Environment

Changes in the work environment over the past two to three decades have significantly altered how we trust organizations, our bosses and our coworkers. In the past, there was such a thing as lifetime employment. Corporations and businesses assumed responsibility for career development, and employees believed that their employer would act in their best interests. Then, due to large inefficiencies, companies began developing a low dependency on employees, leading to restructurings, mergers, and downsizings. Now, companies encourage employees to be concerned about their own career development. Employees' views of work have also changed. Employment has become more transactional. Richards (1998) attributes this to a decline in trust between employer and employee. Employees know they are expendable and employers owe little allegiance to their workers. Furthermore, many employees identify themselves more with their roles than they do with their companies. This free ownership leads employees to see themselves as free agents; they stay on the lookout for the next opportunity. Richards (1998) describes how GTE launched a recruitment effort for a project in Latin America, listing positions on more than 20 Web sites. Within a 30-day period, GTE had more than 1,000 external resumés. Richards has characterized today's work force as multicultural vagabonds. Mutual trust between employer and employee is the casualty.

THE CULTURE OF TRUST

As we participate in a variety of organizations we carry with us our early personal experiences with trust and distrust. An organization is a purposive aggregation of individuals who exert concerted effort toward a common and explicit goal. The organization where we spend the majority of our time is the work organization, and that is the focus of this chapter.

Few concepts have captured the attention of scholars and practitioners as has that of organizational culture. The reason for studying culture is the presumed relationship between organizational culture and performance (O'Reilly & Chatman, 1996). For example, Kotter and Heskett (1992) hypothesized that strong culture firms would perform better over the long term. They argued that the presence of a strong culture, which they define in terms of the values and norms shared by members of the organization, should be associated with higher goal alignment among organizational members, promote an unusual level of motivation among employees, and provide needed controls without the stifling effects of a bureaucracy. Using a sample of over 200 large public firms in the United States, they surveyed managers to assess the strength of culture in their organizations. They then related culture strength during a ten-year period to the firms' economic performances over that same period. They found strong associations between firms' culture strength and performance, but only when the strong culture was also strategically appropriate and characterized by norms that permitted the culture to change. They concluded that even appropriate cultures will not promote excellent performance over long periods unless they contain norms and values that help the firms to adapt to a changing environment.

Culture may be a more important determinant of performance in certain types of organizations, e.g., health care and service, and less critical in others, e.g., manufacturing (Wilkins & Ouchi, 1983). The culture-performance link can be ambiguous, in part, because there is no agreement on the meaning of organizational culture. Some argue that it is the same as organizational climate (Reichers & Schneider, 1990). Others define culture as what an organization *is*, while still others argue that it is what an organization *has*. A few authors believe that culture is subjective and cannot be empirically described (Martin, 1992). Yet, no one would dispute that organizations, like tribes and families, have their own ways of doing things, ways that work for them and ways that don't (Handy, 1995). Whiteley (1995) has said that the culture of an organization is a homemade blueprint for seeing the world in a particular way.[2]

Usually, one type of culture characterizes an organization. This can be efficient for managerial control, but organizations are linked to a larger societal culture which is continually changing. As societal culture changes, organizational outcomes need to change and as an organization grows, its members need to change their attitudes and behaviors. Much of the trouble in organizations comes from the attempt to go on doing the same things in the same way and a reluctance to change the organization when it needs to be changed (Handy, 1995).

Cultural change does not mean abandoning cherished core values that give an organization its uniqueness and reason for existence; it could, however, mean adding new values. The CEO of a large corporation told the author that his corporation had four values: ethical behavior, accountability, service to others, and, a new one, valuing its people. While the last value has always been implicit in the organization, change has caused him and his management team to make it an explicit core value with accompanying rewards to reinforce it.

Core Values

Organizational values are the beliefs shared by organizational members share that defines what is important and set out what attitudes and behaviors are appropriate in the workplace. Shared values lead to a shared culture (Whiteley, 1995). Core values are the organization's essential and enduring tenets, not to be compromised for financial gain or short-term expediency (Collins & Porras, 1994). For example, at Southwest Airlines, Hewlett-Packard and Nordstrom, the recruitment process involves multiple steps, requiring applicants to escalate their investment in the firm. At Tandem Computer and Cypress Semiconductor, there is a deliberate attempt *not* to discuss salary before hiring. Instead, candidates are asked to commit to join the firm before discussing the specifics of their salary. At Southwest, the hiring and firing process is based explicitly on whether an individual has the "right attitude." Procedures enable insiders to learn whether candidates fit the culture of the organization. For example, Southwest pilots hire other pilots (O'Reilly & Chatman, 1996).

Values determine behavior and perceptions. To the extent that behavior and perceptions can be managed, values and culture can be managed. The degree of success in managing behavior and perceptions depends on the extent to which an organization's leaders are in touch with its members' values (Bruhn, 2001c). Collins and Porras (1994) state that a visionary organization needs no external justification for its core values. Nor do values sway with pressures from outside the organization. Nonetheless, values are living things. They need continuous reaffirmation to keep them alive, especially in organizations with a high turnover in personnel, or in those undergoing restructuring or a merger (Stewart, 1996).

Covey (1990) talks about the importance of "natural principles" which pertain to human relationships and organizations, such as fairness, equity, justice, integrity, honesty, and trust. Our values or beliefs reflect the degree to which we adhere to or follow these principles. When leaders institutionalize these principles in their organizational structures and symbols, they express the kinds of attitudes and behavior they expect of members. Trust is an essential core value.

Trust, or the lack of it, is the basis of success or failure in relationships and bottom-line results in business, industry, education, and government (Covey, 1990). Schein has referred to trust as a "psychological contract."[3] Trust is an expression of faith and confidence that a person or organization will be fair, reliable, ethical, competent, and nonthreatening (Carnevale, 1995). According to Carnevale, trust performs three key functions in organizations. First, trust is an integrative mechanism. Trust is a form of conditional faith that employees and management will do what they say they will do. It provides predictability to the organization. Second, trust is social capital.[4] It enables employees to work at their full potential, gives them greater control over their jobs, and promotes independence, participation, open communication, and learning in a context where defensiveness and fear are minimal. Third, trust is a positive mindset. It means that the organization's leaders want to maintain an environment where everyone in the organization believes that the organization has faith in its employees and is willing to let them do their jobs. Trust frees people to be open (Zand, 1997).

Zand (1997) points out that people express trust in three ways, through information, control, and influence, what he calls the "spiral model of trust," i.e. trust is reciprocal and incremental. Trust tends to build greater trust among more people. Effective leaders understand and employ three components of supportiveness that build trust: acceptance, tolerance for disagreement, and constructive use of people's openness.

Organizational trust has been found, in studies, to be associated with many factors, including productivity, group performance, cooperation and conflict, leadership styles, managerial assumptions about workers, need satisfaction, organizational change and development, participation, communication, stress and burnout, and the quality of labor-management relations (Carnevale, 1995). Without trust, organizations cannot be healthy and might not survive. But organizations, like people, are dynamic, attempting to maintain a homeostatic balance. Some organizations are better than others at maintaining a high trust balance.

High Trust/Low Trust Organizations

A high-trust culture brings together idealism and pragmatism. It becomes the basis for both empowerment and quality (Covey, 1999). In a low-trust culture more control has to be used, and people cannot be empowered because that will result in loose cannons all over the place (Covey, 1999). There is an inverse relationship between the number of controls and trust in either the competence or the motives of people in the organization. Excessive controls in organizations are sometimes a residue of past traumas. If organizational members agree that controls are necessary and fair, they will be effective, otherwise, people will disregard them, subvert them, or nibble them to death (Whitney, 1996). In high-trust cultures, parties resolve their disagreements by a process of problem-solving (as opposed to power tactics) made possible by a joint assumption of shared goals and values (Fox, 1974). Trust is developed out of the context of shared respect for differences, not out of dependency (Fairholm, 1994). High-trust organizations are those with optimally permeable group boundaries and high levels of relationship mutuality (Shaw, 1989). Uniformly high levels of trust are difficult to maintain among individuals and in organizations. It is more realistic to view organizations as maintaining optimal levels of trust where moderate levels, not extremes, are desired (Gamson, 1968). Indeed, Covey[5] points out that "organizations are organic, not mechanical. They live and grow because they are composed of living, growing people. You can't 'fix' people. You have to nurture them, like plants. You have to create the right conditions and climate for growth .... it takes time. You can't rush it." Trust is a process. It is multidimensional. And it needs the constant care and feeding of all members of an organization.

It is difficult to characterize high and low trust organizations in terms of traits and behaviors because these are not static or absolute, they vary in degree or quality, and often are situationally determined. However, Tables 3.1 and 3.2 attempt such a portrayal to dramatize the extremes between high and low trust cultures.

Certainly this picture of contrasting high and low trust cultures has become somewhat muddied by recent downsizings, mergers, layoffs, salary raises for CEO's during the recent stock market turndown, and with corporate governance being pressured by shareholders to be more responsive to their owners (Miller, 2001). After in-depth studies with individuals of different generations in the computer industry, Clancy (1996) concluded that trust in management had

Table 3.1. Some Characteristics of High Trust Organizations

Leader Behaviors	*Employee Behaviors*
• consensus often reached • problem-solving atmosphere • creativity • minimum of controls • charismatic, inspiring • sensitive to employee concerns (fairness) • highly visible • provide trustworthy information (credible) • reward performance appropriately • flexibility in rules to accommodate changing needs • responsive to external community • visionary; values reinforced • mergers/acquisitions done openly with planning involving employees	• open, participative, accept responsibility • highly productive • loyal to organization • not defensive • cooperation, work teams • high job satisfaction • problem-solving attitude in disputes and differences • involvement in decision-making • sense of pride in work

Table 3.2. Some Characteristics of Low Trust Organizations

Leader Behaviors	*Employee Behaviors*
• issue edicts, establish rules	• blame leaders and others
• attack, blame, threats, pressure	• feel defensive, fearful
• protect administrative actions	• unwilling to accept responsibility
• control, little or no delegation of responsibility	• suspicion, jealousy, gossip
• manipulation of people and motives	• adversarial, file grievances and lawsuits
• favoritism	• high absenteeism
• power tactics, intimidation	• high job turnover
• see employees as dispensable	• no identification with organizational goals
• untruthworthy information/integrity failure	• loss of loyalty
• misalignment of performance and rewards	• performance meets minimal expectations
• tolerance of incompetence	• unhappy in job
• high degree of supervision	• distrust, "put it in writing"
• little or no connections with larger community	• employee disputes with other employees
• little, if any, philanthropy	• sabotage, theft of organization supplies
• inaccessible to employees, use staff to control access and information	• boundary fighting
• use of organizational moles	
• mergers/acquisitions done secretly	

substantially eroded in the last twenty to twenty-five years. All of the recent changes in work organizations, especially in the last decade, have heightened distrust among the labor force in general, including those who continue to be employed in high-trust organizations.

Mergers and acquisitions reawaken and cause individuals to relive their early life conflicts with trust and mistrust and disrupt their sense of security and well-being. Such loss reactions are normal, but if they are not well-managed they can lead to protracted periods of dysfunctional depression. Leaders must facilitate the process to assist employees to regain their sense of security and trust if they are to revitalize their organizations (Gilkey, 1991).

Betrayal of Trust

Caudron (1996) points out that many people believe trust disappears because of downsizing and the resulting loss of job security. But the major reason trust disappears is that leaders have handled workplace changes poorly. Management may espouse open communication, but some employees hear or read about their layoffs in the media. The Board talks about the need to trim costs, while the CEO gets a million dollar bonus. Work teams are encouraged, but individuals are rewarded. Mixed messages cause employees to stop listening, stop believing, and stop trusting. Employees' perceptions of employer's credibility and fairness have been found to be the strongest predictors of trust (Courtney, 1998). Some leaders and managers think it is Human Resource's job to become trust mechanics and restore trust. Some even believe that once downsizing and other organization transitions are complete, trust will return on its own.

There are many examples of violations or betrayals of trust in organizations such as changing the rules after the fact, breach of contract, broken promises, lying, stealing of ideas, wrong or unfair accusations, and disclosure of secrets (Elangovan & Shapiro, 1998). In addition, there are a range of supervisor behaviors that employees have identified as entailing varying degrees of betrayal of trust. These include coercive or threatening behavior, withholding of promised support, blaming employees for personal mistakes, favoritism, sexual harrassment, improper dismissal, and the misuse of private information. As a result, "betrayed" has many meanings and definitions.

Elangovan and Shapiro suggest several key characteristics of betrayal. First, betrayal is seen as a voluntary act. Second, betrayal involves the violation of expectations of the trustor. Third, both parties must be mutually aware of the questioned expectations. Fourth, betrayal involves a behavior rather than just the thought of betraying. Fifth, betrayal has the potential to harm the well-being of the trustor.

Although betrayal involves a violation of personal trust, it is not necessarily unethical or antisocial. Betrayal, for example, may involve disclosing a coworker's padding of his expense account or misleading of a supervisor about the status of a project, both of which may be damaging to the coworker and supervisor, but they have no effect on the organization.

Why do people betray trust? Elangovan and Shapiro adopted the betrayer's perspective in answering this question. They suggest that the lower the degree of satisfaction a person has with the organization, the greater will be his/her motivation to betray. Therefore, betrayed involves a degree of self-satisfaction and an attitude of "getting back" at someone or the organization. Indeed, the culture of an organization and its trust practices have a great influence. For example, betrayal behavior is more likely to occur if the penalties for betrayal are minor or nonexistent. If the organization has a lot of conflict and internal politics with shifting coalitions, goal incongruence, and breaking of norms, betrayal is more likely. How the organization dealt with prior incidents of trust violation also influences a betrayer's assessment of a probable penalty and its severity. Elangovan and Shapiro suggest that "opportunistic betrayal," when an initial act of betrayal serves as an antecedent to subsequent revenge-seeking behaviors, when the opportunity presents itself, is the most common form.

Once distrust has occurred, it is difficult, if not impossible, to facilitate the return of trust. Outside consultants, trainers, workshops, and "good feeling activities" will in themselves be distrusted by employees. If the leader practices trust during good and bad times, there will be no need to spend time, money, and energy to replenish lost trust.

LEADERSHIP BEHAVIORS AND TRUST

Just as values shape culture, culture shapes leadership. Leaders are selected to head up a specific organization because they are "a good fit for the culture." Leadership is not so much a function of the individual leader as it is a condition of the culture (Fairholm, 1994). Indeed, leadership is not so much what individual leaders do as it is what the leader and the led do collectively. Leaders can only be effective when they work in a culture of trust based on shared vision, ideals and values (Fairholm, 1994). Leaders create and maintain a trusting culture through the example they set and through listening. The culture of an organization and its leader are mutually reinforcing.

It is erroneous to think that a single leader can transform a culture from a distrusting to a trusting one, especially in the short-term. Some may see this transformation as one that only requires changes in the organizational structure and/or its employees, which the leader can make easily. This kind of thinking is reflected in the readiness with which many Boards or members of an organization are prepared to change leaders when things do not go as they expected. A high turnover in leaders does not occur in organizations where commonly shared values are the foundation of trust between individuals.

Four of the most common errors leaders make, leading to their downfall, involve their misunderstanding of what trust means. Some leaders think it means being friendly and open, believing that if they exhibit these behaviors, others will follow and trust will occur (Zand, 1997). Another error, at the opposite extreme, is for leaders to think they can control their way to a trusting culture. Leaders with the highest control scores have the lowest personal credibility (Kouzes & Posner, 1995). A third error of leaders is to view trust as an outcome of specific actions or activities, e.g. hosting special events to create an atmosphere of trust. A fourth error leaders make is assuming that trust can be created and strengthened by getting employees and management to work together on a strategic plan for establishing organizational values. It works the other way around. Trust must be established before employees feel comfortable about openly discussing values and plans. Often if trust has not been established, employees will merely go through the motions and ignore or avoid bringing up sensitive issues. Thus, while management perceives involving employees in such processes as being open and inclusive, the process may create employee distrust (Annison & Wilford, 1998). For example, a survey of state public welfare executives and local welfare employees in two states explored respondents' views about participation in planned organizational change. Respondents in both states believed that employees should be permitted to participate to a greater extent in implementing change. Executives were concerned, however, that participation might result from frustrated expectations (Bruhn et al., 2001). If a base of trust had been established first, executives and employees would have known each others' expectations in planning from the onset. As a result, employees see their involvement in organizational planning as a *fait accompli*. Trust is a mediating, or process variable, which links leader behavior to members' behavior (Whittington, 1997; Simon, 1994). Trust mediates the choices (provides the context for messages) that leaders make. Trust is what makes leaders' actions reasonable, believable, and acceptable. When leaders establish a track record of trustful choices, they are regarded as having earned the trust of members in their organization.

The topic of transformational leadership has received a great deal of attention in recent years. The literature suggests there are at least six key behaviors associated with transformational leaders (Podsakoff et al., 1990):

- identifying and articulating a vision of the future
- providing an example for employees
- promoting cooperation and team work among employees
- communicating expectations of quality and excellence
- respect for employees' needs
- reexamining and rethinking work functions

Podsakoff and his colleagues examined the effects of transformational leader behaviors on organizational citizenship behaviors, and the potential mediating roles of trust and satisfaction in that process. Measures of transformational leader behaviors, trust, and satisfaction were obtained from 988 employees of a large petro-chemical company, and measures of these employees' citizenship behaviors were obtained from their leaders. They found that the effects of the transformational leader behaviors on citizenship behaviors were indirect in that they were mediated by followers' trust in their leaders.[6]

In the 1991 Annual Report of General Electric Company (1991), Chairman of the Board and CEO John F. Welch, Jr. clearly communicated his behavioral expectations for senior leaders relative to GE's values. He categorized leaders into four groups:

1. Leaders who deliver on commitments—financial or otherwise—and share the values of GE, his or her future is an easy call. Onward and Upward.
2. Leaders who do not meet commitments and do not share GE values. Not as pleasant a call, but equally easy.

3. Leaders who miss commitments but share GE values. They usually get a second chance, preferably in a different environment.
4. Leaders who make their commitments but do not share GE values. These individuals typically force performance from people rather than inspire it: they are autocrats, big shots, tyrants. Too often, all of us look the other way and tolerate these managers because they always deliver in the short term. This type may be more acceptable in easier times, but in an environment that requires good ideas from every man and woman in the organization, we cannot afford management styles that suppress and intimidate.

Shaw (1997) thoroughly studied Kineo Corporation to determine why employee distrust of management was so common. He found that distrust was sustained at Kineo by impermeable boundaries around management. Employees perceived that management was isolated. Management violated the boundaries around employee groups also contributing to distrust. Distrust was especially high at the lower levels of Kineo. Distrust was managed by pushing negative employees down and out.

In Kineo, employees trusted their supervisors more than they trusted those above their supervisors or the organization as a whole. Employees believed the higher up the ladder, the less faithful they could be to their own values and beliefs. A "we/they" (management vs. non-management) attitude prevailed. Management was paid differently, given different benefits, often brought in from the outside, they were rewarded differently, and had more autonomy. Low status employees did not know the managers, who were seen as isolated and inaccessible, and had a limited understanding of what managers did. Management had a resistance to negative information, disagreements, and negative feelings and talked about "opportunities for improvement" instead of problems or issues. Communication was predominantly downward and employees perceived that the upward sharing of information could have negative consequences for those involved. Employees perceived that honesty did not help one to get promoted. Management was reluctant to expose the fact that they were struggling to find answers to difficult problems. Managers believed they were sharing more information than employees believed to be the case. Therefore, the grapevine became a reliable source of information.

Employees did not feel valued by management. Some felt that Kineo was a no-win environment. Employees often found negative intent behind well-intentioned management behavior. Shaw concluded his study with these findings: trust cannot grow unless all members of an organization are free to take risks and fail occasionally; excessive distrust exists in organizations that are over or under-bounded;[7] distrust is a conceptual boundary that serves to separate individuals and groups; distrust is more likely when employees view management as having little regard for them and as being incongruent in their words and behavior.

Kineo is an example of how leaders of this corporation abdicated any responsibility for engendering trust (Kouzes & Posner, 1995). They took a "no problems here" approach to management by pushing problems down the hierarchy for supervisors to resolve. It was as if management operated the corporation encapsulated in an opaque bubble. The Kineo example vividly illustrates what leaders should *not* do in organizations.

Another example illustrates how leaders can completely misunderstand trust and their responsibility for it. ABC Corporation had a turnover in personnel of 60 percent. To find out why, the leadership distributed a questionnaire to employees. The employees' suggestions included: create an employee lounge with television and vending machines, provide areas where employees can take breaks, consider flexible work hours and job sharing, and many other ideas expressing employees' needs. Management responded with a memo saying that if they knew employees were not going to take the questionnaire seriously they would not have distributed it. Not only were employee needs ignored because management considered them frivolous, but the corporation was involved in many inequitable policies. Women were paid less than men for the same job and experience. Some employees' salaries were higher than those of their supervisors. New employees were given more responsibility than employees who had seniority.

The leaders of ABC Corporation looked externally for answers to their high turnover rate. They said it was difficult in this age to find people who wanted to work hard and who were responsible; that people were willing to change jobs readily for more money; that employees no longer had loyalty to employers; that employees' demands of employers were excessive. What the leaders of ABC Corporation did not understand, or were not aware of, was that trust and loyalty involve a reciprocal relationship. The more trust and loyalty expressed by leaders toward their employees, the more positively the employees will behave (Atwater, 1988).

Bennis (1984) says that he often observes people in top positions doing the wrong things well. Like incompetent doctors, incompetent managers can make life worse, make people sicker, and less vital (Bennis, 1984). Leaders may be fully competent in terms of ability, experience, and credentials to lead, but they may lack what Yamagishi (2001) calls "social intelligence." Yamagishi suggests that high trusters are more sensitive people than distrusters, and more accurate in judging the trustworthiness of others. On the other hand, distrust breeds further distrust since it prevents people from exposing themselves to opportunities to develop social intelligence. It is perhaps not surprising that distrusting leaders are more apt to have "closed doors" and stay aloof because they lack a sense of trust of others. By doing so (or by delegating problems to staff), they protect themselves from the risk of being victimized (or used) in social interactions.

One of the limits of candor is self-protection. Like all people, leaders and managers behave according to their assumptions of how the world works—whether it is a kind or a cruel place. A pattern develops when leaders hold three assumptions that prevent trust from forming (Barnes, 1981). One assumption is that leaders must make "either/or" ("do or die") decisions. Barnes claims this way of thinking limits options. It becomes a "win/lose" choice with the leader regarding his choice as good while some individuals or groups will feel the opposite.

A second assumption that leaders may make is what Barnes calls "hard is better than soft." A leader who makes an either/or or do or die decision then has to defend it. To defend his/her position the leader needs facts rather than feelings. Consequently, some leaders become tough-dealers in situations that need more flexibility.

A third assumption that leaders may make is that the world is a dangerous place requiring a position of pervasive mistrust to survive. When a leader holds this assumption, it dominates and blots out situational factors. Barnes concluded "Like the other two assumptions, mistrust can be very useful when well-being is at stake. On other occasions, our own mistrust helps set the stage for either/or thinking and hard-drive-out-soft behavior." Bartolemé (1989) points out that overcoming the limits of trust and the fear of candor is an on-going challenge for leaders.

FOLLOWERSHIP AND TRUST

According to Kelley (1992), we often engage in "leader worship" and ignore the power of followers. He describes how employees build and use networks to accomplish their jobs and help the organization to reach its goals. Followers are extended eyes and ears of the leader. They are close to the action and have information the leader doesn't have access to. Exemplary followers can help a leader do a better job by offering potential solutions to problems. Exemplary followers increase the odds that their voices will be heard by creating trust. They gauge how much they can trust their leader and their co-workers. Sizing up the leader's trustworthiness helps determine how they can use their networks in a positive manner.

Kelley stated that lack of trust is a major issue for followers. In one survey he found that followers could identify only two out of five of the managers in their work experience as being able to instill trust. Followers trust their direct supervisors about two-thirds of the time and top management only about half the time. Leaders, Kelley suggests, can create environments where exemplary followers can flourish. Both add value and both have contributions necessary for success in the organization. Leaders are partners who do different things than followers.[8,9]

Trust: An Exchange Relationship

Many theories of trust are grounded in social exchange theory (Blau, 1964) which assumes that trust emerges through the repeated exchange of benefits between two individuals. Managers and followers are engaged in this kind of relationship (Whitener et al., 1998). Organizational culture is a phenomenon derived from social interactions among members of the organization. Through social learning culture may directly influence managerial trustworthy behavior. Managers observe how their organization responds and learn what behavior is rewarded and punished, and they experience rewards when they behave in a manner consistent with organizational values. Also, the organizational culture encourages (or discourages) managerial trustworthy behavior through patterns of communication and decision making. For example, an organization that values risk taking will reward managers who delegate to an employee, regardless of the outcome. Similarly, organizations can value inclusiveness, open communication (input and feedback), and discussing (and disagreeing with) issues. Cultures that support these behaviors will also encourage and reward trustworthy behavior (Whitener et al., 1998). Managers may be willing to initiate trustworthy behavior, but this is not sufficient for a trust relationship.

Employees may observe their manager's trustworthy behavior, but are unlikely to trust if they lack a predisposition to trust others. Other factors in addition to their manager's behavior and the culture of the organization influence employees' propensity to trust, for example, the nature of the task for which trust is asked, whether the task involves others or not, and whether a single task or multiple interdependent tasks are involved. Managers need to initiate trusting relationships and reward employees by reciprocating. In this way, a foundation can be established for a trusting organization.

TRUST-BUILDING AND ORGANIZATIONAL CITIZENSHIP BEHAVIORS

One of the paradoxes that today's leaders face is how to give up control (or increase the participation) of employees in an organization without losing control. Managers trust employees when they believe employees are competent to make good decisions, concerned about the needs of the organization, reliable, and open to sharing sensitive information (Spreitzer & Mishra, 1999). But trust takes time to develop, so the use of financial incentives and performance information have been suggested as substitutes for trust that can help align employees with the goals of the organization. Nyhan (2000) found that participation in decision-making, feedback from and to employees, and the empowerment of employees can lead to increased trust between supervisors and employees, which, in turn, leads to increased organizational commitment and productivity.[10] Empowerment of employees helps to loosen the reins, allowing them to work without over-supervision. Indeed, it has been found that employees who have more control in their jobs have fewer health problems.[11] As an organization becomes more egalitarian it increases its potential for satisfying the need of employees for esteem and furthers their progression toward self-actualization (Hart et al., 1986). The more an individual trusts his workgroup, and the more he generally trusts others with whom he interacts during work, the greater will be his self-actualization (Kegan & Rubenstein, 1973).

Trust is essential to team effectiveness and managerial problem-solving. Zand (1972) found that it is useful to see trust as behavior that conveys appropriate information, permits mutuality of influence, encourages self-control, and avoids abuse of the vulnerability of others. It appears that when a group works on a problem there are two concerns: one is the problem itself, the second is how the members relate to each other to work on the problem. In low-trust groups, interpersonal relationships interfere with and distort perceptions of the problem. Energy and creativity are diverted from finding comprehensive, realistic solutions, and members use the problem as an instrument to minimize their vulnerability. In contrast, in high-trust groups there is less socially generated uncertainty and problems are solved more effectively (Zand, 1972).

At the group level, trust is essential to group effectiveness (McLain & Hackman, 1999). The degree to which people trust each other determines the degree to which they will share relevant information, allow others to control their behavior, and permit others to exercise influence over their decisions. People often are hired because of their technical or professional ability and are terminated because of their inability to work effectively with others (Boss, 1977).

Nearly two decades ago, a new construct called "organizational citizenship behavior" was introduced in the organizational sciences. It was defined by two criteria: behavior above and beyond role requirements for which there is no formal reward, but behavior that is organizationally functional (Graham, 1991). Good citizenship is a product of organizational culture and its psychological structure and members' interpretations of them (Baum, 1991). Every organization has a "shared reality" which sets certain patterns of behavior and influences members' beliefs about expected behavior. In other words, standards of moral behavior, professionalism, and good citizenship involve the transaction between an organization and its members (Morgan, 1997). Graham (1991) identified three categories of citizen responsibilities—obedience, loyalty, and participation. She points out that responsible citizenship requires a balance between these three behaviors. Smith and her colleagues (1983) suggest that citizenship behavior includes the dimensions of altruism (helping others) and conscientiousness. Podsakoff and his colleagues (1997) found that helping behavior and sportsmanship had significant effects on performance quality, but civic virtue did not influence the quality of performance.

Trust protects citizenship behavior. The fairness of supervisors was found to lead to good employee citizenship behavior (Konovsky & Pugh, 1994). Employees' perceptions of the effectiveness of the organization's reward practices are also related to trust (Costigan et al., 1998). Good citizenship, therefore, means more than going to work everyday and fulfilling one's contractual obligations. It means exhibiting characteristics of what Organ (1988) has termed "the good soldier syndrome" and is characterized by these attributes: altruism, helping, conscientiousness, prosocial behavior, neighborliness, sportsmanship, and civic virtue. It has been noted, however, that there may be discrepancies between the organizational citizen image that an individual believes others hold of her and how she wishes to be viewed. Bolino (1999) warns that some "good soldiers" may be good actors.

Good citizenship is tied closely to trust. Members of organizations who trust their organization seem to put more into it, they appear more satisfied and participate in its activities (Driscoll, 1978). Indeed, the more good citizens an organization has, the more social capital it enjoys (Leana & Van Buren, 1999). Integrity appears to be the key to all types of relationships in organizations, whether between supervisors, peers, or subordinates (Schindler & Thomas, 1993). Locke (1997) said that there are three essentials an employer needs to know about a job applicant: (1) does the person have the knowledge, skills, and abilities to do the job; (2) will the person exert the necessary effort; and (3) does the person have good character; will she be a good citizen? Good character means that the person has integrity. And integrity is the basis of trust.

CEO'S AND CULTURES CHANGE: WHAT ABOUT TRUST?

The interrelationships between the culture of an organization and its leader are key to building and maintaining trust. CEO's can carefully guide culture change in their organization to maintain trust. But what happens when a CEO leaves her organization? Cultures survive leadership changes, but what happens to trust?

A president of a large national trade organization who had worked for the company for 30 years, the most recent 12 years as a CEO, was planning his retirement in conjunction with his Board. He gave the Board three years notice of his retirement because he wanted enough time for a smooth transition in leadership. He also wanted to help in designing a values-driven search to find his successor. He had crafted a healthy, productive, trusting company and wanted to do his part to ensure that his successor would be a "values-sensitive" person. He was not looking for a clone of himself, but he was concerned about the values that had come to distinguish the century-old company.

Organizations are used to culture change as they continually change in evolving through their lifecycles (Grenier, 1972). Just as with the growth of persons organizations experience all of the problems typical of each stage of growth (Schein, 1992). CEO's help to shape and direct organizational change to keep the organization moving forward. When CEO's leave, the pacesetter for the organization is gone. If the CEO has fostered the growth of a trusting organization, the impending change can be quite disruptive. This is particularly acute if the CEO is the founder of the organization (Schein, 1992).[12] Will the next CEO be as trusting? Which, if any, parts of the culture will the new CEO change? These questions become critical to the members of an organization, especially if the organization is anticipating, or undergoing, a merger, takeover or other major structural changes.

Cultures can be managed, but trust must be modeled and inspired (Bennis, 1993). Trust is the result of a relationship. When a CEO leaves, the relationship is changed; hence, trust must be remodeled and reinspired. The entire process of risk-taking must be replayed in selecting another CEO. The President of the trade company just mentioned wanted to minimize the risks of making a wrong or poor choice of his successor by having a values-driven search, that is, the advertisement for the job would emphasize that the company is values-driven, and during the interviews of finalists, management and employees would specifically probe for examples of how the applicants have used the specified values in their actions.

The search for a CEO replacement is a process that continues even after the person has been named. Trust is a relationship that evolves, it is dynamic, it occurs in a context (Mayer et al., 1995). Therefore, how trustful the new CEO will be will be determined well into the future, after the search firm and the retiring CEO have turned their focus to other efforts. Successors can be selected with care, values can be protected, and trust can be espoused, but trust is a fragile gift that needs the test of time and context.

SUMMARY

Organizations are known for their cultures; their values and beliefs unite their members and tell non-members who they are. Culture has a predominate effect on the performance and productivity of its members and, in turn, it influences the feelings of loyalty, pride and commitment members have for the organization. Culture is the glue that keeps an organization together; it is what makes one organization different from other organizations. Because of the strength of its glue, culture is difficult to change. Most of the difficulties in leading and managing organizations are due to resistance to change. One of the factors that make organizational change possible and palatable is trust.

Shared values lead to a shared culture. Core values are part of culture. Values are reminders of what the members of a culture believe in. Trust is such a value. Trust is an integrative mechanism in a culture, it helps create social capital, and it creates a positive mindset among members. Some organizations are more trusting than others. Among the factors influencing how trusting an organization is, are whether the leader models and encourages trust, empowers members to do their jobs fully, by using their talents and abilities, and facilitates their personal and professional growth.

Just as values shape culture, culture shapes leaders. Leaders alone cannot transform organizations from non-trusting to trusting ones. It takes the involvement of the Board of Trustees and the effort of the total organization to effect desired cultural change. Sometimes, cultures are unhealthy and members too entrenched in them to change or even to see possible alternatives. Sometimes, leaders who like control do not want to create more change than they can manage and discourage all change that they don't create themselves. Sometimes, there is too little trust to mobilize the total organization to reframe itself.

We all have worked in organizations whose cultures and leaders needed changing, where member turnover and dissatisfaction were high, and where the core values have been forgotten. Often, members feel helpless to do anything to change the organization and leave it. There are no blueprints for change in such organizations as each has a unique history and story. There are blueprints for creating and maintaining a trusting organization. A leader who inspires trust, models it, rewards it, and reinforces it on a daily basis takes the first step. It takes time to evaluate how trusting a leader will be. Lack of trust can be a major issue for the followers in an organization. Leaders and followers need each other to build trust in organizations. Leaders need to learn how to properly use control and empowerment, and followers need to learn how to participate and be open to sharing information. Trust is essential to team effectiveness and managerial problem-solving. The degree to which leaders and followers trust each other determines the degree to which they will share information, allow others to control their behavior, and permit others to influence decisions.

Good citizenship is a product of healthy, trusting organizations. Being helpful to others and conscientiousness have been shown to be two aspects of citizenship that help to build trust and social capital. One of the essentials an employer needs to know is whether an applicant will be a good citizen. Good citizens have integrity, and integrity is the basis for trust.

Organizations and their leaders change. The trust history of an organization is important in guiding organizational transformations. Organizational cultures and core values are inherited by a new leader. Trust is not inherited; it has to be modeled, inspired, and put to the test of time. Trust is a fragile gift that cannot be insured or replaced.

Chapter 4

Trust and the Lifecycle of Organizations

"Trust is the pulse of an organization; its strength varies with the time it is taken."[1]

INTRODUCTION

A friend related the following story. He had accepted a position as a Vice President in a large corporation but would not assume the position officially for approximately six months. During this period, the President of the corporation, whom he greatly admired and to whom he was to report, became ill and announced that he was stepping down. A vice president who was a member of the leadership team accepted the Presidency of another firm. Searches for two management executives were suspended pending the naming of the President's successor. My friend was dismayed to learn that the organization he was eager to join would change substantially before he got there. He was especially concerned because his boss and some of his future associates were people whom he believed he could trust and work with effectively. His expectations of the trustfulness of the organization he had committed to join were influenced by people who were no longer there. An organization is like a moving train which takes on and drops off passengers at various points en route to its destination. Establishing and reestablishing trust is what passengers do as the train moves from point to point.

ORGANIZATIONS AS PERSONS

Organizations are living organisms in a continual process of adapting to their environment and satisfying their needs (Morgan, 1997).[2] The people who are members of the organization are engaged in the same processes; the organization and its members depend upon each other in a symbiotic relationship; as such, they comprise an open system. A system is a set of interrelated elements. Because these elements are interdependent, changes in the nature of one component may lead to changes in the nature of the other components. Another way of looking at a system is to see it as a mechanism that imports energy from its external environment, transforms it, and produces an output back to its external environment (Nadler & Tushman, 1995). Most organizations are open systems, but some organizations, such as prisons or monasteries, wish to minimize contact with their external environment and therefore maintain a highly structured and controlled internal environment, guided by uniform goals. Some family businesses maintain a partially closed system, although they are dependent on the external environment for survival.

Organizations, whether open or closed, continually change. The speed and types of change depend upon each organization's need for input and output from other organizations in its environment. In addition to these external influences, organizations change internally as they progress through their lifecycles. In this sense, organizations like individuals, move through a series of phases or stages of development from birth to death (Bruhn, 1997). Not all organizations die, many merge or are reinvented and so may experience some lifecycle stages more than once. Backer and Porterfield (1998) point out that change hurts because we lose something. Loss, or the anticipation of it, is the root of the hurt of change. Change can also increase anxiety about the future. In a distrustful environment change of any kind can create fear, anxiety and resistance, and reduce creativity and innovativeness. Trust is often the key factor in determining the degree of ease with which an organization moves through its lifecycle, how it copes with, and whether it survives threats to its viability.

ORGANIZATIONAL LIFECYCLE TRANSITIONS

Tichy (1980) has said that organizations do not follow predictable biosocial stages of development because the laws of social systems are not the same as those of biological systems. However, there is fair agreement that organizations have lifecycles and, irrespective of their size and complexity, share some common characteristics as they move from point to point in the process of growth and development. Quinn and Cameron (1983) reviewed nine models or organizational lifecycles and found that, although the models were based on different organizational phenomena, all nine suggested that organizations progress through four lifecycle stages. Stage 1 is the *entrepreneurial stage* with an emphasis on marshaling resources, some planning and coordination, forming a "niche," and entrepreneurial activities. Stage 2 is the *collectivity stage* in which a sense of mission is developed, innovation continues, there is a high degree of commitment, long hours, and a sense of collectivity. Stage 3 is the *formalization and control stage* in which rules are formalized, the structure is stabilized, institutional procedures are developed, the emphasis is on efficiency and maintenance, and the mode of operation is conservative. Stage 4 is the *elaboration of structure* stage in which the organization undergoes adaptation, renewal, expansion, and decentralization. Interestingly, only one of the models included organizational decline and death as a lifecycle stage. Death is not an inevitable stage for all organizations; rather, it is a choice that results from the action or inactions of the organization's leadership. The length of time that organizations are expected to remain in particular stages was not specified by the authors of the models. Since there are no markers for development, as there are in the human lifecycle, it is not possible to clearly identify the beginning and end of each stage. Also, the criteria used to evaluate an organization's success in each stage was unspecified. This is because an organization's success will be judged differently by people inside and outside the organization, and one lifecycle stage does not complete closure before the next one begins. The evaluation of success is usually a more global judgment that is made as an organization reaches its maturity. Finally, organizations tend to pursue strategies or choices in their lifecycle progression that have proven effective for other organizations, e.g., best practices. Some of these strategies may be ineffective or inappropriate when applied to other organizations. Rather, what appears to be an important factor in an organization's maturity is the strength of its culture. It is evident that organizations with strong cultures and strong social control systems experience success earlier than might be expected and mature organizations with strong cultures remain vibrant and vital longer than might be expected (O'Reilly & Chatman 1996).

Even healthy organizations are not healthy all of the time. Ouchi (1980) has pointed out that all organizations are in a state of at least partial failure because new technologies, the rate of change, and the ambiguities of performance evaluations tend to overwhelm attempts of rational control. In order for leaders to minimize failure and maximize healthiness in their organization, it is important that they be able to conceptually separate stages of the lifecycle and understand them individually and collectively (Tichy, 1980).

Schein (1992) has proposed three broad organizational stages: founding and early growth, midlife, and maturity and decline. These stages provide a useful structure for understanding the development and maintenance of trust throughout the lifecycle of organizations. Trust begins with the relationship of the founders of an organization have with each other. The founders, in turn, help to create a culture of trust.

Before we begin our discussion of organizational lifecycle and trust, we should point out that beginning in infancy, new organizations develop trust through the influence and modeling of their founders. While all organizations have an origin or birth, many become "reborn" or reconfigured as a result of mergers, acquisitions or buyouts. Trust is not inherited as part of these changes, but distrust is. Organizations that change leaders, missions, and values have to begin anew in their quest for trust. Organizations that merge, are acquired, or bought out, especially in hostile takeovers, have to deal with distrust. Efforts to establish trust in a new organization are complicated by the fact that the former organizations are usually at different lifecycle stages. The iterations of the building of trust in reconfigured organizations are many and beyond the scope of this book. Our focus will be on organizations that follow a fairly predictable sequence of growth and development, beginning at their birth.

Founding and Early Growth

A Spencer Stuart survey of 10 multinational corporations indicated that most technology companies favored internal hiring of executives who would head start-up ventures (Smith, 1997). These companies believed in the existence of a higher level of trust and confidence in executives who had been with the company for years. Some companies hire executives from within the organization because they have knowledge of the internal complexities. If there is a significant investment, a company may find it better to bring in someone it already knows and trusts, someone who has proven himself to the organization. Trust is usually highest at the times of the founding and early growth of an organization.

Several factors are essential in building a culture of trust in new organizations (Cufaude, 1999; Cangemi et al., 1989). (See Table 4.1)

1. *Depth and Strengthening of Relationships*. Quality relationships are essential among the people involved in the early stages of forming an organization. You can't trust people you don't know. Knowing means more than familiarity with credentials and experience. It means understanding an individual's values, aspirations, talents, beliefs, fears, and shortcomings. Executives, board members, and staff need to know each other as individuals. They need to understand each other's work styles, strengths and weaknesses. They need to agree on how they will work with each other. Roger Sherwood, executive director of the Society of Teachers of Family Medicine has said that trust allows the Board to focus on the macro while the staff manages the micro (Cufaude, 1999).
2. *Understanding Roles and Responsibilities*. Without a clarity of roles many ambiguities can erode trust. A clarity of roles is crucial for all members of the organization. Organizational charts are not substitutes for dialogue and frequent communication to clear up confusion about roles and responsibilities. Boundary management is important in keeping frustration to a minimum and

properly recognizing employees for accomplishments in their areas of responsibility.

3. *Frequent, Direct and Timely Communication*. Timely communication that offers full-disclosure, and is shared appears to engender a culture of high trust. The absence of communication, on the other hand, often causes suspicion and creates rumors and gossip. Department heads, directors, and other staff are key messengers of communication from the CEO and executives. Middle managers help to sustain the leader's credibility and trustworthiness. Therefore, they must feel secure about how they are trusted by their superiors. To trust others with full disclosure of information requires that you feel secure and confident with yourself. During the early stages of the formation of an organization, it is essential that all employees be involved in forming a culture of trust. It is important for members to know what is happening at all phases of early growth. When trust has been established and members have bought into the organization's goals, objectives and *modus operandi*, the seeds of loyalty will be sown. One way to help ensure a constant flow of information to members is to involve them in decision-making as appropriate and continually solicit their input. Knowing that people perceive information as power can be used to create trust. When information (power) is shared, members are likely to feel entrusted and respond accordingly. Sharing also creates self-esteem and self-awareness (Cufaude, 1999).
4. *Clarity of Shared Vision and Purpose*. One major aspect of a culture of trust is knowing what the members of the organization have in common, what holds them together. Schein (1992) has pointed out that the main cultural thrust comes from the founders when they outline the organization's specific competence and the psychosocial glue that holds the organization together. The purpose and vision of the organization should be known by all members. In this way, members can articulate the organization's purpose and goals to new members when turnover occurs. Every member should understand how and why his/her particular job contributes to the success of the organization. Gaining this clarity about shared purpose, direction, and vision helps to create and maintain a high trust environment.
5. *Honoring Promises and Commitments*. It is important that promises and commitments made during the early stages of development of an organization be honored. It is not unusual, as a young organization grows rapidly, for executives to find that some of the original promises and commitments can no longer be honored. Certainly there may be realistic constraints on finances in the early stages of an organization's life. Inevitabilities should be clearly outlined and discussed among members at the onset of their joining the organization. It is always advisable to follow verbal agreements with written verifications. One way to erode trust among members of an organization is to allow inconsistences between what leaders say and do (Cangemi et al., 1989).

6. *Understanding and Respecting Diversity*. Multiculturalism is a goal for our society, its organizations, and its institutions, involving a continuous process of education and change within organizations. Multiculturalism begins with diversity and requires various steps to achieve changes in attitudes, behaviors, and values. The leaders of organizations must not only commit to diversification, they must participate in it and reward its efforts. Diversification should be managed by creating a climate of open participation, feedback, and control at lower organizational levels. To micromanage the process of becoming diverse increases resistance and paranoia and counters educational efforts (Bruhn, 1996b).

   One of the challenges of a new organization is to create a culture of trust which is inclusive of the differences among its members. Members of different cultural, ethnic and religious groups have different interpretations of the meaning of trust; therefore, their expectations and perceptions of what they experience will differ. This makes the ability to acknowledge and seek to understand diverse views even more critical. It may mean bringing into a dialogue the opinions or individuals with whom many may disagree. Creating a multicultural organization of high trust requires good listeners, respect for differences, and a willingness to explore rather than win.
7. *Connectedness and Public Face*. While organizations need to develop a strong internal culture, the total culture of an organization must also embrace its external environment. Unless they are closed systems, most organizations depend, in varying degrees, on their external environment. How an organization goes about developing external ties, and their degree of success, will influence how the organization is perceived by other organizations. Perhaps the best example is that of initial stock offerings (IPOs) which involves assembling a strong group of entrepreneurs, seeking an investment banking firm which will underwrite them, and timing the initial public stock offering. The personal chemistry must be excellent within the IPO and between the IPO, underwriters, and the public for the effort to succeed (Wise, 1990). The interface between these components will determine the degree of trust that the IPO will be able to maintain.

Therefore, building and maintaining trust in organizations is a daily endeavor of reinforcing and strengthening the elements of trust to sustain a healthy homeostatic balance between the sometimes competing internal and external forces of change.

Midlife

The second broad organizational stage proposed by Schein (1992) is the midlife stage (see Table 4.2). This stage has also been referred to as high-growth

Table 4.1. What Leaders Can Do To Develop Trust During the Founding and Early Growth of an Organization

Establish a Baseline of Trust

- CEO and leadership team need to meet with the entire organization in person or by video and state the leadership's philosophy, mission, goals and expectations. Explicitly state that a culture of trust will be the highest priority. Ask all employees to help build such a culture. Outline specifically what organizational citizenship behavior is, explain accountability, the importance of working together for the common good, specify that rewards will be tangible and intangible, emphasize the need for communication horizontally and vertically. Leaders should outline expectations for their own behavior regarding keeping promises, commitments, doing what they say they will do, and consistency.
- All of these issues cannot be addressed at a single meeting. Indeed, there should be frequent organizational meetings, not all planned by management, to discuss and explain the above issues.
- It is important to convey to the organizational members that problems should not consume agendas. Problem-solving should occur at the earliest time and at the point of the problem. Preventing problems by clear, frequent, and timely communication enables the organization to focus on positive agendas.
- A strong support and reward system must be put in place for members. They must have clear channels for input for ideas and grievances. Participation in the life of the organization is essential.
- CEO and leadership team must be visible, people-centered, offensive (as opposed to defensive), responsive, enthusiastic, and practice trust.

Establish Processes for Maintaining Trust

- Trust cultivation is an ongoing, daily effort. It is the responsibility of everyone in the organization, but must be modeled by the leaders and managers.
- For trust to be maintained, those who are trustworthy need to be rewarded and those who are not need to be held accountable.
- The biggest factors in maintaining trust are communication and follow through. Members may understand that they have a voice, but who hears them and what happens next?
- A work climate that permits learning by mistakes and tolerates occasional failure is essential to trust.
- At all levels of the organization, members must be given the emotional safety to be themselves.

(Smith et al., 1985), Prime (Adizes, 1979), and growth through delegation and coordination (Greiner, 1972). When the organization has reached this stage of development, the strength of its culture and level of trust is well-developed, but trust is not the only factor determining whether an organization survives to midlife. Low trust organizations can also be productive and responsive to change, but they will not be as *effective* as high-trusting organizations. If an organization has maintained stable leadership and low turnover in personnel, new members can be socialized into a strong organization with minimal disruption in trust. The culture of an organization is continually undergoing some learning and change. This does not disrupt trust in the organization as long as the core values, goals and mission do not change. Organizational culture provides a stabilizing effect for its members. As long as trust is practiced, the priority of organizational members will be to remain loyal, productive and participative (Schein, 1981). Not all organizations survive to middle age, and those that do have experienced problems, crises, and sometimes revolutions. The organization at midlife is concerned with results, but as Adizes (1979) points out, staying in Prime is not assured.[3]

Table 4.2. What Leaders Can Do To Maintain Trust During the Midlife of an Organization

Maintaining Trust in an Environment of Change

- An organization that has reached some of its goals and objectives, is growing, meeting needs, establishing credibility for its products, etc. could be said to be at midlife. Midlife can be a time of many challenges and pressures, some at cross purposes. If an organization focuses too much on its successes, or on expansion, or other issues, it is easy to neglect the maintenance of trust.
- As new members come on board, they need to be oriented and mentored to "fit" into the culture.
- As organizations grow they need to change roles and responsibilities, adjust boundaries; all employees need to have clear and frequent communication about changes and their rationale if appropriate.
- Members need to be asked for ideas, suggestions; as citizens of the organization they need to be involved in its evolution.
- During periods of change, growth and re-structuring, it is especially important that the organization's mission, goals, and basic values do not change. This will undermine trust. Members need to be especially supported and reassured during transition periods.
- Promises and commitments made earlier must be kept; change or its consequences is not an excuse for leaders to become flexible about trust.

Renewal and Strengthening of Organizational Values

- Organizations that have shown success are good candidates for takeovers. Fears, apprehensions about takeovers among members erode trust and decrease productivity.
- Leaders should deal directly with rumors or gossip about mergers, downsizing, buy-outs.
- Members need to be reminded about the purpose of the organization, told that they are the reason for its success. Ask members how success can be expanded and failures turned into learning for success.
- The basic values of the organization need to be reaffirmed. New values can be added, but "old" values should not be dropped—they might be the very values that many members hold dearly.
- Members should be asked how the organization can be improved.
- Members must be rewarded and publically acknowledged for good behavior, ideas, etc.

With time, leadership changes and aspirations also change. Smith and his colleagues (1985) conducted a field study and a simulation to determine how top level management priorities changed at different stages of an organization's life-cycle. As organizations matured, top-level managers became less concerned with coordination, integration, and synergy and focused more on their subordinates' commitment, morale, and opinions when they made decisions than they did at early stages. This also raises the possibility that trust can be taken for granted at midlife, especially if it has been successfully established as part of the culture. Trust is fragile. A single violation can erode or destroy it. Therefore, an organization has to work at maintaining trust as it ages.

The transition to midlife is complicated by cultural issues because succession problems force cultural assumptions to be openly addressed (Schein 1992). Core aspects of culture are embedded and usually do not change with new leadership unless there is a take-over or merger. Trust is not a core aspect of culture and is not transportable or inherited. While the effects of a trusting predecessor do not carry over to a new leader, the effects of a distrusting predecessor confront a new leader with an immediate challenge.

One of the time-consuming, but necessary tasks of leaders and managers is to manage trust as an organization changes. While a leaders' job is to maintain a high trust culture throughout the organization, the level of trust in units within the organization will differ. This is expected as personnel and managers change at the unit level. From time to time, one or more units may become dysynchronous from other units in the organization. Leadership's job is to correct dysynchrony before it spreads to the total organization. Ouchi (1980) notes that although an organization (or a part thereof) may fail to build (or maintain) trust, it may continue to exist and remain productive by relying on the close monitoring of performance. When building trust in the early stages of an organization, it is important for leaders to attain as much homogeneity of trust as possible. When maintaining trust as an organization ages, it is important that leaders monitor the synchrony of trust between and among units within the organization to prevent seeds of distrust from spreading throughout the organization.

The midlife stage of an organization often is a paradox of stability and change. On the one hand, organizations that have survived to midlife usually have attained a high degree of efficiency, productivity, cohesion, and recognition. They want to continue doing what has led to their success, and do it even better and longer. Yet, the natural forces of change from within and without the organization will not permit it to sail smoothly for long. Especially in the current world, forces of change occur fast, frequently, and often unexpectedly. In the past ten years, there have been over 23,000 registered acquisitions in the U.S. (Deetz et al., 2000). Mergers are common, but do not have good track records. It is estimated that 90 percent of mergers fall below expectations (Bruhn, 1998, 2001d). Downsizing, reengineering and restructuring also are used commonly to improve organizational efficiency through organizational change. The organizational culture, level of trust, type of leadership, and stage of lifecycle all are factors that profoundly affect the outcome of organizational change strategies (Appelbaum et al., 1999). Kotter (1995) reported the results of a decade-long study of more than 100 companies that have engaged in significant organizational transformation. The change programs Kotter studied included the implementation of total quality management, reengineering, rightsizing, restructuring, organization-wide cultural change, and corporate turnarounds. He concluded that while a few of these corporate change efforts have been successful, a few have been complete failures, and the majority fall in between, toward the lower end of the scale.

A low level of trust appears to be common in most organizations in the U.S. at the beginning of the 21st century (Appelbaum et al., 1999). Yet, some organizations succeed in managing and directing change. An organization that has a strong supportive culture, a high level of trust, and strong leadership committed to a clear vision and mission is likely to maintain viability over the long term (Appelbaum et al., 1999). No single program or set of practices can assure that an organization will cope well with all changes. It is evident that successful organizations do a lot of little things a little better than most (Kotter, 1988).

Maturity and Decline

A mature organization is not mature because it has successfully attained a certain age, size, or reputation (Schein, 1992). A mature organization is one that has met its long-term goals and objectives and is faced with several options: (1) revitalize and restructure with new goals and objectives and seek new opportunities and challenges. This could be done by bringing in new members, through partnerships or coalitions with other organizations; (2) become a candidate for a buy-out, takeover, or merger; (3) spin off a part of the organization for a totally new venture; or (4) continue with minimal responsiveness to change and opportunities until the decision is made to cease existence. A mature organization is a survivor, and usually healthy, although a few unhealthy organizations reach maturity (see Table 4.3).

A mature organization has coped successfully with change, crises, and transitions over a period of time. One has the image of a small family business or a neighborhood grocery or gas station, that has survived multiple generations of leadership, as a prototype of mature organizations. It is tempting in today's world to think of organizations that have achieved great financial success rapidly as mature organizations. However, measures of maturity have more to do with the intangible, but observable, aspects of organizational life. Maturity involves experience in managing change, anticipating problems, creating and maintaining a healthy culture for members, and producing quality output that meets the expectations of clients, users or customers.

Table 4.3. What Leaders Can Do To Prevent Distrust During the Maturity and Decline of an Organization

Trust Is Taken For Granted

- One of the problems with organizations that have grown large, complex, and successful is that many of the more personal aspects of the organization become bureaucratized. Trust becomes synonymous with the organization's name even though it and the leaders have changed. Often, long-term organizational members expect the same behavior they encountered when they joined. When they encounter a changed organization, they may become cynical, distrustful, angry and/or depressed. Indeed, new leaders do not have the benefit of the zeal, energy, and enthusiasm the founders did, but they may still buy into the basic values. One of the key activities of the leaders in a mature organization is to keep it vital, forward-looking, and affirm new and old values. New leaders will need to earn trust.
- Leaders' visibility, frequent communication, honoring of promises and commitments, consistent behavior, and involving members to participate in the life of the organization help to prevent distrust.
- In many respects the same activities that were suggested for the birth and early development of the organization are appropriate here.
- Concerns about future options should be discussed openly and directly.

Trust May Need To Be Established Anew

- Since mature organizations have options that involve revitalization, spin-off, merger, buy-out, or death, trust is likely to have to be developed anew whatever the choice. It is also likely that given these options, many members of the organization may leave, including leaders and managers, hence trust will have to be developed by new founders.
- Organizations can always go into decline; decline is not limited to the end of the lifecycle. However, the erosion of trust is often one of the reasons organizations decline at any stage. While we tend to think of organizations that decline and die as those that cannot sustain their financial viability or quality products, the bottom line is the inability to attract and retain members who are loyal and trustful. This, in turn, often is connected to the lack of a strong mission, goals, and basic values. When members of an organization view their participation only as a way to get a paycheck, it is unlikely the organization will reach the later stages of the lifecycle.

Some of the greatest assets of mature organizations are also problematic at this stage of the lifecycle. Members of mature organizations usually have a strong commitment to the organization, substantial longevity, and a high degree of loyalty and trust, but they often are resistant to change. Many members of mature organizations have personal obligations and commitments with their employers that define their working relationship. For these organizational members to buy into change they would need to change their personal relationships. This is why radical efforts at organizational reengineering have success rates ranging from 50 percent to 20 percent (Strebel, 1996). Change in mature organizations is particularly problematic because the uncertainties surrounding change generate feelings of loss and perceived insecurity about the future among many long-term, loyal, and trustful members (Backer & Porterfield, 1998). Therefore, it is not unusual to see strong resistance to change at this lifecycle stage (Kets de Vries & Balazs, 1999).

There is very little in the published literature about organizational death. There are discussions about organizational decline and the regeneration or rebirth of organizations. Morgan (1997) explained that we understand organizations in terms of a quest for immortality. Organizations often survive for generations and as we identify with them, we find meaning and longevity ourselves. We invest ourselves in organizations, especially work, therefore, it is not surprising that organizational survival has personal meaning for us.

Schein (1992) pointed out that little is known about the process of reorganization and rebirth in organizations. Most organizations, like committees, don't die, they outlive their usefulness; that is, their cultures or rationales for existence are no longer in tune with the constituencies they propose to serve. Sometimes. organizations become so out-of-touch with their external environment that they become dysfunctional, ineffective, and non-productive. In this sense, they decline and die. Some organizations die when their original culture is transformed through a merger, acquisition or buy-out. They become "born again" in a new culture; remnants of the old culture usually disappear as personnel changes. Often, as "old" organizations disappear, former members and clients lament the loss of a trusting enterprise.

Individuals and organizations are social organisms and are dependent upon other individuals and organizations for survival, neither are self-sufficient. Trust or distrust is formed during the founding, entrepreneurial or infancy stages of individuals and organizations. Trust is essential to the healthy functioning of both; trust can be lost and attempts to regain it are equally challenging for individuals and organizations. Finally, individuals and organizations must meet their needs in order to survive and flourish. Therefore, individuals and organizations need others (networks) to help them accomplish their lifecycle tasks. Individuals marry or join organizations; organizations merge or expand. While organizations do not have a biological component to their lifecycle, their progression is influenced by the behavior of the members who are moving through their own individual lifecycles.

Figure 4.1 illustrates comparisons of conceptual parallels between the lifecycle stages of individuals and organizations.

The key differences between the lifecycles of individuals and organizations are: (1) there are biological, psychological and social markers for the healthy development of individuals, while there are expectations for the progressive next steps for organizations; (2) there are time frames that coincide with the markers for development for individuals, however, while organizations may develop at different speeds, there are only expectations of how long is long enough in each stage; (3) individuals have a life expectancy and ultimately die, organization's don't always die; (4) the aspects of the lifecycle stages of individuals are incremental and

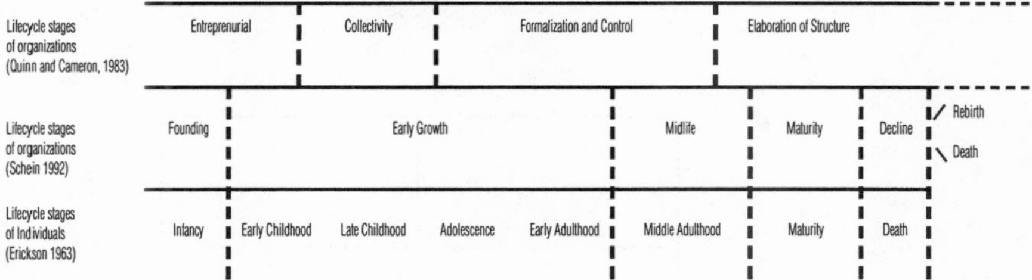

Figure 4.1. Comparisons of Conceptual Parallels Between the Lifecycle Stages of Individuals and Organizations.

synergistic while organizations (since they are not dependent on physical phenomena) can perform many different activities without the need to complete specific steps or stages, and synergy can be planned and implemented as needed; (5) an individual's lifecycle is unique and focused on one person, while in an organization the leader must meld the similarities and commonalities of many people (each of whom has a unique lifecycle) to create a life for the organization.

RELATIONSHIPS BETWEEN TRUST, ORGANIZATIONAL CULTURE, AND LEADERSHIP BEHAVIOR

One of the major factors determining the degree of ease or difficulty of an organization's ability to continue to trust or distrust during its lifecycle are the trusting or non-trusting orientations of its leaders. Figure 4.2 depicts four general paths that result from the interaction of an organization's culture with its leader. Cell A shows a "good match" between an organization's and its leader's trust orientation. This is an ideal fit. While such a fit has its ups and downs, both the leader and the culture (and its members) trust each other. Cell B shows a distrusting leader taking the reins of a culture that is trusting. It is likely the leader will pursue a management style that is protective, cautious and controlling. It also is likely that the leader will be careful about making cultural changes that take away authority from members or restrict their input after they are used to functioning in an environment of trust. The leader may prove to be too great a mismatch to survive in a culture's that is more trusting than he is. Cell C is when a trusting leader inherits a culture that distrusts. This organization's members are likely to welcome openness and trust, yet the culture has not experienced trust and members will be wary of the leader's actions. A trusting leader will have limited success in this organization. Cell D is when a distrusting leader heads a distrusting culture. This is likely to be a successful match unless either the leader or members want the organization to become more trusting. This negative match,

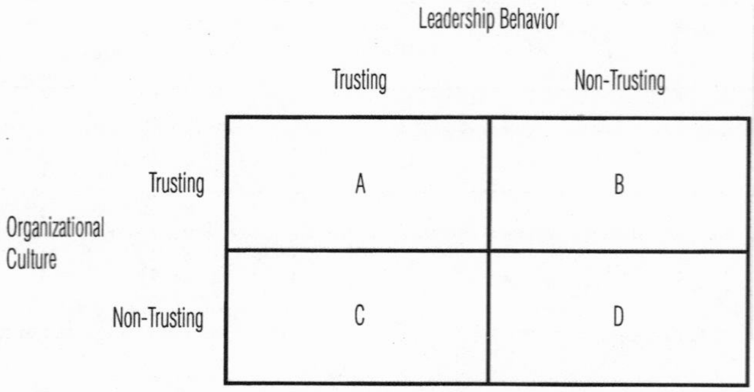

		Leadership Behavior	
		Trusting	Non-Trusting
Organizational Culture	Trusting	A	B
	Non-Trusting	C	D

Figure 4.2. Relationships Between Trust, Organizational Culture, and Leadership Behavior.

similar to the positive match in Cell A, satisfies the needs of both the leader and the culture.

Organizations have a lifecycle of trust that relates to their lifecycle of growth and development. Trust, as well as the overall growth and progression of the organization, will be enhanced or repelled by the personal and managerial beliefs and style of its leader. The longer the duration of a trustful leader, the more likely it is that the organization and its members will support a trusting culture. On the other hand, the longer the tenure of a distrusting leader, the more likely the organization and its members will support a distrusting culture.

CHARACTERISTICS OF A TRUSTFUL ORGANIZATION

Respect for Persons

The comedian, Rodney Dangerfield, has been successful in his routines, which center around the theme "I don't get no respect." There is a pathetic aspect to his stories and vignettes which portray situations in which he is taken for granted or overlooked; he is not appreciated. The psychologist, William James, said that the deepest principle of human nature is to be appreciated[4]. Persons must be appreciated and respected before they can be trusted. Ouchi (1981) describes the substance of the Z organization "... relationships between people tend to be informed and to emphasize that whole people deal with one another ... this wholistic orientation ... inevitably maintains a strong egalitarian atmosphere that is a feature of all Type Z organizations ... if people deal with one another in segmented ways ... rather than as one human being to another, then these dehumanized relationships easily become authoritarian."[5] In other words, the Z organization respects people. Rosen and Berger (1991) pointed out that there is a lot of lip service given to respect in organizations, but in practice, people spend more time protecting their turf than forming productive partnerships or promoting good ideas. Organizational members attend to their own needs first. When things do not go their way, members are quick to seek other job opportunities. Rosen and Berger (1991) stated that respect is the first step in building a trusting organization and must be made explicit through the practice of: (1) trust; (2) appreciation; (3) communication; and (4) ethics.

Adherence to Explicit Values

A trusting organization is characterized by explicit values and consistent adherence to them. An organization's set of values make up its culture. Values show how a culture is unique, what it stands for, what its members believe in, and why it exists. The values that the organizational leadership stand by and reward need to be communicated to organizational members continually. For example, if collaboration and teamwork are to be highly valued, the organizational environment must be one that balances empowerment with collaboration. Members must be encouraged to think for themselves, but to work with one another. Team members must be involved in maintaining loyalty to the team and to their manager (Hirschhorn, 1991). The value of the team must continually be reinforced, and teams, rather than individuals, rewarded. If management rewards individuals rather than teams, members will ask "why", and revert to values that serve themselves. When values are explicit, everyone inside and outside the organization knows what the organization stands for and how they relate to it. When there is consistency in adhering to values over time, people inside and outside of the organization believe that its values are real in practice. The organization becomes credible, dependable, predictable, and therefore, trustworthy.

A People-Centered Leadership Team

A third characteristic of a trusting organization is a leadership team that practices respect for persons and the values of the organization. The leaders and managers of the organization must work as a team. The CEO's job is to make sure that there is evenhandedness and fairness throughout the organization. In other words, the CEO maintains balance within the organization while facilitating its growth and development. While profits and products might be outcomes for the organization, money is not a good motivator for members. Studies have shown that what employees miss is appreciation. People need to feel valued for their talents and what they contribute to the organization.[6] Organizational members at all levels must practice personal recognition with intangible and tangible rewards tied to performance. Trust, self-esteem, and loyalty are the rewards for the organization.

Members Actively Participate in Organizational Life

A fourth characteristic of a trusting organization is its members' participation in the life of the organization. Organizational members can be respected, feel valued and rewarded, yet not trusted if they are passive observers to what is happening to them and their environment. Rosen and Berger (1991) state that employees in an organization have a right and a responsibility to contribute, to stay informed, and to share in the benefits of their participation. Real participation makes people feel that they are in control and in charge of their destiny. Ownership is the consequence of participation. Ownership arises when members see that their efforts can make a difference and that they are part of the process.

The degree of participation and ownership among members of an organization defines their levels of commitment to a job. When the feeling of ownership is high, everything matters; when ownership is low, nothing much matters (Rosen & Berger, 1991). The form and extent of member participation will vary with the type of organization. De Pree (1989) points out that at Herman Miller Co., employee stock ownership ensures that, as owners, everyone is accountable for personal performance and is committed to do everything to grow, both as employees and as owners. De Pree believes that participation has more to do with trust than with organizational structure. Trust cannot be built into a contractual relationship but must be developed and fostered by the leader of the organization, using participatory processes (Carnevale & Wechsler, 1991).

The survival of nonprofit organizations depends on public trust. The recent ouster of the CEO of the United Way of America and the mishandling of funds led to a period of substantially decreased giving to the annual campaign. There was an obvious gap between participation and ownership at the national office and local communities. Nonprofit organizations need to maximize participation from the increasingly diverse make-up of communities if an organization is to survive and flourish.

Public institutions are broadening their bases of participation. The health care industry is one example. The histories of most health care organizations have been marked by turf and boundary conflicts. Physicians and managed care organizations are frequently at odds, with patients in the middle having minimal say in their care plans.

Universities pride themselves in practicing participation. Yet, participation is carefully controlled. For example, participation in strategic planning at all levels of the organization is usually mandatory, yet there is little ownership of the plan by all levels of the organization, hence little commitment to the plan.

Zajac and Bruhn (1999) described how participation differs in different types of organizations and offer guidelines for participating. Participation begins with a respect for the opinions of others and a belief that growth and strength can result from an organizational climate that cultivates a diversity of ideas and opinions. Several guidelines are offered for effective participation:

- respect and encourage existing channels of constructive communication
- offer opinions and solutions, not simply criticisms and vague suggestions
- be willing to invest personal effort and to be accountable for your participation
- be willing to work honestly with others and to assume responsibility for tasks
- support fundamental organizational goals and mission
- be willing to change your own attitudes and behavior
- trust and respect the *process* of participation

Participation, no matter what guidelines are employed, is not always a smooth and productive process. Participation can go sour. The process of participation must continue throughout the organization's lifecycle. When member participation stops, trust is sacrificed.

Uniform and Consistent Accountability

A fifth characteristic of a trusting organization is uniform and consistent accountability. There probably is no single managerial action that will destroy trust in an organization faster than treating members of the organization differently with respect to accountability. The synonym for accountability is responsibility. When a trusting organization has been established, members believe they have a dual responsibility, one to their specific job and one to the organization as a whole. When members do not trust the organization, their immediate supervisors, or their coworkers, they feel responsible only for their narrow turf or territory. One symptom of a distrusting organization is members who say, "It's not my fault," "that's not my job," or "who cares?"

Sometimes leaders and managers talk "double speak" about accountability, members become confused about what's expected of them, and begin to distrust what leaders say. For example, leaders of an organization may say that they value teams, but feel that group decisions take too long and may be inconclusive; therefore they seek the team manager's opinion without the benefit of group input. Team members begin to doubt the value of their opinions and, perhaps, become tentative about the team, engaging in self-protecting behavior.

Perhaps the most extreme violation of accountability in an organization is the encouragement of organizational moles by a leader or manager (Bruhn & Chesney, 1995). Moles flourish in distrustful organizations. Organizations whose leaders are paranoid, controlling, distrustful, and insecure are likely to be receptive to information from moles. Information from moles is welcomed and encouraged by leaders who see enemies everywhere. A controlling leader, on the other hand, seeks information to keep members in check. Moles feel free to cross boundaries and violate organizational norms because they have the protection of the leadership. Mole behavior is well known throughout all levels of organizations and creates an atmosphere of suspicion and tentativeness in all aspects of an organization's daily operations.

Accountability is directly linked to boundaries and boundary management. Boundaries determine where responsibilities begin and end. Organizations with too rigid boundaries discourage innovation and autonomy. Organizations with too fluid boundaries discourage taking responsibility and following through (Hirschhorn, 1988).

Members of an organization need to know that the leaders of the organization will ensure that accountability applies uniformly to all members and that there is consistency over time. Accountability is currently an "in" word. Leaders and managers all espouse accountability, especially during tough economic times. If members of an organization are promoted because of their ethnicity or gender, it is certain that the meaning of accountability and trustworthiness will be diminished in the eyes of organizational members who were denied promotion or who are working towards it. Accountability is more than language, it must be packaged with trustworthy decision-making by leaders and managers (Elsbach & Elofson, 2000).

Citizenship and Win-Win Behavior

The sixth characteristic of a trusting organization is citizenship and win-win behavior. In a trusting organization, every member has rights and responsibilities. There is no need to defend or fight for one's rights. Rights are explicit and protected. When members are responsible citizens, they do not have to worry about their rights. Everyone at every level of the organization has equal rights, even though their responsibilities differ. To be the recipient of rights, one must be a responsible person. A win-win environment is created when members of an organization accept the consequences for their successes and failures. Blaming is replaced by learning how to correct and improve. Promoting organizational citizens promotes organizational loyalty and trust. There should be explicit tangible and intangible rewards for good citizenship. Rewards need not be in the form of a check or a plaque; public recognition of members who are good citizens at all levels of an organization is an award that is reachable by everyone.

One organization started a monthly "Good Idea Contest" whereby anyone connected with the organization could submit an idea of how to improve its effectiveness, or make it more cost effective. Winners were selected by a small committee, representing management, staff and employees, which evaluated the brief proposals anonymously. Each winner received a $50 savings bond, a write-up in the organization's newsletter, and saw their idea implemented. There could be more than one winner each month, but over a period of a year, 12 members of the organization were rewarded for 12 new ideas. The contest was kept alive by the fact that winning ideas were actually implemented and everyone could have input into improving the organization. The contest dispelled the idea that only management has good ideas and showed that good things sometimes happen when employees express an opinion, thus everyone in the organization was encouraged to make it better.

Risk-taking to Become Better

For many years we have heard about learning organizations, leading edge organizations that have a special capacity to learn, adapt, and change. Learning organizations are supposed to continuously analyze and monitor how they are doing with the aim of making them better. The organization creates, captures and moves knowledge easily and quickly so that members can use it. Members are encouraged to think in new ways (Gephart et al., 1996). In essence, an organization attempts to shape itself as it evolves, recycles, and benefits from real-life experiences. A learning organization allows members to take risks and, instead of a single prescription for success, learning organizations use many. There are many arguments about the beneficial nature of organizational learning. Argyris and Schön (1996) suggested that organizational learning is not only beneficial, but meaningful. Popper and Lipshitz (2000) state that the productiveness of organizational learning depends on the organizational culture.

A trusting organization is likely to benefit from organizational learning as trust enables members to take risks in a protected environment. Nonetheless, since learning and change ultimately take place at the individual level, individual members of the organization must be able to cope with criticism and be willing to make personal changes. A firm commitment to individual responsibility and accountability also is needed. The method or processes by which the organization conducts input and feedback are key to organizational learning. Facilitators and interviewers must be skilled and the issues of confidentiality respected while, at the same time, openness is maintained, sharing of information is encouraged, and feedback is provided to others. A trusting/learning organization's leaders must be willing to participate in the process, not just to be the recipients of reports. Finally, the rationale, processes, and use of organizational learning should be unique to the organization.

Tolerance of the Out-of-Equilibrium Organization

An eighth characteristic of a trusting organization is that it has leaders who are able to accept the fact that stability (equilibrium or homeostasis) is not equated with excellence (Stacey, 1992). Stacey suggests that instability is not always bad, indeed, instability goes hand in hand with growth and development. While it is often common lore that leaders need to maintain stability in their organizations in order to reach goals, organizations, like people, are never totally stable, but are always in motion as are the people who lead them and work in them. Stacey points out, there always is a blend of order and disorder in organizations. Therefore, the degree of trust in an organization is variable, depending on what is occurring in the organization at any specific time. The key is to manage the blend of stability and instability while maintaining a trustful culture. The culture must be resilient. Managing organizational change is not just technical skill, experience, and trust, nor, is it the sole responsibility of the leader. The organization has to have "hardy" members who have a clear sense of their own and the organization's goals, values and capabilities, are optimistic, task-oriented, and problem-focused, have a broad network of social support, and are actively engaged in shaping their environment (Klarreich, 1998).

Leaders in organizations face a choice; they can initiate change (take risks) knowing that it will be accompanied by some degree of conflict and disorder and unknown outcomes, even with planning, or they can initiate those changes they believe they can control, which usually are small and of short term. The first option is more dangerous because it could result in failure. The second option is least risky and likely to result in small successes. Risk-taking and trust go hand in hand. When there is little or no trust, a bold move, if it is unsuccessful, could cause a leader's demise. On the other hand, in a culture that trusts, leaders and members are permitted to fail.

Trusting Leaders Carry Few Keys

A ninth characteristic of a trusting organization is that the leader of such an organization has few keys. Dauten[7] related how a business leader first learned to delegate. The leader said he was trying to solve a complicated systems problem when an employee walked in complaining that he'd just lost a quarter in the Coke machine. "Why are you telling ME?" he asked. "Because you've got the keys to the Coke machine!" the employee answered. Dauten pointed out that wise bosses have very small key rings. They understand that leaders don't unlock potential, rather they allow people to unlock the best in themselves.

Empowerment can only work when an entire organization buys into it—when formal systems and the informal culture support it (Covey, 1999). Managers need to be rewarded for delegating decisions and developing people. Otherwise, the degree of empowerment will vary according to the practices of individual managers. The most important aspect of empowerment is effective delegation, and that depends on a trusting relationship between a manager and his subordinate.

Subordinates are the persons who should have the keys so that leaders can spend time with the real gorillas in their organization (Covey, 1999; Oncken & Wass, 1974).

Leaders who cannot let go often are seen as having a positive management style. Such leaders often receive accolades for their intense commitment to and involvement in every aspect of the organization (i.e., hands-on managers). They usually have intense loyalty to the organization. These leaders cannot delegate because their personal need for success requires that they maintain a high degree of control. They become supermanagers rather than leaders (Bruhn, 1993).

Collective Pride, Loyalty and Spirit

Maslow (1998) observed that one indicator of the degree of health (and trust) of an organization is the degree of grumbling among its members. No organization is free of grumblers, but grumbling that is extensive and of the type that indicates that members' basic needs are not being met is significant. He also indicated that humor is an indicator of healthiness. Organizations that are so stiff and formal that they can't act human are unlikely to tolerate mistakes and missteps of members. It is unlikely that people in grumbling, humorless organizations trust each other.

Maslow also notes that enlightened management and humanitarian supervision is a form of patriotism in which every member is transformed into a partner rather than an employee. This creates pride and loyalty among organizational members. The best managers seem to be psychologically healthier than poor managers. The best managers increase the health of the workers they manage. The healthier the members are to start with, the more they profit psychologically from enlightened management, and the healthier they become. Maslow believed there was a reciprocal relationship between psychological health and Douglas McGregor's Theory Y style of management.[8]

Pride, loyalty, and spirit (or morale) are outcomes of a trusting organization. These feelings usually result in high productivity, low personnel turnover, low absenteeism, few grievances and conflicts, and an enthusiasm for the organization conveyed to people outside of it. Bolman and Deal (1995) point out that most leaders and managers concentrate on the rational side of the organization, neglecting its spirit. Yet, it is the spirit of members that keep organizations energetic, resilient, and willing to go the extra mile. Leaders and managers look almost exclusively at "hard" measures to explain success or failure. Pride, loyalty, and spirit are indirect measures of trust that are usually ignored, dismissed, or cause smiles among managers.

Table 4.4 summarizes the characteristics of a trusting organization. This is not a definitive list but includes some of the most critical elements necessary to

Table 4.4. Characteristics of a Trusting Organization

- Respect for persons
- Adherence to explicit values
- A leadership team that is people-centered
- Members actively participate in the life of the organization
- Uniform and consistent accountability
- Citizenship and win-win behavior
- Risk-taking to become better
- Tolerance of the out-of-equilibrium organization
- Trusting leaders have few keys
- Collective pride, loyalty and spirit

create and maintain trust along an organization's lifecycle. The characteristics are attributes of the entire environment and not exclusively the responsibility of leaders, managers, or members, but of all.

The structure and lifecycles of most organizations, as well as the way they conduct business and how members communicate with each other, are profoundly influenced by technology. In addition, the world has enabled organizations to expand cross-culturally presenting new challenges in how to accommodate members with different beliefs and values.

Virtual organizations have virtual lifecycles as well as virtual members who establish virtual trust. Trust will always be a part of organizations, even virtual ones, as there needs to be a "glue" that bonds members together so that they "stick" with an organization. Trust is necessary to start a new organization and, if it is a business or professional organization, trust is necessary to attract members and clients.

Perhaps one of the biggest challenges facing virtual organizations is how to form virtual communities cross-culturally and how to do so without excluding people who do not have access to technology. Virtual organizations have the possibility of becoming elitist if they are restricted to skillful users of technology. It will be interesting to see if loyalty and commitment to a virtual organization are strong enough to retain members over the long term without a sense of place and face-to-face interaction to personalize loyalty and commitment.

VIRTUAL TRUST

Estimates from early 1996 are that 60 million people in 160 countries were using the Internet. In a separate estimate, 6 months later, it was found that 65 million Americans were online (Locke, 1998). Locke has pointed out that as humans we retain a basic drive to connect with others but inhabit a technostructure that provides diminishing opportunities to do so.[9] E-mail is devoid of information about who we are. We cannot guess whether the people we are dealing with are legitimate. There is no way to discern truth from lies.

E-mail helps users become entrenched in an individualistic fortress. It prevents people from seeing each other. A British study of over 1,000 office workers found that 46% of workers said e-mail decreased their face-to-face interactions and 36% said they used e-mail to avoid face-to-face interactions.[10] According to Locke, e-mailers do not expect to meet in the future, and may not actually care to. Without identities, personal reputation cannot operate. "With no access to social feedback and control mechanisms, there will be nothing to keep misunderstanding, incivility, and dishonesty from creeping into our daily lives" (Locke, 1998, p. 167).

Managers of Trust

People are more willing to take risks when a significant amount of trust has been established. The problem with electronic mail is that most people are accustomed to building trust through personal contact, and e-mail deprives users of the psychological benefit of face-to-face encounters. Most people are cautious in their e-mail correspondence, fearing that they might be held more accountable for comments made over a computer than in person (Sanders, 1991). So Internet entrepreneurs are computerizing trust. Using equations and databases, they are creating systems known as "reputation managers." These repositories will help users decide whom to do business with and whose recommendations they ought to accept (Weber, 2000). One of the most sophisticated examples of a reputation manager is Epinions.com. The site provides reviews of, for example, arts and entertainment, televisions, cars, electronics, restaurants, sports, hotels, and personal finance. As you read the reviews you tell the site which ones are helpful and which fellow members you trust. When you return for more review, Epinions prioritizes your ratings on the basis of who has earned a good reputation with you.

Consumers make Internet buying decisions on the basis of trust. Urban and his associates (2000) indicate that the first step in trust-based marketing is to build trust in the Internet and specific web site, then trust in the information displayed, and finally in fulfilling the delivery and in service. Among the ways to establish website trust is to create customer communities that provide feedback to reduce the customer's perception of risk. For example, eBay posts the number of positive and negative evaluations of each person or store that offers an item at auction and allows bidders to contact past customers by e-mail. They also point out the limitations of this approach to trust-building. Urban and his colleagues (2000) point out that the most important element of trust is fulfillment; trust is earned by meeting expectations. They state … trust will soon become the currency of the Internet ... customers will pay a premium price to the companies they trust" (p. 48).

Virtual Organizations and Virtual Teams

Handy (1994) points out that organizations now need to be global and local at the same time, to be small in some ways and big in others, to be centralized some of the time and decentralized most of it. Organizations expect members to be more autonomous yet more of a team, have less face-to-face contact with each other and more by video, e-mail and voice mail, and to work on projects in clusters and with different groups in the same organization. This is what some have called the "virtual organization."

The virtual organization will not be a place to go to, but rather an activity to be accomplished via video, e-mail, or voice mail. We will be working with people we may not see and whom we do not know as persons. Trust is difficult enough to establish with people we know and see every day; it will be even more of a challenge to trust people we can't see, don't know, and may never meet. Managers will need to manage workers without face-to-face meetings. Organizations will need to create a sense of belonging to a community rather than a sense of belonging to a place (Handy 1995). But, as Handy points out, there are principles that need to be followed for trust to work, even in virtual organizations. He lists several principles or rules of trust:

- trust is not blind (even large organizations need stable, small groups to help trust take root)
- trust needs boundaries (trust is not unlimited)
- trust demands learning (organizations need to be flexible to keep abreast of change)
- trust is tough (persons who cannot be trusted should be dismissed)
- trust needs bonding (small units need to have the same goals as the total organization)
- trust needs touch (high tech needs to be balanced with high touch to build high trust)

In order for these rules or principles to work, all members of the virtual organization need to share responsibility for them. In one sense, it might be easier for virtual organizations to enforce the rules or principles of trust and privacy. On the other hand, information in virtual organizations cannot be checked against directly observed behavior and is largely information the members choose to share, which may vary in its accuracy. Leadership in virtual organizations is as important as it is in any other type of organization, but in the virtual organization there needs to be an even greater sharing of responsibility and accountability of members toward each other.

Virtual Teams

The increased need in self-direction and self-control in virtual organizations is exemplified in global virtual teams. A global virtual team is a boundaryless network organization form where a temporary team is assembled on an as-needed basis for the duration of a task and staffed by members from different countries. Coordination is accomplished through trust and shared communication. Trust is pivotal in preventing geographic distance from leading to psychological distance in a global team. Trust is even more essential in global virtual teams. The global virtual context renders forms of social control, such as direct supervision, inoperable. Other factors known to contribute to social control and coordination, such as geographical proximity, similarity in backgrounds, and experience, are often absent.

Jarvenpaa and her colleagues (1998) studied, in a virtual team setting, the effect of factors that have been identified as sources of trust in traditional face-to-face relationships. Seventy-five teams, consisting of four to six members (students) residing in different countries, interacted and worked together for eight weeks. The teams were charged with completing three tasks: two team-building exercises and a final project (a World Wide Web site) presenting information of interest to global information technology practitioners working in a global business setting. Students communicated solely through electronic means. The list processor archived mail messages and team members were sent an electronic survey to complete immediately following the second trust-building exercise. A second survey was sent to the team members the day following the completed final project.

The two week trust-building exercises were found to have a significant effect on the team members' perceptions of the other members' ability, integrity, and benevolence, but they did not have a direct effect on trust. Team trust was predicated more strongly by perceptions of other team members' integrity, and least strongly by the perceptions of their benevolence. Members' own propensity to trust had a significant effect on team trust. High-trust teams exhibited a high level of optimism and excitement, task orientation, rotating leadership, good time management, a clear sense of task goals, and high levels of individual initiative and accountability. The three high-trust teams also exhibited a form of "swift trust," that is, members acted as if trust was present from the start. Swift trust enabled members to take action, and this action helped to maintain trust and deal with uncertainty, ambiguity, and vulnerability while working on complex interdependent tasks with strangers in a situation of high time pressure (Jarvenpaa, et al.,

1998). Yet, swift trust appears to be fragile and temporal. In swift trust, unless one trusts quickly, one may never trust at all. In a second study, Jarvenpaa et al., (1999), found that only four out of 29 teams shifted to a high trust condition from a low trust condition. The first messages by the team appeared to set the tone for how the team interrelated. The adage, "You can never give a second first impression" seemed to apply to electronic impressions as well (Jarvenpaa, et al., 1999).

The results of these studies suggest that trust might be imported in global virtual teams, but it is more likely created by communication behavior established in the first message. Communication that rallies around a project and tasks appears to be necessary to maintain trust. Social communication that complements rather than substitutes for task communication may strengthen trust. Finally, initial behaviors such as members' verbalizing their commitment, excitement, and optimism and their own propensity to trust has an effect on establishing team trust.

SUMMARY

Organizations, whether open or closed, are systems of change. In closed organizations, change can be more carefully controlled; in open organizations change must be anticipated, planned for, directed, and managed, if the organization is to shape its growth and development. Organizations are living organisms and, as such, are continually adapting to their environment. Those organizations that are successful in satisfying the needs of their members and furthering their collective goals are more likely to be healthy and trusting organizations.

As living organisms, all organizations have lifecycles. Organizational lifecycles differ from those of humans because they do not have a biological dimension. Theorists and researchers of organizational behavior have different perspectives about the number of stages or phases organizations go through and what these stages or phases should be labelled, the amount of time organizations are expected to stay in each stage or phase, and the criteria that should be used to judge whether an organization has been successful in completing the various stages or phases. All scholars of organizations agree that organizations do have lifecycles, and that understanding which phase or stage an organization occupies at any one time is critical in understanding that organization's behavior. For example, all organizations have a birth, or founding. At this phase or stage the founders are concerned with building an organizational culture. In order for the founders to be effective they have to trust one another; how they make trust a part of the total culture of the organization will influence the health of the organization, and possibly, its survival.

In addition to the founding and early growth stage of organizations, Schein has suggested that organizations have a midlife, and finally a phase of maturity and decline. By midlife, organizations that have reached this stage are experiencing results. It is a stage of growth, an entrenchment of organizational values, stable leadership, and a high degree of efficiency, productivity, cohesion, and recognition. However, organizations at this stage are also prime targets for mergers, buyouts, and takeovers. Therefore, leaders of organizations during midlife have to steer a course which incorporates on-going change, but is futuristic and realistic. No single program or set of practices can assure that an organization will survive midlife well. It is evident that successful organizations do a lot of little things a little better than most. Midlife has the enticement of security and complacency with past success.

A mature organization is not mature because it has reached a certain age, size, or reputation. A mature organization has been successful in meeting its goals and objectives. Now it is faced with several options: (1) continue as it is; (2) revitalize itself; (3) become a takeover target for competitors; (4) become a new organization; or, (5) cease to exist. This latter option is often the case in family businesses where there is no family successor. Maturity is a difficult stage of the lifecycle; the major choice is whether to keep the organization viable and adapt to change, or whether to let it either take a new form or die.

Little is known about why or how organizations die. The most obvious reasons are an inability or unwillingness to change, failure to maintain a culture attractive to members, and various unresolvable problems. One major factor determining whether an organization will continue is its leadership. If an organization's culture is healthy and trusting, and the leader reinforces these values, the organization is likely to continue. On the other hand, if a leader of a mature organization wants to maintain stability in the face of change, is not innovative, creative, or trusting, it is not likely that that organization will have an extended lifecycle.

Trusting organizations have several characteristics which set them apart from other organizations. They: (1) adhere to explicit values; (2) have a people-centered leadership team; (3) have members who actively participate in the life of the organization; (4) have uniform and consistent accountability; (5) encourage citizenship and win-win behavior; (6) engage in risk-taking to become better; (7) tolerate the out-of-equilibrium organization; (8) have trusting leaders who carry few keys; (9) demonstrate respect for persons; and (10) display collective pride, loyalty and spirit. Leaders of trusting organizations are effective in maintaining these characteristics as their organizations mature and change.

Electronic technology is transforming many organizations to those where members have little or no face-to-face contact and need to establish "swift trust." Little is known about the lifecycles of electronic organizations, but they certainly begin with a founding phase in which founders have established sufficient trust to launch the organization. Internet entrepreneurs are computerizing trust by using "reputation managers" to help users to decide who to do business with and whose recommendations one ought to accept.

Virtual organizations are both global and local and create a sense of belonging to a community rather than a place. Although trust is difficult to establish between members we don't see or know, and may never meet, there is some evidence that trust can be established in global virtual teams whose members are assembled to accomplish specific tasks. High-trust teams act as if trust was present from the start and members exhibit a high level of optimism and excitement, task orientation, rotating leadership, good time management, a clear sense of task goals, and high levels of individual initiative and accountability. Virtual team trust appears to be created in the first electronic message by members' verbalizing their commitment, excitement and optimism and their own propensity to trust. We do not have information, as yet, on the lifecycles of virtual organizations and the long-term maintenance of trust in these organizations.

Chapter 5

How Trust and Distrust Work in Organizations

"To try to do everything possible to create trust is a mistake. You need to be authentic and fair. You cannot change anyone but yourself."[1]

INTRODUCTION

When a person meets a neighbor's new dog, it is customary to bend down and extend an open hand so the dog can smell it, become familiar with, and accept that person. When people are introduced, a handshake is an expected courtesy, and the nature of the handshake can impart a lot about the personalities of the two parties and how interested they are in meeting. Similarly, when an organization is telephoned the response of the person who answers the phone can tell a lot about the spirit and level of morale in the organization. A conversation with a CEO's administrative assistant can give a caller insights into the management style of the CEO and the trustfulness of the organization, e.g., whether the assistant has to get approval from the CEO before making appointments. Trust or distrust have a way of saturating organizations. As one CEO told the author, "culture drives trust. All members of an organization, including staff, collaborate in a trusting organization—one leads the other. It starts with culture and values."[2]

Building a Culture of Trust

I asked some CEO's and former CEO's what they considered to be the major factors in building trust in their organizations. All of the CEO's mentioned one or more of four factors. Table 5.1 presents these in order of the frequency in which they were mentioned. An environment of openness and sharing was the most

Table 5.1. Building Blocks of Organizational Trust

Dialogue of openness and sharing
- honesty with self and others (sharing humanness)
- no hidden agendas
- no need to worry that what you say will be used against you
- people feel valued for their contribution
- people feel safe to express honest opinions
- people do not withhold information for power
- basic belief that all people have good potential
- willingness to listen
- willingness to be vulnerable

Consistency in behavior
- say it and do it
- do the right thing
- consistency in how decisions are made
- keep promises and commitments

Everyone committed to the mission
- know where the organization is headed
- people know and believe in organizational goals
- teamwork
- sharing similar values

Trust: a process built on practice
- trust built upon key decisions made at key times
- need to see it and experience it
- trust is a learning curve

frequently mentioned, consistency in people's behavior the second most frequently mentioned and so on.

1. *Dialogue of Openness and Sharing*. Isaacs (1999) points out two essential aspects of dialogue: the atmosphere or "field" in which it occurs, and the conditions that are likely to encourage it. He outlines four practices or conditions that promote dialogue: (1) people listening; (2) people respecting one another; (3) suspending judgment; and (4) speaking one's own voice.

   The atmosphere or field could be regarded as the culture of the organization and the conditions are the organizational rules that provide boundaries for trust. First, there needs to be permission to trust from the CEO. CEO's help to create an atmosphere, field, or culture of trust by being honest with themselves and others; by espousing a belief that all people have good potential, this organization will value their contribution, and that this organization is a safe one in which to be themselves, i.e. that it is safe to share opinions and feelings. Second, the CEO encourages sharing information by personally doing so. By voicing and modeling sharing and safety, the CEO indicates that there is no need for hidden agendas, no need to worry about being stabbed in the back, or that people will withhold information for their own power. Third, the CEO *encourages dialogue* and conveys the idea that members of a trusting organization *learn from each other*. All good ideas are not reserved for management. Fourth, the CEO and managers *continuously reinforce the conditions* for trusting behavior by *managing boundaries and monitoring the total environment* (or the "acoustics" as Isaacs has called the various settings for dialogue).

A new generation of management consultants, trained as psychotherapists, is making its way into corporate offices. Unlike traditional consultants who try to analyze and improve an organization's business strategy, these consultants focus on emotional impasses at work—from competitive executives who waste time undermining each other's work to autocratic bosses who squash employees' initiative. Instead of individuals as patients, the organization becomes the patient. Most of the problems are related to the lack of openness and sharing. Dialogue often doesn't fit in a competitive environment where the bottom line matters more than the process of achieving goals (Hymowitz, 2001).

A superintendent of schools shared how she is going about turning a severely dysfunctional and distrustful one hundred year old school system into a trustful one.[3] She was the fourth superintendent to head the system in four years. Her four predecessors either resigned under pressure or were fired. The system was under an Attorney General's order because of bid rigging, violating the open meeting law, and other illegal activities. She told her Board, "You can't move forward by looking in the rear mirror." Her first steps in establishing an open and sharing culture was to *listen*. She said people wanted to unload, "it was like a divorce, people needed validation."

She said people needed to vent and she needed to learn, but, she told her Board and constituents she dealt only with facts and did not want to hear rumors, gossip or about what might have been. She made it clear that she could not solve problems by herself, her role was to assist in a team effort. She pointed out that time was her enemy in turning the culture around, people wanted fast fixes, but, she noted, "the longer the violation of trust, the longer it takes to reestablish it." After a year on the job, the superintendent has received high marks from her Board and constituents for her management and leadership style.

One of the biggest obstacles in establishing a dialogue of openness and sharing is a highly bureaucratized or layered organization. If people you want to dialogue with are inaccessible or protected, no matter how much the CEO talks about trust, the environment contradicts it. The Chairman and CEO of General Electric, John F. Welch, Jr., expressed this clearly when he said, "Layers insulate. They slow things down. They garble. Leaders in highly layered organizations are like people who wear several sweaters outside on a freezing winter day. They remain warm and comfortable but are blissfully ignorant of the realities of their environments. They couldn't be further from what's going on."[4]

Another common blind spot of leaders in building a culture that stresses openness and sharing is that they forget the dialogue part. Communication and sharing are expected to be from the bottom up, but leaders can pick and choose what they want to share. A professor in a small college illustrated this point with a statement his President made to a faculty group, "I can't tell you everything, but I'll tell you some things."[5] As the professor said, what the President told us was not what we had on our minds, and what he didn't tell us what was what we considered to be most important. Choosing what to talk about is not a way to generate trust. A high ranking officer of a distinguished military operation said the guidelines he uses for deciding what to talk about and share are: (1) be honest; (2) use candor without being hurtful; and (3) don't hide the bad news but don't paint it blacker than it is, deal with it up front." He continued, "if the people respect the leader as a person then the leader need not be concerned about how information will be received."[6]

In order to build a culture of trust based on openness and sharing, the CEO and his/her team need to be good communicators. As the Vice President of a large brokerage firm said, "The CEO needs to step up and take ownership of issues."[7] The ability of the CEO to do so is based on organizational members' perceptions of his/her personality traits, "presence," and leadership style. How effective the CEO is in communication affects judgments about his leadership ability and how effective he is in representing the organization in the community. The CEO is responsible for clearly and continuously articulating the organization's mission. He must be able to convey a belief, commitment, and enthusiasm for the mission through his communication abilities.

There is an interesting contradiction between trust and likability in a leader. One respondent put it this way, "A trustful leader may not be likable as a person but will do what he says he will do. On the other hand, a distrustful leader might be a likable person who never gives a straight answer to a question." Therefore, the ease of establishing rapport with a leader might be not always a reliable indicator of their trustfulness. Trust and likability are not natural bedfellows.

2. *Consistency in Behavior*. The Vice President for finance in a large corporation said, "People are perceptive in deceptions, runarounds, and qualified statements. The higher in the organization you are, the more situations there are to be tested. People take a look at how the CEO acts." Another CEO commented that "the top people in an organization set the behavioral standards." It's not just the CEO but the behavior of her team.

The new President of one of the largest health care systems in the U.S. said that he and his managers needed to cut 10% of their workforce by reducing hours, not filling vacancies, and encouraging voluntary retirements.[8] He said, the system had experienced two other reductions in force by his predecessors, in the previous two to three years and "People have long memories." He wanted to conduct this reduction differently. The prior reductions almost brought the union in so he decided to minimize the impact of the planned reduction by telling employees this would be the only reduction, that there would be no others. This CEO felt that this approach would minimize fear among the remaining employees. Furthermore, he said the previous reductions were not done in a caring way. He felt that *how* the reduction was accomplished was key to retaining trust in the organization. Employees were talked to individually and in small groups. They were assisted in finding other jobs.

The dean of a law school said, "the way messages come from the CEO is key in trust....My predecessors had different management styles than I do. There was a lot of confusion regarding people's roles—a lot of finger pointing, confusion over who dropped the ball ... .I have promoted trust by seeing each person as an essential process. I have spent time with each person in the school, giving them a sense of the big picture and where their responsibilities fit with others. I share information in individual meetings, group meetings—I share good and bad news, dispel rumors, and keep people talking through things.... I feel an obligation to remember that the effects of what I do has a profound impact on people."[9]

Consistency in CEO behavior is complex because all employees are not at a single site. Furthermore, as the President of a major insurance company pointed out, his and his managers' behavior needed to be consistent for employees, the Board of Trustees, and a host of independent insurance agents.[10] This President held weekly staff meetings which were informal, relaxed, and created camaraderie. He held annual meetings for all employees and went on field trips to visit employees in various locations. He used his Vice Presidents to keep communication open with management and assembled small groups of people in the organization "to run ideas by them." Newsletters and e-mail ensured that what was said was followed by action. Since the insurance business is paper intensive, the CEO would walk around and drop in on various groups of employees unannounced to interact on a personal basis. Indeed, paper flow was an indicator of how well management was working with their staffs. If the flow of paper was bottled up, there was a problem.

One CEO of a large health care institution said he learned that "it is not a matter of whether you speak the truth but how you go about day to day decision-making."[11] He said he found out that while he was speaking out about values and openness, his immediate vice presidents were practicing control. "I took for granted the value match I felt with people, now I have sent 70 of my leaders and managers to a workshop on organizational values and how we match personnel with organizational values."

The Executive Director of a Chamber of Commerce summarized the importance of consistency in behavior when he said, "You can feel it—you know when people trust you and when you let them down. We can build mistrust and when we do, we know it (feel it)."[12]

3. *Everyone Committed to the Mission*. The CEO of a large non-profit hospice said that one of the major reasons for trust in her organization is, "We have employees committed to the mission.[13] They want to do the mission up, down and sideways." This was expressed in another way by a respondent, "If you believe in the organization's goals and are willing to do organizational work, trust is essential; if none of that matters, and you don't trust, you don't get much done."

Several CEO's told stories of what had happened, historically, to trust in their organizations when members took their eyes off the mission, ignored or dismissed the mission, or a new leader radically tried to change the mission. One story was told about the new president of a small, private college whose term lasted 18 months. He set out to change the culture from that of a teachers college to that of a liberal arts college by hiring only doctorally prepared faculty. He approved serving liquor in the Student Union. And, feeling that faculty administrators could not be trusted to follow Affirmative Action guidelines, he outlined a new faculty hiring process involving 41 steps. His abrasive, military manner led the Board of Trustees to conclude that "the shoe didn't fit" and they fired him.[14] In this case, the organization's original mission was ignored by the incoming CEO. The question might be raised as to why the Board of Trustees hired such a person to be CEO. We do not know how candid and honest the prospective CEO was about his views and plans during the interviewing process, and the Board may not have been clear about the expectations and boundaries of a CEO. This example clearly illustrates the importance of hiring people who will be true to an organization's mission.

The newly elected mayor of a moderate sized city described how she inherited a local government of cynicism and negativism where people had their own agendas, were not inclusive, and looked over their shoulders.[15] Her new city manager elaborated further, pointing out that the city council doesn't trust the staff.[16] Council members think the staff has hidden agendas. The staff, on the other hand, doesn't want the city council to make certain decisions because they do not think the council will make good decisions. While there is a mission statement and goals for the city, this growing area has new concerns about no-growth and environmental preservation, which have caused much divisiveness in the community. The city manager explained that the culture of the city is difficult to change. The higher level executives of the city have been in place for 15 to 25 years; they only know one way. They don't know how other cities work. When the city manager raised the issue of making changes in basic business practices with the executives she inherited, they asked, "What's wrong with the way we're doing things?" The city manager said they acted like their competencies were being questioned. She began to hold retreats for her staff and she required them to read "*Who moved my cheese?*"[17] as a means of creating a dialogue about change. In addition to consolidating trust among her staff, the city manager also must establish trust with the citizens of her community. She explained, "The public today doesn't trust government. We have to prove ourselves." Her challenge is to establish a level of trust with her coworkers and constituents that will enable the community to move ahead together.

A CEO's dream might be to be able to develop a new organization from scratch and be free from tainted history, memories of prior leaders, and cynical members. This opportunity presented itself recently to a new dean of a new school in a large university health sciences center.[18] The senior leaders of the university had developed a mission and vision for the school, and after conducting a national search, hired the new dean to carry out the mission. The dean began to recruit a leadership team by obtaining input about exceptional candidates from experts in the field as well as advertising following established university guidelines. A senior team of academically qualified and experienced leaders was recruited based on their concurrence with the new school's mission and the dean's vision; the ability to get along with each other and work together for the benefit of the school; and their awareness of and willingness to work in a larger environment of distrust. At the time the new school was established, the CEO of the health sciences center was not open to dialogue, only a few people controlled university resources, and the leaders did not keep their word. As the health sciences center expanded, the School of Medicine, which had previously dominated the budget, was forced to share with new emerging schools. When budget planning time came around, it was always a struggle, and not always above board, to get financial resources. The dean of the new emerging school, therefore, established his new school, based on trust, within a larger context of distrust. The dean and his team, however, took this as a challenge to establish a well functioning school that stayed loyal to a shared vision.

The dean and his leaders proceeded to recruit faculty who were loyal to the new school's mission and vision. They established an organizational structure that decentralized power and authority; developed a system of rewards; an evaluation and feedback process for identifying problems as well as monitoring performance; and built relationships with organizations and constituents in the community and state, nationally, and internationally.

While the larger culture of the health sciences center is distrustful, primarily because of tight finances ("everyone is fighting for bits and pieces"), the new dean and his school, after a few years, have begun to prosper. When I asked the dean how he was able to do this he said, "It helps to circle our wagon so we can feel good about what we are doing; it gives us a sense of unity." As for the larger environment in which he works, he said "You can't change suspicion until you change the people."

INDICATORS OF TRUST

I asked the CEO's and former CEO's, if they were asked to visit an organization for a day to make a cursory assessment of how trusting that organization was, what were the major things they would look for in making that assessment? They all mentioned a combination of five indicators, shown in Table 5.2.

Table 5.2. Indicators of a Trusting Culture

Comfort Level
- the way people carry out their job (degree of pride in one's work)
- ease of interaction (quality of how people interact, *how* people treat each other)
- the organization has a sense of right and wrong and responds with just and fair decisions
- the organization acts out what it promises
- affect of members; smiles on faces, optimism, sense of humor, positive conversations

Responsiveness
- immediate response to problems
- accessibility of leaders and managers
- willingness to make changes, consider alternatives
- problems are not bureaucratized to death

Loyalty
- low turnover
- selectivity in quality of people recruited to the organization
- overt expression of values, goals
- people say they feel valued

Quality of Product or Service
- positive, helpful attitude toward customers/clients
- has standards and affirms and practices them
- organization acts out what it promises
- client/customer retention

Reward System
- rewards are considered fair and equitable
- satisfaction with method for evaluating performance

The five indicators in Table 5.2 each have sub-indicators which can be observed, asked about, or deduced from listening, to help the visiting CEO make his/her assessment. One CEO said that she could gain an initial impression of how trusting an organization was by the way she was treated from the time she entered the lobby of an organization, and watching transactions between people, hearing the receptionist handle telephone conversations, striking up a conversation with the receptionist, and noticing the convenience and friendliness of the waiting area.

These observations are the first insights into how trustful an organization might be. The first indicator in assessing trust is the degree of comfort, that is, how people are treated, how they carry out their jobs, and their general demeanor. The CEO of a customs brokerage family business described the comfort level in his organization as follows:

> "Employees take pride in their work, in not making mistakes. We have certain standards; we accept only clean-cut people, we are a drug-free environment, and we do not tolerate any type of sexual harassment. We set a standard for service. If employees get three complaints, they are fired. All employees have the same benefits. We have had no grievances or lawsuits. Many employees have been here over 12 years. My motto is, 'if we take care of our people, they will take care of us.'"

Responsiveness is another indicator of a trusting culture. Responsiveness refers to how willing and ready the organization is to deal with problems, the organization's willingness to make changes, to consider options, and how accessible key people are to respond to daily issues as well as crises. How the organization is organized gives a clue to its degree of trustfulness. In a highly bureaucratized organization it is likely a problem will either resolve itself or worsen by the time appropriate persons deal with it.

Loyalty is another indicator of a trusting culture. Organizations where members spontaneously express their feelings of pride and satisfaction are usually trustful places. Low turnover in members is often a good indicator of loyalty; however, low turnover must be considered along with the age of most members of the organization and the availability of options in the area, e.g., some members may be long-term employees because of concerns other than loyalty. A CEO of a large travel agency described loyalty in her firm as follows:

> "We have 60 employees at three different sites. We have little turnover and have not had any layoffs in 35 years. I am open with the employees about the state of the agency, I empower them, they participate in profit-sharing, have full health benefits and flexible hours. I tell them that I count on them to help me keep clients. We build a relationship with each other."

The quality of an organization's service or product is another indicator of trust. Trustful organizations will have standards and act out what their values are regarding quality and service. As one CEO expressed it, "The main part of trust is not to patronize people. My father taught me that people are never above me and never below me."[19] His emphasis on quality and service has seen the company expand to 14 plants in several countries. He has been able to establish trust cross-culturally by being sensitive to different values and methods of transacting business in different cultures.

An organization's reward system provides an important clue about its trustfulness. How people are rewarded provides insight into how they are valued. The Acting Vice President of Research in a large university expressed his frustration with the reward system of his university as follows, "I'm tired of doing good and then covering it up." He obviously felt that what he was doing in his job was unappreciated and that talking about the good he did was frowned upon. An organization can have people of great integrity, but the organization can decrease their effectiveness. In some distrusting organizations, leaders, managers, and coworkers are vindictive toward employees or members who do a good job. Politics, favoritism, jealousy, competition, resentment unfortunately seem to be common emotions and behaviors surrounding the ways of evaluating and rewarding organizational members in many organizations.

One approach to helping reduce paranoia and suspicion about evaluation and reward is to make the processes open; ensure representation, participation, and input from various constituents; and continually review, refine, and improve the processes.

The CEO of a large national professional organization said that the reward system of an organization is tied to its espoused values. He said that four major values have been the mainstay of his organization for over a century. These are: (1) ethical behavior; (2) accountability; (3) service to others; and (4) we value our people. He described how numbers 3 and 4 are carried out. "We have a lot of staff meetings where we share information about our organization, particularly success stories, what we are doing right. At these meetings, we give bonuses to people, who the staff has recommended, for 'above and beyond' behavior. We have a budget for this and I give out the bonuses and give a speech about each recipient. We added the fourth value, 'we value our people' recently. It was the recommendation of a committee which acts as an ombudsman for our organization to continually take the pulse on our humanity."[20]

The CEO of an 11-year-old laser printer service which remanufactures toner cartridges, says that she invests in her employees. "I show them that I trust them (all supervisors have keys) and that I care. Each employee has a growth plan to get a college degree. We pay for all their education in full. We send all employees to a Dale Carnegie course. We have an annual performance reward package for all managers which includes a vacation for them and their spouse anywhere in the U.S. Periodically,we take managers out for breakfast to reward them if their employees have produced our product defect-free. We also pay all benefits for our employees in full. Our philosophy is that it would be hard to leave someone who gives you so much."[21]

BUILDING A CULTURE OF DISTRUST

No Board of Trustees or Directors, or CEO, intentionally goes about creating a culture of distrust, or do they? According to Kets de Vries (1991) there is a substantial body of knowledge to support the contention that organizational leaders are not necessarily rational, logical, sensible, and dependable human beings. Research findings show that executives are prone to a fair amount of irrational behavior. Within organizations we find both irrationality and intentional destructiveness (Kets de Vries, 1991, p.3). For example, why would the Board of Trustees of the small, private college mentioned earlier in this chapter hire a President who was obviously a mis-match for the college culture, and then fire him 18 months later after a campus rebellion? Why would a Board of Trustees promote an executive who was second in command in a large corporation, and who was distrusted widely and known for his vindictiveness, to President when the position became vacant, resulting in an exodus of many loyal, productive employees? Why is a President of a large multi-million dollar corporation, who makes knee-jerk decisions, has had a high turnover of executives, carried out lay-offs and then re-hired some of them back at higher positions and salaries, and recently received the results of an in-house survey that indicated the lowest level of trust in more than 20 years, continued in his position? As one CEO who I interviewed would respond, "Some people don't care about democracy as long as they are taken care of."[22] Another CEO commented, "People have learned to be opportunistic, the short-run goal is what is important."[23] Still another CEO said, "Sometimes it takes a massive, visible challenge to trust to get people's attention."[24]

When talking to my interviewees about distrust in organizations, they pointed out some building blocks that lead to (or create) distrust in organizations. Table 5.3 summarizes the five most prominent factors that can create distrust.

1. *Character of Leader and People Chosen for the Organization*. The character of the person chosen to become leader of an organization, and the people he might bring with him or recruit, is key to whether the organization will be trusting or distrusting. Most of the CEO's who described previous unsuccessful CEO's in their organization or in organizations they knew, told of character flaws or difficult personalities. CEO's who had difficulties and short tenures were often characterized as "doing what they wanted to do without input from others," "whimsical," "made massive organizational changes upon arrival," "vindictive," "aloof," "not open to dialogue," "controlled resources," "didn't keep his word," and "not a good communicator." One CEO said one of the failings of CEO's is that "some are ego driven as opposed to giving credit away to allow other people to be the center of attention."[25] Indeed, a CEO's character extends beyond his work, there needs to be respect for the CEO as a person; as one CEO expressed it, "even though

Table 5.3. Building Blocks of Organizational Distrust

Low Trust of Leader and People Chosen for the Organization
- some people bring a low level of trust with them
- people have their own baggage, ego issues and personality
- people who are not open and operate behind the scenes
- some people are hired for expediency; their backgrounds not checked thoroughly

Uncertainty of Leadership
- power struggles, undercutting among leaders/managers
- values of organization and leaders covert
- mission, goals unclear, vision not articulated
- frequent turnover in leaders, difficulty attracting quality leaders

Members Living in the Past
- sacred cows protected
- fantasies about what might have been
- unwilling to change
- obsession with previous mistakes, grievances, fault finding

Anti-Problem-Solving Climate
- point fingers, blaming
- gain attention by creating chaos
- "we/they" games
- many rules, inflexibility

Anti-Involvement Climate
- factions, lack of cohesion
- no loyalty or commitment
- attitude "I'll leave" rather than change
- following an agenda they don't believe in
- "it's their problem"

a member of the organization may be engaged in affairs, members don't expect the leader to—they hold the leader to a standard different from their own."[26]

Some leaders bring people with them from their previous organization. Leaders who do this assume these folks will be accepted as part of the new team, but organizational members tend to evaluate team members individually. Therefore, some people who worked well with the CEO in a previous organization may not fit well in the new culture. New CEO's like to have the security of working with previous colleagues in a new environment and to call upon the expertise of colleagues they know to accomplish specific tasks in the new organization. Yet, organizational members may resent a new CEO's bringing in outsiders he feels comfortable with rather than calling upon existing talent in the organization he is inheriting.

2. *Uncertainty of Leadership.* A second building block of distrust is uncertainty in leadership. Leaders who are unable to articulate a vision, or whose goals for the organization are unclear, become a topic of conversation in the organization. Of course, some organizational members might not agree with the vision or goals of the leader and attempt to undermine his effectiveness from the onset. CEO's who had difficulties in their organizations had difficulties in communication. Leaders who are aware of their communication problems may resort to written communication, withdraw from, or avoid face-to-face encounters, using team members to represent them. This helps to create mistrust in the organization. Members are sensitive to a leader's visibility and accessibility; avoidance of contact is certain to generate gossip and rumors about decision-making behind closed doors.

   Some leaders and their teams never seem to "gel." A new leader who takes an exceptionally long time to assemble a team may create leadership gaps in some parts of the organization; when the team does come together, a period will be needed to develop some synchrony between team members. It is not wise for leaders to keep interim leaders in positions for long periods of time as this encourages rumors and gossip about the CEO's intentions, which may impact other related aspects of the organization. CEO's often can save money by using internal people to fill vacant leadership slots in an organization, but long term "interims" and/or many "interims" help to create a trust gap in the culture.
3. *Members Living in the Past.* Some members of an organization always seem to look in the rear view mirror. If this number is significant it can trap an organization in its past, irrespective of a new leader and a fresh vision. Every organization, including trustful ones, has a few sacred cows. Sacred cows, especially if there are many of them, can create strong resistance to change. Sacred cows can be changed, but the planning, timing, and support needed to change them are key—some sacred cows survive CEO's!

   One set of attitudes that helps to keep a culture of distrust strong over the years is that certain past leaders failed to do certain things, or missed windows of opportunity, or might have selected someone different for CEO, making things different. Some members feel the past has created a destiny for the organization from which it cannot escape. Malcontents and cynics usually are long-term members of the organization who were passed over for promotion or in some way, feel victimized by persons who had control over their future and are determined to "take it out on the organization." More often than not, these people have few, if any career options, so have made a career of creating barriers for whomever is CEO. The CEO of a large health care corporation said, "Some organizational members will be unhappy whomever the CEO is. They don't know any other way to behave. They believe by complaining they can get a power base; they gain by creating chaos."[27]

4. *Anti-Problem-solving Climate*. Some members of organizations don't want problems solved. Some gain satisfaction by playing we/they games, pointing fingers, and creating uncertainty. Some have problems with authority figures or harbor jealousies or resentments which they conceal by keeping their complaints generic and illusive. These frequently are the less productive members of the organization. If an organization does not resolve its problems and more forward to new agendas, it cannot be proactive; strategic planning becomes an exercise and the plan never is permitted to become a reality. The same issues keep being raised and there is an unwillingness to reach consensus for the benefit of the organization. When organizations need to rely on outside consultants or mediators to resolve their disputes, it is a sign that the organizational structure lacks flexibility and the members lack the ability to heal and move on. Organizations that continually expend energy on keeping old problems alive are chronically sick and distrustful.
5. *Anti-Involvement Climate*. Most members of organizations want input into decision-making, they want to be involved in as much of the life of the organization as possible, yet often, members shun the responsibilities of leadership or opportunities to give their time and talents to certain activities. Organizations that have more observers and commentators than workers for the total good are certain to be unhealthy and distrusting. Some members of organizations have been conditioned not to trust management. It is safer if one does not participate constructively in the life of an organization because one avoids disappointment. Without loyalty or commitment to organizational goals and objectives, and a willingness to work together for the benefit of an organization, there can be no cohesion or trust. Too often, members do not see things as "their problem" and take a hands off attitude, yet they expect things to happen that will benefit them. It's easier to say "I'll leave" than to ask, "how can I help to make things better?"

Distrustful cultures are either inherited or created. They do not happen by accident; they take time to develop, and, like distrust among people, are very difficult to turn around. The CEO is important in helping to create distrust or in helping to turn the culture around. More powerful than the CEO, are the attitudes and willingness of the members of the organization. Usually, new leaders are recruited to make forward changes (or help heal a sick organization), not to keep the organization *status quo*. However, poor choices in leadership can help steer a healthy organization towards distrust. Distrustful organizations tend to recruit, knowingly or unknowingly, distrustful leaders. While there may be complaints about distrust, it does satisfy needs. The public language of most searches for new leaders indicate that healthy, trustful leaders are sought to lead healthy, trustful organizations. Herein is the rub; what is healthy and trustful lies in the perception and expectations of the beholder. It is my contention that, with the tenure of most CEO's in the United States currently averaging five years, this short time span is not sufficient to create a healthy, trusting culture in an organization. It is too short to make a distrustful organization trusting, and too short to establish a firm base of trust in a new and developing organization. On the other hand, five years is enough time for a CEO to turn a trusting organization into a distrusting one.

INDICATORS OF DISTRUST

Distrust in an organization differs from distrust between individuals, which can result from a single encounter. Distrust in organizations is cumulative unless, for example, a major moral or illegal action that would take down a CEO occurs. As Morgan (1997) explains, "bad systems allow members to leave some of their own badness in the system—the system has a strange way of tying them in—even though some members want to, they cannot change it."[28] Distrust often develops in segments of an organization and spreads as new instances of distrust occur, eventually consuming the culture. The obvious outcome of accumulated distrust in an organization is the ouster of the CEO, by a petition from members, pressure from clients, or other vested interest groups, yet many distrustful organizations become immobilized or give-up, and live with distrust. Some organizations may have been distrustful for so long that members have abandoned hope that the organization could be any different, even with a new leader. In some instances, an organization and its leader may be oblivious to distrust, especially if the organization has little contact with other organizations. All organizations have some pockets of distrust at sometime in their life cycles; what is key is recognizing and reversing distrust before it spreads. Some obvious signs of distrust are summarized in Table 5.4

1. *Excessive controls*. Excessive controls, which limit the input and output of an organization, can be deleterious. One CEO said, "organizations that become overly bureaucratic reduce justice."[29] Controls on information flow in an organization might make it easier for leaders in the organization to make decisions, but if members have limited information about how other organizations do a particular thing, and have no input into decision-making in their own organization, they feel railroaded. When leaders ask for input in the future, members will see it as an exercise in futility. Some respondents told of experiences with the control of time, information, and resources in the various organizations they worked for previously. For example, the development officer for a major Big 10 university said her supervisor questioned her about how she spent her time and required her to keep a record of her time, even though her employment record at the university had been outstanding for over a decade. This development officer

Table 5.4. Indicators of a Distrustful Culture

Excessive Controls
- micromanagement
- monitor time, activities
- minimal risk-taking, lack of innovation and creativity
- minimal autonomy, delegation
- rigid boundaries

Antagonistic Interactions
- cynical, critical, blaming, uncivil, anger
- overly cautious, protective behavior
- grievances, vindictiveness
- reactive behavior

Distancing Behavior and Communication
- aloof, no enthusiasm for the organization, few friends
- pessimism, low morale, no loyalty
- passive-aggressive behavior
- do the minimum required

Lack of Spirit, Vitality and Vibrancy
- appearance and behavior of members shows unhappiness
- difficult to recruit, quality of employees decreased
- no long-term commitment

was recruited away by a large national medical organization that permitted her to work at home half time—as she said, “they trust that when I am home, I am working.”

Stories of excessive control were more prevalent in state or public organizations that were under scrutiny by legislatures. It was often at budget time, when resources were allocated in publically funded organizations, that the dynamics of distrust became acutely overt. Leaders of publically funded organizations are rewarded for frugality and measurable outcomes, not for how trusting an organization they maintain.

Controls usually originate with the CEO of an organization. Controls often reflect the CEO’s personality and management style and frequently are imposed without recognition of how they will affect members’ perceptions of the leader and the organization. There are two opposing views of CEO’s who encourage members of their organizations to send them e-mails. One view is that the CEO wants to be seen as an accessible listener who responds promptly to any inquiry. The other view is that direct e-mail contact between a member and the CEO can bypass members’ direct supervisors who may or may not know (or have the opportunity to know about a problem before it is taken to the CEO) of the e-mail contact. The opportunity to talk to any member of an organization at will is a dream for a CEO who is controlling and paranoid. E-mail information lies in the hidden motivations of the users.

2. *Antagonistic Interactions*. An organization where members spend a great deal of time being cynical, critical, uncivil, blaming, looking over their shoulders, obsessed with their own resources and benefits, take most things personally, volunteer for nothing, and are absent from organizational meetings and social affairs, is a distrustful organization.

   Organizations are microcosms of the world. As such, they have personal agendas that carry over to work. Others have had agendas with individuals in the organization that persist over time, and still others use the organization as a forum to hear their disappointments or conflicts about anything. These are found in any human group. Organizational distrust, brought about by antagonistic interactions among members, however, is more insidious. Organizational members who are intentionally undercutting, destructive, engage in vicious gossip and rumor mongering, are verbally abusive, vindictive, discriminatory, dishonest, and recruit others to join them, help to destroy trust in organizations. While most people who engage in these behaviors have problems needing professional attention, they create and perpetuate problems for the organization. One CEO expressed it, "there are people who will reframe whatever is said and paint it a different color, and there is nothing you can do."[30]
3. *Distancing Behavior and Communication*. One indicator that distrust has a foothold in an organization is when members no longer show enthusiasm for the organization's mission and goals, criticize the mission, talk about leaving the organization, actively look for alternative employment, and distance themselves from coworkers, not attending meetings and events. Some members might disconnect themselves from the organization but stay because of benefits or age. Disenchanted and disenfranchised members often are chronic critics and complainers; some even attempt to sabotage new activities and ventures out of spite or resentment. Often these members outlast CEO's.
4. *Lack of Spirit, Vitality, and Vibrancy*. Some organizations seem to exist to do the minimum. Organizations that are minimally productive are not always so because they have a distrustful culture. They may resist change, have an uninspiring leader, and are secure enough that competition may not overpower them. However, you can tell when distrust has drained spirit and a willingness to excel from an organization. You can feel it when an organization glides along. Smiles are gone, the vibrancy is missing from voices, and movement has become unenergetic, it is difficult to fill vacancies, and the quality of interaction among members has deteriorated. These indicators in a young or developing organization are especially diagnostic of distrust. A member of an organization that has had three different CEO's said the organization has not been comfortable with any of the three, and that initially members were vocal; now they accept whomever is selected as CEO as an inevitability. Sometimes, the historical grounding for distrust is so strong that members feel apathetic and helpless and doubt that any leader could make a difference.

POCKETS OF TRUST AND DISTRUST

I asked the people I interviewed to rank how they perceived the trustfulness of their organization on a scale from 1 to 10, with 1 being the lowest and 10 the highest. No one ranked their organization a 10. Fifty percent of the CEO's ranked their organization in the 7 to 9 range, 35 percent ranked their organization in the 4 to 6 range, and 15 percent ranked their organization between 1 and 3. Many CEO's said that their total organizations had improved in trust since they became CEO, but that they still dealt with some units or sections of their organization that were distrustful and problematic. Often these pockets of distrust were comprised of employees or members who had been with the organization a long time and were resistors of change. Some CEO's who were responsible for divisions or schools within a larger umbrella organization told of their difficulties in maintaining a trusting organization when they did not regard the umbrella organization (their employer) as trusting. Therefore, some CEO's would rank their component as a 7 or 8 and the umbrella organization of which they were a part as a 4 or 5. This was especially true in universities where the dean of a college or school was one of many CEO's on the campus or in the system who reported to a Provost or Senior Vice President. In the case of universities, if the senior leadership changed, it profoundly affected the CEO's of the various components.

No organization is ever a 10, even for a few minutes. In some organizations, where growth and change might be a high priority, the organization may never be stable. Indeed, it is impossibile to "maintain" trust in an organization in today's world where the forces of change impact even the most "balanced" organization.

The President of a large national insurance company in the United States described his job as the juggling of three balls: profit, expense, and growth. He was responsible to a Board of Directors whose members included insurance executives with strong opinions about how these balls should be juggled. He had to develop trust with his Board, the external community, and the 750 or so employees of the company. As CEO of a public company, he had to create trust in his company's performance in order to draw investors. He had to build trust with the hundreds of independent insurance agents who were selling insurance products by providing quality service. And he had to maintain the trust of current policyholders. Pockets of distrust may emerge periodically as attention and resources focus more on some aspects of the organization than on others. Therefore, the CEO described the trust level of his organization as varying according to what the organization is doing at various points in time.

Some pockets of distrust in organizations may survive a succession of department leaders and CEO's. A new CEO was warned to expect trouble from one of the departments in his organization. Members of the unit were quite vocal about how they organized a successful petition drive to oust the previous CEO. The department had 12 members, the majority of whom had been with the organization for over ten years, and some since its founding 30 years ago. The department had had a series of leaders over the years, three of whom remained in the department after their unsuccessful tenure as leaders. Departmental meetings were typically characterized by argumentative, contentious, uncivil behavior, with rare consensus on agenda items. Some members of the department were chronic complainers to the Department of Human Resources. The new CEO met with the Department numerous times to hear issues from the group, and met with individual members regarding their grievances. Dissension and distrust in the department continued as it had for nearly 12 years. The department established a reputation for dysfunction within the organization and externally, which affected its ability to attract people to fill vacancies and to develop connections with other organizations.

At the opposite extreme, in the same organization, there was an exceptionally productive, positive, proactive department headed by an energetic, innovative leader. This department was comprised of two sub-units which had successfully been merged. There was enough turnover among the professionals and staff that there was a continual influx of new members. The 30 some members were involved in many activities outside the department; many were engaged in team projects, and there was a high degree of productivity in the department as a whole. While there were dissenters among the members, the department was able to reach its goals and a consensus on issues.

Why was there trust in one department and not the other? The distrusting department had recruited members who were difficult personalities; certainly the three people who had been recruited as department heads and then had to step down, had hidden agendas of not wanting their successors to succeed either. The previous CEO had exempted this department from an organization-wide workload policy, permitting certain members in the distrustful department to have reduced work loads under certain circumstances. This created deep resentments within the department, between the department and the other components in the organization, and between the bulk of the organization and the CEO. This exemption enabled the distrusting department to successfully accumulate sufficient signatures across the organization for the CEO's removal. A third factor was that the majority of members in the distrusting department had tenure, securing their jobs. Therefore, they were vocal about their beliefs and opinions, often finding that any new members did not meet their standards to receive tenure. Hence, they often voted against tenure for members when the time came for that decision. These same individuals also refused to act as mentors for new members or for changes in their work assignments when they were short-handed and overloaded. A fourth factor encouraging distrust was that one or two members of the department were accused of making personal use of departmental resources; and the department leader did not act on the complaint. The leadership styles of the leaders of the trusting and distrusting departments were different. The leader of the trusting department was scrupulous about equity and establishing policies and procedures to which all members of the department were held accountable. The leader of the distrusting department tended to make decisions informally, over a lunch or a drink. The perception by some members was that decisions were made prior to department meetings. Issues tended to be resolved on a personal basis, hence, accusations of favoritism and unfairness were constant. Over the years, members protected their way of doing things in their unit, which they tried to expand to the organization as a whole. The distrustful department supported or criticized the CEO, depending on how the CEO's actions or inactions affected them. They always seemed prepared to organize another petition drive for the newest CEO's removal.

A regularly occurring event in organizations that tends to crystalize trust and distrust is budget allocation. Money, resources, and space are the sacred indicators of value, individually and collectively. It is a given that there is never enough money or space, but that every leader asks for more with the expectation of getting some. The worst scenario is undergoing a budget cut and having to give up space for another part of the organization that is growing. Leaders take their budget and space personally, and so do the members of an organization. It is rare that there is not some grumbling in organizations over monetary rewards, the quality and/or quantity of space, and the amount of resources available. The tighter the budget, the more scrutiny members give to their perceptions of the use of funds, how they are allocated, and the rationale underlying the allocation. The less open leaders are about the budget and allocation process in an organization, the more speculation and judgment there is among members about the trustfulness of its leaders, and a criticism of their compensation, benefits, and lifestyle. Parts of an organization that might be borderline distrustful may become full-blown after budgets are allocated.

One weapon members of an organization can use when they become dissatisfied with their organization's reward system is the union. Several of the CEO's interviewed mentioned that they considered it a vote of confidence when unions were not voted into their organization. Unions are seen by many employees as guardians of trust, equity and fairness.

TOUGH AND EASY CULTURES

Arsenian and Arsenian (1948) observed that some cultures are tough on their members while others are easy. They engaged in a conceptual analysis that led them to derive the conditions requisite for tough and easy cultures, to demonstrate a continuum by characterizing polar or extreme cases, and to determine how cultures could be evaluated for their toughness or easiness. Cultures were judged as tough or easy depending upon the ways and means (paths) they provided their members for meeting needs and reducing tension. When a culture's paths made for easy tension-reduction for its members, the culture was easy. When a culture's paths were tension-producing or tension-sustaining, the culture was tough. The authors did not advocate that easy cultures were "the best," but they did suggest that very tough cultures were expected to be pathogenic.

This scheme for understanding the mental hygiene of cultures can be applied to organizations. Tough cultures would be expected to ignore, minimize, or be out of touch with the values of their members and suppress value conflict. Easy cultures, on the other hand, would be expected to incorporate, maximize, or be sensitive to the values of their members and to deal with value conflict openly. It should be pointed out that how demanding the culture is on its members is not a major issue in toughness or easiness. A tough culture can be positive and an easy culture negative. The key point is that a culture that is out of touch with its members' values will be a tough culture to work in because the way of working, interacting, and dealing with conflicts in values will not be people-sensitive. Conversely, a culture that is in touch with its members' values will be an easier culture to work in because the way of working, interacting, and dealing with value conflict will be open, mutually reinforcing, and more fulfilling of needs.

Either toughness or easiness can be extreme; organizations should be blends of toughness and easiness. A police force needs to enforce laws, but it can be service-oriented and people-sensitive. Many organizations, such as the health care and airline industries, are becoming increasingly tough cultures where clients' needs are not being met. Tough and easy cultures at their extremes can become non-trusting organizations; for example, a tough culture can be excessively controlling and an easy culture can give members so much autonomy that they feel no loyalty to the organization.

NO ORGANIZATION IS A 10

Trust is only one piece of the organizational puzzle, albeit a critical piece. CEO's and managers do not singularly and intentionally set out to develop trust in their organizations. As Isenberg (1984) said, "most successful senior managers do not closely follow the classical rational model of first clarifying goals, assessing the situation, formulating options, estimating likelihoods of success, making their decision, and only then, taking action to implement a decision. Nor do top managers select one problem at a time to solve."

Some CEO's are fortunate to be chosen to lead an organization that has had a long history of excellence, and to follow in the footsteps of model CEO's, such as John Welch of General Electric. Most CEO's do not walk into organizations that have a history of trust. More often, as the CEO's interviewed in this study affirm, they are recruited to bring a different leadership style to an organization, to make changes in an organization's structure, goals, and mission, or to modify its culture. Trust is like quality, an expected by-product of these changes. CEO's are not rewarded for building trusting organizations. They are rewarded for profits, productivity, and growth.

As elusive as trust is to quantify, the CEO's all knew what trust was, and when it was present and absent. Trust and distrust can be seen, and felt, and have permanent effects on an organization's well-being. Trust can be the bottom line. As one CEO said, "Trust is a fine line between leading and getting run out of town."[31]

INTUITION AND TRUST

Efforts to create trust and combat distrust are not always planned, deliberate, and rational. CEO's talked about trusting their intuition and experience to make decisions, to go with their "gut" feelings, especially when they did not have all of the facts and had a difference of opinion among their staff. Sometimes, trust is "sensed" (Rowan, 1989). One CEO described his working relationship with his Board of Directors as one based on intuition. He said, "I *know*, I sense it, I feel it, I know the Board's limitations. I know when I need to go to my Board, when to run something past the Chair, or when I can just FYI everyone by e-mail. They trust me to provide them with the information they need to make a decision."[31]

Similarly, a CEO of a closely held business said that he "sensed something was wrong" when one of his new employees, who was a recent graduate from a local university and highly recommended by the College of Business Administration, started coming to work late, not showing up for staff meetings, using the restroom frequently to talk in Spanish on his cell phone. He found out that the employee had a business of his own and was conducting business on his employer's time.[32]

Repetition in one's mind seems to bolster intuition. Continual rehearing is a crucial part of verifying information. Rowan (1989) describes how the CEO of Cunard Line conducts rehearsals with his staff, discussing "gut feelings," which then lead to new ideas and approaches. Another CEO periodically conducts what he calls "stray-bullet drills" to make sure that he has his pulse on his organization and "can identify all of the unlikely bad news." (Rowan, 1989).

HOW CEO'S LEARNED TRUST: MENTORS AND MODELS

CEO's practiced the kind of trust they had experienced and seen modeled in organizations they had been members of earlier in life. For example, one CEO told the story of being late for a meeting (he had overslept) when he was a staff member to the CEO of the organization he now headed. When he told his boss that he was sorry he missed the meeting, that he overslept, his boss said, "Tom, you were where you needed to be." The CEO said he has applied that philosophy;

he never checks up on his staff to see what they are doing or why they missed a meeting. In his view, "they are where they need to be."

Several CEO's said that their experience in the military influenced how they practice trust in their organization. They learned that in times of conflict, trust is essential at all levels of a military organization. CEO's pointed out that they learned that leaders and members of a military organization need to be committed to a goal and be willing to sacrifice for that goal; there is a need to achieve something together. CEO's also pointed out that they learned that it was important to find ways to solve problems and not expect others to fix them or compromise on solutions. While CEO's with military experience did not run their organizations as a military organization, they did benefit by establishing a clear mission and goals, a functional structure, and procedures that ensured fairness and equity.

CEO's of family businesses usually pointed to their fathers as important mentors influencing their leadership behavior. A few young, new CEO's said that they were helped by being involved in organizations like a local Young President's Association where older, experienced, successful CEO's shared experiences through speeches and workshops on specific issues.

Many CEO's were conversant with the latest books on management and organizational dynamics. Some attended workshops sponsored by their professional organizations on specific topics such as how to manage conflict and change, accountability, planning, and mergers, acquisitions, takeovers, downsizing, etc. And a few learned about trust (or the lack of it) from observing or being a part of failed ventures.

SUMMARY

Trust is not a natural part of an organization's culture, nor is trust a natural part of leadership. While leaders usually do not set specific agendas for trust-building, trust (or distrust) is created both by what they say and do not say and what they do and do not do. Leaders must be aware of what trust and distrust are and how they work in organizations in order to be effective. Building trust and distrust are both conscious efforts with unconscious motivations. While a leader would not be expected purposely to create chaos in an organization, some leaders enjoy chaos and the control behaviors associated with restoring order to the organization. The majority of leaders expect some degree of chaos with change and try to contain and direct the effects of chaos.

The CEO's in this study mentioned four building blocks of organizational trust: (1) there needs to be a dialogue of openness and sharing; (2) there needs to be consistency in behavior, especially at leadership and managerial levels; (3) everyone in the organization needs to be committed to the organization's mission; and (4) trust is an on-going process that is built upon experience. Building trust requires leadership, but it takes a partnership between leaders and followers to make trust work.

How do you know when an organization is trusting? Some indicators provide insights into an organization's degree of trustfulness, even to a short-term observer. Five such indicators are: (1) the comfort level in the organization, that is, how people in the organization behave toward each other and to outsiders; (2) how responsive the organization is to resolving problems and how willing it is to make accommodations; (3) how loyal members are and what they say about the organization; (4) what attitude is prevalent in the organization about the quality of service or the product it provides—Is there pride?; and (5) what is the reward system for members? Do members feel valued and rewarded?

Distrust is not just the neglect of trust; it too, must be built. The building blocks of distrust mentioned by the CEO's interviewed include, foremost, the character of the leader and the people chosen to join the organization. One CEO said that leaders need to judge people exceedingly reliably—a good leader knows a good person. But CEO's do not select all the people in their organization, and some people are hired for expediency. "Bad or poor" hires can live with an organization a long time, especially in the educational system where there is the protection of tenure. One educational leader said, "tenure shows the failure of leadership in an academic environment, but we need tenure in today's world as a protection of free speech in academia." A second building block of distrust is uncertainty in leadership. Power struggles, people undercutting each other, working on their own agendas, and expressing no loyalty to the organization are symptoms of uncertainty from leaders. Leadership may turn over frequently or leaders may be unable to articulate where the organization is headed; values are covert and poor behavior sometimes is overlooked or ignored. This helps breed distrust.

A third building block of distrust is members who live in the past. It's hard to look ahead when you are looking over your shoulder, wishing for what might have been. Many people in an organization who are unwilling to change, look back and talk in the past tense. People who are unforgiving about how they were wronged by someone in the past are unwilling to free themselves to look forward. A fourth building block of distrust is an anti-problem-solving attitude. Some people like to blame, point fingers, and play we/they games. This can consume a great deal of time and energy in an organization. Sometimes, problems or issues seem too complex to solve and it is easier to let them ride "for someone else to solve." The lack of accountability in an organization can become a chronic disease. The fifth building block of distrust is an attitude of non-involvement. It is easy to look for another job (or threaten to do so) when things do not go one's way. Some people find it easy to "show up to do one's job and then leave," don't volunteer, and don't take on added responsibility. For example, response that is commonly heard by the author when seeking volunteers to serve on committees in church is, "that's something I would like to do in the future, but now my plate's full."

Obvious signs and symptoms of distrust can be observed without engaging in an in-depth study of an organization. These include: excessive controls imposed by leaders and managers; cynical, critical, antagonistic relationships in the organization; members of the organization who "don't want to be bothered," are aloof, don't attend meetings, and have no loyalty to the organization; and the lack of spirit, vitality, and vibrancy in an organization. These are indicators of a culture of distrust.

All organizations have pockets of trust (even distrusting organizations) and distrust (even trusting organizations). Using a dental analogy, some pockets of infection can be isolated and with proper treatment can be healed, other pockets worsen over time, even with treatment, and must be surgically corrected. The causes of pockets are often unknown and can be due to a number of factors working together over time. Therefore, it is hard to prevent pockets because just as individuals genetic make-ups differ, so too organization's histories differ. However, just as individuals are responsible for monitoring one's health needs, a CEO is responsible for monitoring the needs of all parts of his/her organization.

Organizations can be labeled as "tough" or "easy," depending on the ways and means they provide for their members to meet their needs. Some organizations are "tougher" to be a member of than other organizations. Either tough or easy organizations, at their extremes, are likely to be distrusting.

It is important to remember that trust is only part of an organization's culture, but it is a critical piece, often referred to as the "glue" that keeps a culture intact. We all know of organizations that function, some productively, with little or no trust. They usually have unhappy members, as many members of distrustful organizations have no other options, or some choose to remain, thriving on chaos and dissension.

No organization can capture trust as an attribute permanently. Social change and the unpredictability of human behavior do not permit organizations to reach perfection. This is the challenge for CEO's, to manage change and trust concurrently so that the organization remains at the healthy, trustful end of the continuum.

Chapter 6

Challenges to Trust During Change and Crises

"Speed exhilarates and energizes ... Speed helps force an organization 'outside of itself' and prevents an inward focus."[1]

INTRODUCTION

Among the values espoused by General Electric's leaders throughout the company are two that deal with change. These are:

- "Stimulate and relish change ... are not frightened or paralyzed by it. See change as opportunity, not just a threat.
- Have enormous energy and the ability to energize and invigorate others. Understand speed as a competitive advantage and see the total organizational benefits that can be derived from a focus on speed."[2]

At the other extreme, the CEO of a large manufacturing company told his employees to be patient. He said, "They want things to change too quickly." These two companies illustrate opposite views on change, one wants faster change and one wants slower change. While change is ongoing and has its own speed, we can try to speed it up, or slow it down. When the changes are the ones we want, we often try to speed them up; when changes are viewed as possible threats, we try to slow them down or we resist them. Whether change is seen as "good" or "bad" is related to whose idea the change is, how change will be managed, and who will be responsible for its effects. In some organizations, change often is imposed by leaders, and members have to deal with the effects, whether they like them or not.[3] Most organizational leaders equate change with progress, and progress means growth or expansion. Most of the CEO's interviewed said that expansion and growth were changes they planned for the future of their organizations.

PLANNED CHANGE AND TRUST

Change can affect trust, especially if changes are imposed, rapid, pervasive, and unexpected by members. This is best illustrated by the personnel problems that usually follow mergers, hostile takeovers, buyouts, acquisitions, and demergers. On the other hand, change which is slow, focused, and planned can strengthen trust. An example might be a spin-off group of church members who form a new church in a new suburb with the help of their former pastors. There usually is considerable pride on the part of the parent church in helping "grow" a new congregation and loyalty from the spin-off members to the parent church. But, change extends along a continuum, from hostile mergers to assisted change. The important factor in these examples is the degree to which the leaders engage the members of their organizations in discussions and decisions about change and its implementation. The possibilities range from leaders' exclusion of organizational members to leaders' partnership with organizational members in planning and implementing change. The more trusting the organizational culture, the more likely change will be a partnership; the less trusting the organizational culture, the more likely change will be an ordeal, resented, and resisted. Nyhan (2000) has proposed that participation in decision-making, feedback from and to employees, and empowerment of employees lead to increased interpersonal trust between supervisor and employee in a public organization. Trust-building practices between supervisors and employees can lead to increased productivity and strengthened organizational commitment.

Figure 6.1 shows the relationship between the extent to which leaders involve members in planned change and the level of trust in the organization. A high trust organization is one in which the leader and members jointly engage in organizational planning. This could be called a *proactive organization*. It is likely there will be a great deal of mutual support, wide participation, cohesion, and enthusiasm in such an organization, especially if members participate in the full spectrum of planning from initial input to implementation.

Another high trust organizational culture is one in which the leader and his/her inner circle dominate organizational planning and members participate perfunctorily. This could be called a *focused organization*. It is likely to be structured, and task oriented, with members responsible for carrying out the leader's agenda. Members have a high degree of loyalty and commitment to this type of organization, such as the military.

In low trust organizations, where the leader may encourage the involvement of the total organization in planning in an effort to "turn the organization to a

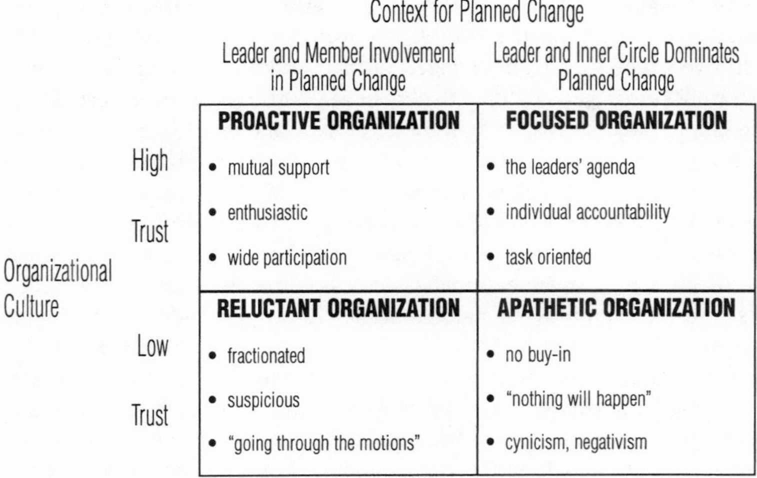

Figure 6.1. Relationship Between Context for Planned Change and Level of Organizational Trust.

more trusting one," there may be more trust in the leader than in the culture. This could be called a *reluctant organization*. In this organization, members like what they hear but they remain suspicious about whether their involvement will entail more than "going through the motions." This is often an organization that has a history of distrust. This low trust culture is characterized by members who dismiss planning as a bureaucratic exercise and believe that change will happen whether it is planned or not. Oftentimes, members in low trust cultures have seen change other than that planned for imposed upon them so they are cynical about planning. Perhaps the most ineffective organization is the *apathetic organization*. The leader and the leader's inner circle engage in planning and members follow, reluctantly. There is no buy-in to most things in the organization because it is believed that "nothing positive will happen." Cynicism and negativism are common, fed by a cycle in which leaders make decisions without involving members, and members say, "I told you so." A great deal of withdrawal behavior (lack of participation) takes place in such an organization.

Planning involves changing the mind-set of an organization.[4] Leadership style and philosophy, as well as the past and present level of trust in the organization, affect members' attitudes about and willingness to invest in planning change. As Kets de Vries & Balazs (1999) point out, planned change is a cognitive *and* emotional process, which can lead to more pain than pleasure unless planned change and the total organization's participation in it is a core value of the organization. Trusting organizations are more likely to regard change as positive, have established ways of coping with change, and encourage members to create change.

Many leaders of organizations will say, "sure we involve our members in planned change." This was the attitude uncovered in a survey of state-level executives in two states who were engaged in restructuring their agencies following the Welfare Reform Act of 1996 (Bruhn, et al., 2001). Employee participation in planned change was seen as a right by executives and employees at the state and county levels in both states. However, the actual levels of employee participation in planned change within these agencies were low. There was concern among executives that employees would limit their views of change to their level in the organization and would want quick fixes to problems, and to have them participate in all phases of organizational change might raise employee expectations unrealistically. The employees stated that they know and understand client needs and therefore, their input is important. All of this said, the agencies did not involve their employees as fully as they could have in all phases of organizational change. Not all employees wish to participate in planned change to the maximum extent. Organizational leaders in trusting cultures are more likely to provide the opportunity for participation and permit members to choose the extent of their involvement. Organizations need to provide training for members in how they can participate effectively in planned change. Organizational leaders may also need to be trained in how to involve a total organization in planning change.

UNPLANNED CHANGE AND TRUST

Planning change must include contingencies for unexpected change. Unexpected events and actions can set-back or dismantle the most carefully designed plan for change. Therefore, planned change must include several options for meeting goals and objectives, including the possibility that some goals and objectives may have to be abandoned. Plans need to be developed in steps and evaluated periodically so tremendous time and energy will not have been wasted should an unexpected event foil the plan. Unexpected events are usually, but not exclusively, external to the organization. For example, a CEO, at the direction of a Board of Trustees, may take an action that conflicts with the organization's plan, or an event at a university main campus may lead to the creation of a policy that affects all of its satellite campuses. Unexpected events can be very demoralizing to an organization that has invested a great deal of time and resources in planning. Even in a trusting organization, morale is put to the test when unexpected events make new possibilities impossible.

The generally accepted view is that stability in organizations is necessary to build trust. Instability in organizations often is considered the result of an ineffective leader. But organizations, like individuals, are living, dynamic organisms, they are never completely stable or unstable.[5] It is the fact that organizations are constantly changing (creating as well as responding to change within and without the organization) that can make the effects of unplanned change so acute. This is where the experience and skills of a trustful leader come into play. The leader's response to unplanned change influences how organizational members will respond to it. This is why it is important that leaders and members have a consonant relationship which may be put to the test during an episode of unplanned change.

TYPICAL ORGANIZATIONAL CHANGE AND TRUST

All of the CEO's interviewed were involved with managing change of various magnitudes ranging from that of one manufacturing company, which had been doubling sales annually for several years and opening new plants in Mexico, to that of a health sciences center which was restructuring after a demerger with an HMO. One of the most common types of change, was that of a transition in leadership. Either the CEO was a recent hire, or the umbrella organization of which the CEO was a part had hired a new president. Many of the organizations adapting to a new leader had had an interim CEO while a search for a new CEO was underway. This meant that some organizations had been in a leadership transition for one to two years.

1. *Leadership Transitions*. According to a recent Harvard Business School study, CEO's are getting older, with 44 percent of them over 60, and today, their average tenure is slipping to slightly less than eight years.[6] A study by a New York consulting firm found that leading executives in distressed companies, had been in their positions for eight years, on the average, compared to 5.2 years at healthier companies. The CEO turnover rate, in general, is fairly substantial and accelerating, and one-third of current CEO's at major companies, today, have come from outside.

   Leadership transitions in family businesses are often stressful as the founder usually has a difficult time "letting go." Among the CEO's of second generation family businesses interviewed, it was not uncommon for 85–90 year old fathers to still come to work. Several of the CEO children of the founders said that they inherited trusting companies whose industry had changed, but that their fathers didn't have the interest to change. Often, this meant the new CEO had to restructure and downsize. In addition, employees had gotten used to working with the new CEO family member in another role, such as sales or marketing, before the founder retired. The new CEO often was distrusted by members because the organization wasn't doing things as they had been done in the past.

   Whether a CEO is chosen from outside an organization, or is a family member who succeeds the founder in a family business, the "halo effect" of the trustfulness of the organization is only temporary. CEO's have to earn their own trust.

2. *Personnel Turnovers*. Personnel turnovers are also likely to occur when CEO's turn over or when the organization undergoes major structural changes like mergers, acquisitions, and buy-outs. Turnovers may also occur involuntarily, through downsizing by not filling vacancies when they occur, and through early retirements. The New York consulting firm mentioned previously reviewed data from 107 of its clients who were in financial distress and found that 40 percent of the companies had extraordinarily low employee turnover. Low employee turnover at many companies causes a lack of creativity, stale management, and failure to adapt to change.[7] For example, one manufacturer bought an expensive software package to improve its operations, but never used it because middle management was comfortable with the existing system. The study found that people at distressed companies not only had longer tenure, but stayed in the same job category longer than those at healthier companies. There are always exceptions, however, such as the CEO of a 35 year old travel agency, founded by her mother, which has grown to three offices and annual sales of $24 million. The CEO said that the general manager, who has been with the firm for over 20 years, "is like a daughter." Her husband joined the firm a few years ago for a second career and one of her sons is the manager of one of the three offices. The CEO said, "No one looks after a business like a family member." This business has had no layoffs in 35 years and very little turnover.[8] The CEO prides herself in maintaining open communication, loyalty, and truthfulness among the 60 employees. Long tenure among employees does not always mean resistance to change and stagnation. It depends on the nature of the business and its leader.

Whenever turnover occurs in an organization, it disrupts patterns of established trust. The CEO of a data processing and consulting firm expressed frustration at the high turnover rate of his employees, despite his efforts to establish a trusting culture. With some anger he said there was a work ethic difference in the young generation—"tell me what you are going to do for me; not, I'll show you what I can do." He said younger employees "don't trust our technical knowledge, it has to be state-of-the-art." He said young employees had no loyalty, no career focus, and little up-front commitment despite the fact that the firm fully pays for the advanced education of employees who make A's and B's, pays $10 an hour for internships for students studying for business degrees, pays annual bonuses, gives merit increases as they are recommended during the year, and provides profit-sharing for long-term employees. They have difficulty in filling management positions because, the CEO said, "they don't come for the long-term." He concluded "we want a true work ethic in our firm."[9] When turnover is frequent and pervasive, it gives no time to "connect" employees to a culture.

3. *Budget Planning and Allocations*. In large, complex organizations the annual budget process tests trust in the organization. Often, a budget committee that conducts budget hearings with major units of the organization to hear their projected plans and financial needs for the next year or so. At the conclusion of these hearings, the CEO and decision team put together a budget. In public universities, the budget goes through various bureaucratic layers, ending up at the state legislature. In private organizations, it is usually the Board of Directors or Trustees that makes final budget plans with the CEO. Budgeting is a process every organization goes through every year, yet budget processes, the players in the decisions, and the available resources change. This makes the budget process an on-going concern in organizations. It is not simply a matter of making a good case for more money. The budget process is highly politicized in most organizations; there never are enough resources, so some, or even all requests usually will be cut; the bottom line concern for most organizational members is that regarding their own salaries.

   In one large university, the President made a comment at a campus meeting about the annual budget being developed. He was questioned closely by the faculty, indicating their distrust of the existing process. In order to demonstrate trust, the President revamped the process, including the President of the Faculty Senate and two Vice Provosts on a large politically representative campus committee. The President said, "We are going to keep this process open." As one of the Vice Presidents told the author, "He followed through on what he said he was going to do. The process is uniformly accepted—he has been President for 9 years. In addition, when our budget was cut last year, the President recommended that the percentage of merit available for administrators and faculty be reduced in order to give a cost of living raise to the staff."[10]

   Yet, at a major health sciences center, the CEO of a college told the author that budget time was always a crisis on their campus, especially when resources were tight (which was all the time). He said that budget decisions often were made and never *fully* explained. College CEO's eventually learned about each other's budgets and there was always resentment about whatever amount each college received. The CEO said that the college CEO's always felt decisions were made by a few, that their input was *pro forma*, and that no one outside of the President's inner circle actually knew how final budgets were put together.

   Budgets, to those who are responsible for them, are highly personal. Therefore, budget cuts are taken personally. Usually, it takes only one budget cycle to sow the seeds of trust or distrust in the process. Usually, the budget decision-making process is a good barometer of the overall trust level in an organization and of members' feelings about how powerful their CEO is in negotiating for their organization.

The Superintendent of a major public school system said, "When people deal with issues of the heart, namely money and children, they are not objective. That's why a CEO should not make promises. This community has never seen a CEO deliver on promises. I tell them, "I can't tell you what I can't deliver."[11]

Leadership transitions, personnel turnovers, and budget planning and allocation are typical changes encountered by the majority of organizations. All of these have direct implications for the trust of the organization, but are not as potentially devastating as the crises we will discuss next.

ORGANIZATIONAL CRISES AND TRUST

Probably the most significant thing about a merger, hostile takeover, or buyout is not that they happen, but *how* they happen, and their effects. Most occur quickly, often after covert planning and denial from the leaders, so that the rank and file members are surprised, stunned, and greatly angered. Corporate trust and loyalty to a company offer no protection against these intrusive types of organizational crises. Indeed, after 34 years with a company, an employee dismissed rumors that it would close. His bosses, who he knew personally, had promised him the rumors were not so, but in the months leading up to the company's closing the company's public statements retreated from "never" to "it all depends" to "probably so." The prizes the employee had won for perfect attendance and promotions for dependable work were overwhelmed by his anger. He believed that the company owed him something. "I trust them," he said.[12]

Organizational leaders have been warned to be vigilant about increasing layoff rage.[13] Recently, the manager of information management systems, one of 50 employees laid off by a chemical company, used an executive's computer password to tap into the company's computer system from home and delete critical inventory and personnel files, causing $20 million in damage and delaying a long-planned public stock offering. While attacks on computer systems by outside hackers generate most of the headlines, the results from a survey conducted online by *Security Magazine* in 2000 indicate that a significant number of companies experience insider security breaches such as sabotage or intentional destruction of computer equipment; electronic theft, sabotage, or intentional destruction or disclosure of proprietary data or information, and abuse of computer access controls. One company executive said that it is not just the laid-off employees who pose a threat. Employees who survive a lay-off also can vandalize company property to avenge their departed coworkers.

According to an annual survey of Fortune 1000 companies by Pinkerton, Inc., two of the most common acts of revenge are theft of company property and breaches in the company's computer network. Estimates are that employee retaliation occurs in only 1 percent of dismissals, but could be as high as 5 percent at companies that do not handle layoffs well or that have a hostile corporate culture. Disgruntled employees have found it easy to take their frustration out by spreading false information in the chat rooms, sending out fake news releases, or badmouthing their former employer. Some companies help increase the anger of laid-off employees by using security guards to watch them pack their personal belongings and then escort them out of the building.

It is not surprising that the literature indicates that mergers are most likely to be successful when they are the result of choice, and communication processes are in place. Yet, major difficulties can arise when trying to merge two different organizational cultures even within the same industry. Merger success often depends on choosing good strategies of negotiation, yet the significance of the human side of the merger appears after the merger has occurred. When attempts to resolve potential operating difficulties and to facilitate the values of employees from both cultures are not completed before the merger, employees may work to sabotage the merger after completion. The success or failure of a merger rests on the ability of the merger's planners to negotiate a new, blended culture from the previously distinct ones. Schein points out, "If we understand the dynamics of culture, we will be less likely to be puzzled, irritated, and anxious when we encounter the unfamiliar and seemingly irrational behavior of people in organizations, and we will have a deeper understanding not only of why various groups of people or organizations can be so different but also why it is so hard to change them."[14]

Much of what we know about mergers comes from their failures. Yet, mergers can be successful politically and financially, even if they fail culturally, at least for awhile (Bruhn, 1998, 2001). However, it is not possible to build a new trusting organization from a merger if the two cultures are too different. Usually, one of the merged cultures fades away, possibly leaving behind a few remnants of its traditions and customs.

Mergers and acquisitions create significant losses for individuals in both of the merged organizations. Levinson (1972) identified four types of loss that occur during times of organizational upheaval. They are: (1) a loss of familiar work relationships, products, and work settings; (2) the loss of support that occurs when ties to valued coworkers are disrupted; (3) the loss of sensory input resulting from changes in the amount or type of information previously received; and (4) the loss of capacity to act caused by destabilization and displacement. Gilkey (1991) makes the analogy of a merger to a blended family when step children and/or adopted children are blended with two parents, both of whom have been married before. As Gilkey says, "it's especially tough if you're not the natural parent and your values are both different and new." There are new issues, all necessary in establishing a new base of trust, such as boundary and territorial alliances to define new roles, responsibility and authority; establishing new bases of power and recognition; and respecting different traditions and beliefs. The blended family must begin to live and work together before all of these functions are worked out. Thus, the development of trust may take longer, depending upon the players and their willingness to adapt.

Demergers

The author had the opportunity to interview the new CEO of a health sciences center who had been recruited to rebuild the health sciences center following a merger and demerger with an HMO.

The merger, which was thought to be a "natural," failed for several reasons. The university hospital was losing money and needed the link with the largest HMO in the state to increase its patient base for income and teaching, and the HMO needed the prestige and benefits it would acquire by linking up with a teaching hospital and medical school. The CEO's of the two organizations, together with an inner circle of five people, planned the merger. Others, who might have had valuable information showing that the merger was not a natural match, were excluded. Indeed, when the faculty and clinical heads were assembled by the CEO of the health sciences center to alert them to the merger, those attending were asked to sign non-disclosure contracts or leave the meeting. Those who attended the meeting and signed the contract were told that if they discussed what transpired, they would be considered disloyal to the health sciences center. The majority of staff and other employees of the medical center learned of the merger the next morning on the car radio, in the daily paper, and on television. The merger was followed by a large exodus of prominent clinical faculty, a threatened strike by the nurses, and the closing of a number of hospital beds. As one respondent said, "the corporate HMO was 'very Soviet' and the head of the medical center 'very patriarchal'—two strong leaders who were soon at loggerheads."

The merger lasted about three years. A new CEO for the medical school arrived following the official demerger. He is working to bring the health sciences center together in common ways in accord with its values. He has established a structure of campus leadership teams of faculty and administrators, he has frequent, open town meetings, and is easily accessible. His goal is to communicate, emphasize values and value fairness, to build trust in him and the organization from scratch.

Downsizing and Restructuring

A less dramatic form of organizational change that still precipitates a crisis is downsizing and restructuring. Downsizing may involve dismissing employees, not filling vacant positions rather than restructuring functions in the organization to improve efficiency, cut costs, and substitute technology for some functions performed by personnel. But these moves precipitate rumors and speculation about what may follow. If these changes are accompanied by budget reductions for programs and resources while there is an expected assumption of additional responsibilities by the remaining employees, trust is also eroded. Employees will complain about work load; there also may be a decrease in productivity, an increase in anxiety and incivility, criticism about the organization's leaders, and cynicism about organizational goals.

Downsizing in a predominately distrusting organization is more serious than in a trusting organization. Leaders in a distrusting organization who do not share information will be scrutinized carefully regarding what they might do next. The new CEO of a large health care organization said, "We have a challenge to repair the bad feelings some of our employees have about the reduction in force we had here three years ago. It was not handled well. It's important that we do this, this time, in a caring way."[15] A poll of senior managers of down-sized companies found that 74 percent believed employees had lower morale, feared future cutbacks, and distrusted management.[16]

The American Management Association found that 47 percent of its 7,000 member firms reduced their work forces in the past several years. Increasingly, downsizings are the result of new strategies to outsource non-essential work to other firms, adopt labor-saving new technology, and realize efficiencies from mergers and acquisitions of other firms. The management association found that companies that view downsizing as an ongoing activity have shown better gains in profitability and worker productivity than firms that downsized only once.[17]

Some dispute whether downsizing pursued to save money really restores companies to profitability because fundamental weaknesses in operations often are not corrected in and, in addition, there is a serious deterioration in employee morale. Downsizing is now becoming a normal, ongoing corporate activity; nonetheless, it has a social cost for organizations. Downsizing indicates to employees that their loyalty is inconsequential to the organization's goals.[18] Employees, in turn, have their eyes on that better job out there. As a result, both employers and employees view each other as a way to meet short-term needs.

Hostile Takeovers and Buy-outs

Hostile takeovers and buy-outs represent extreme forms of organizational crises. Some hostile takeovers begin as friendly mergers that turn sour; other takeover attempts involve name calling and finger pointing from the beginning. The supposed victim in a takeover, if the takeover fails, can, in turn, become the aggressor in a buy-out. An example is the recent $84 per share in cash hostile takeover bid by Union Pacific Resources Group to acquire Pennzoil Co.[19] The Pennzoil Board urged its shareholders not to tender shares, but rather to trust in its strategic plan to increase the value of the company's stock. The fight became public when Union Pacific Resources failed to strike a friendly merger with Pennzoil after negotiating behind the scenes for four months. A dissident, and the largest, shareholder of Pennzoil stock threatened a proxy fight to obtain a seat on the Board. Pennzoil launched a counter-offensive with a number of bylaw changes including reducing the size of its Board. More than 60 percent of Pennzoil's shareholders had offered to sell their shares to Union Pacific Resources, even before the all-cash offer. Many Pennzoil shareholders were unhappy with the management team. Pennzoil fought in court to keep the specifics of their strategic plan secret. Union Pacific Resources withdrew their $4.2 million bid.

A month later, Pennzoil announced that it would buy Quaker State to form the largest motor oil company in the United States. The buy-out came three weeks before Pennzoil's annual stockholder meeting. Pennzoil stockholders were upset about the then $69 value of their stock. A settlement was reached with the dominant stockholder of Pennzoil stock, who said he approved of the Quaker State buy-out. For nearly a year, 5,000 Quaker State employees did not know whether they might have to move or face a layoff.

ORGANIZATIONAL COPING AND SURVIVAL

Organizations change most by surviving crises. Not all crises can be survived but organizations that do survive seem to be better for it (Farson, 1996). Most invasive crises, such as hostile takeovers, are unexpected and can't be planned. Planning has its limitations in organizations. Planning may be more effective in assessing the present than the future in some organizations. It helps to indicate trade-offs, set boundaries, simulate plausible scenarios, integrate ideas, and force people to think about consequences. The process itself is important. Planning is a form of anticipatory, strategic thinking that gives organizations flexibility and readiness (Farson, 1996). Flexibility and readiness are assets in dealing with any crisis.

Organizations that are in touch with themselves and know what helped them survive critical changes in the past usually are well prepared to handle new crises. What often is underestimated is the *personal impact* profound change will have on organizational members. Noel Tichy, a Professor at the University of Michigan has expressed it "most managers are scared to death of emotion. It's a lot easier to put on a macho act and come across as a heartless cost cutter. But if you can't do the 'soft stuff', as well as the 'tough stuff', you'll never get people's total support."[20]

Often organizational leaders have their eye on the organization's long-term future and they and their organizations can be blindsided by sudden external crises. Organizational members often are forgotten while leaders deal with the crises. In insensitive organizations leaders may delegate employee problems to the Human Resources Department. Yet, employee problems do not resolve as rapidly or as easily as leaders might hope. Research has shown that after layoffs and downsizing have occurred, employee productivity and morale decrease, and fear and hostility increase. Organizational leaders often avoid and underestimate the human side of crises.

Two of the key factors that appear to assist organizations in coping with change are communication and caring behavior from their leaders. Michael Blumenthal, former CEO of Unisys, said, "... making sure that gobs of written communication went out and that good people were in charge of that ... and one must not underrate the importance of a personal appearance of someone who has become a symbol of the change."[21] Rosen and Berger (1991) recommend that leaders tell their employees what they know is going to happen, even if the news is unpleasant, suggest ways they can prepare for the change, and regularly share information or facts, even if they are spotty.

CHANGE AND TRUST

Trust can survive change. Change can strengthen trust. It is not uncommon to hear comments in organizations such as, "I don't agree with some of the changes the CEO is making, but I respect the way he is going about them." Obviously, the more the change impacts the individual, the more critical that person will be of the change. Change in organizations requires that members continually adjust their attitudes and behavior regarding trust.

Layered Change and Looped Change

Organizations do not go through one change at a time. Many changes, of different complexities, occur simultaneously and overlap. We could use a fish-scale analogy to illustrate how change is layered and interrelated.[22] Each fish-scale could be considered a single change. The numerous, overlapping scales of the fish call attention to the fact that many changes overlap. Thus, there is both an interrelated and a cumulative effect to change. In this view, there are no gaps between changes, each changes affects all other change in the same organism.

Another perspective on change is that it occurs as loops of interaction as opposed to linear lines (Morgan, 1997). Loops interact with other loops while continually moving at various speeds and creating various configurations. There can be any number of loops interacting at any one point in time, each configuration is unique, but the loops are in constant motion. In this way, we can view change as building upon itself; that is, change begets change, begets change. Change never waits for a clean ending before more change is created. This, of course, makes it difficult, if not impossible, to fully identify the causes of change, understand how it works, and its consequences. What we know about change is drawn from our own observations and experiences and those of others, all of whom are part of the change process.

Because change is layered and looped, it often is difficult to identify the origins of mistrust. Usually, mistrust is additive, that is, a series of actions of a CEO or the leadership team slowly erode trust. Members of organizations often are patient in overlooking mistrustful behavior until the behavior becomes a pattern or an egregious action leads members to abruptly abandon trust in their leaders.

Change does not occur within clear boundaries; hence, its effects usually are not containable despite attempts to contain them. As a result, change in an organization can affect the trust level of members who are not directly affected by the change. This is why CEO's and their management teams must reinforce and strengthen trust continuously throughout an organization, especially in organizations continually undergoing rapid changes.

CHANGE CHANGES RELATIONSHIPS

Bridges said, "it isn't the changes that do you in, it's the transitions."[23] Transitions make trust transitory. Whenever new members join an organization, members leave, or are assigned to new jobs, trust relationships are altered. Two aspects of organizational dynamics, which are key influences in building trust, namely, social and psychological boundaries and social networks, are disrupted when change occurs.

Boundaries are essential in clarifying members' responsibilities, power, and authority in organizations. They determine turf and help everyone define their relationships with each other. Boundaries also have a psychological function. They provide structure for uncertainty and limit anxiety regarding risks and threats (Hirschhorn, 1988). Trust can only be established when boundaries feel comfortable to the trustor and trustee.[24]

A retired army colonel was an assistant to the CEO of an educational institution. He had held positions of substantial responsibility in the military, where boundaries had been clear. In his role as assistant to the CEO, he experienced a great deal of anxiety and frustration with some members of the faculty and staff who did not do what they were supposed to do, did more than they were supposed to do, intruding into others' turf, did not follow guidelines or procedures, and were reluctant self-starters, needing continual handholding. The faculty and staff viewed the assistant to the CEO as too rigid and rule-oriented. There was a great deal of emotional exchange in transactions between the assistant and the faculty and staff, which limited the effectiveness of all parties. As a result, some faculty and staff "went around" the assistant to transact business, which further angered him. The assistant, in turn, belittled those faculty he did not trust to others in the organization when he had the opportunity. Disputes about boundaries and how they were managed interfered with the work of the organization and often required the CEO to mediate between his assistant and members of the faculty and staff. This situation became increasingly intense as, at the same time the organization was being restructured by the CEO, the university was engaged in a massive reorganization, which led to mergers between many campuses. As a result, the assistant to the CEO had increased responsibilities which focused on transacting business across two campuses and helping to meld two cultures.

Establishing and reestablishing boundaries between patients and physicians is occurring so frequently that often there is no time for a trust relationship to form. It is not uncommon for a patient to have several different physicians over the course of a year or two as physicians retire, leave medicine, drop insurance providers, and change employment. Indeed, the physician is the key boundary spanner when services are needed for the chronically ill and dying. Having the same physician is important in providing continuity of care from someone who knows you and your health status. Patients in today's health care system continually must negotiate and span new boundaries of organizations that provide services they need. Some patients, for example, find it easier to buy prescription drugs in Mexico or Canada to avoid the financial boundaries established by pharmaceutical companies in the United States. Patients in non-profit hospices have to negotiate new sources of care when they out-live the six months their physician said they had left to live. And, overcrowded emergency rooms which refuse to admit additional patients, leave boundary-spanning to the ambulance driver who must find an emergency room that will admit them.

A second aspect of organizational dynamics that disrupts trust is changes in social networks. Groups, as well as the individuals within them, have an interest in creating and maintaining the social conditions under which trust can occur (Tyler, 2001). Trust is important because it is a key antecedent of the willingness to cooperate voluntarily. People want resources from others and engage in organizational life to exchange resources. Furthermore, people are motivated to maximize their gain of resources and minimize their losses. To do so, they need to estimate what others will do in response to their own behavior. As they identify with a group and its values, people feel an obligation to the group, leading to cooperation that is distinct from that based on expectations about the behavior of others (Tyler, 2001). People also have another motivation for interacting with others. They use the information they gain from others to define their social identity and their "fit" within an organization. Social networks are modified by losing and adding members, but when the entire network is disbanded by substantial organizational change, members usually have to begin establishing new networks. Their "fit" in the organization often is determined more by their place in a social network, than by their job title. Abrupt, substantial change usually destroys the context in which people derive meaning for their work. This is why mergers, downsizing, and other changes of such magnitude are so devastating to employees; family-like relationships are destroyed each time a network is frayed or eliminated. Under such conditions, the search for trusting relationships is perpetual.

While the positive side of strong social networks is that they give members identity, security, pride, motivation, and psychological rewards, they also have a downside. Dense social networks can become pockets of resistance that are "closed" to accepting even minor changes, even if they are productive. This was the case in one department in an organization where the ten members had worked together for over fifteen years, surviving changes in CEO's, and remaining relatively untouched by major changes in the larger organization. The ten employees had become personal friends, knew about each other's families and off-work activities, and at work, were highly productive and known for their customer-sensitivity. The department received many awards for quality improvement, customer service, and exemplary behavior. A merger required that this department be merged with its counterpart in a location about 50 miles away. Both departments had similar histories of loyal, diligent employees who had formed close social networks. Distance and cost made it impossible for employees in either location to commute. New methods of delivering services needed to be put in place, which meant that jobs needed to be restructured, employees had to learn new technology, and some downsizing would take place. Rather than experience these changes, the employees at one location decided to leave the organization. While this choice destroyed their network at work, they continued to be friends. They did not want to go through the ordeal of having to establish new working relationships and learn new ways of doing their jobs. While this choice is not always financially feasible, it illustrates the point that social networks can be more powerful than loyalty to one's organization.

Another example is that of a social network that tried to prevent change from occurring in an organization. A new pastor and assistant pastor arrived to head a new, growing suburban church affiliated with a larger conservative religious body. The new pastor was young, aggressive, innovative and eager. A small group of about 12 families took a dislike to the new pastor and claimed that the changes he was making were taking the church away from its traditional customs and beliefs. The families began to take different members of the congregation, including the assistant pastor, to lunch to talk them into a movement to remove the new pastor. Over a period of two years, these dissident families attempted repeatedly to oust the pastor. Finally, the families transferred to other churches. Sometimes, social networks, which are out of step with the majority can isolate themselves and become victims to change.

BUILDING, MANAGING, AND PREVENTING ORGANIZATIONAL FIRES

All organizations have fires, some are the by-products of change and some are symptoms of problems that need to be addressed. Leaders and members of organizations help to set, manage, and prevent fires. Organizational fires are deliberately set to call attention to problems. Fires never extinguish themselves; they may smolder for awhile, burn continuously if fueled, and if ignored long enough can, easily spread and become major fires. Organizations and their leaders usually are more experienced in putting out fires than they are at preventing them. Building and managing fires are characteristic behaviors of low trust organizations, while fire prevention distinguishes high trust organizations.

Building Fires

Leaders chance building possible fires in organizations every time they make a controversial or highly emotional decision. Baum (2000) points out that employees work for themselves and evaluate change according to their self-interest. The leader's job is to focus on areas where change offers benefits to everyone and to help employees see the benefits of change, if not for themselves, for the whole organization. This is difficult in low trusting organizations, in which members may not trust the leader or the culture.

When people resist change, it often is because they are comfortable with their own situation and see more benefits in not changing. In this case, leaders may be faced with a dilemma, as resistors to change often are loyal, conscientious, long-term employees, whose resistance may hold back innovation in the entire organization. In this instance, the leader may have to build a fire by reorganizing or dissolving units in order to break up pockets of resistance to change. When a fire is set, the leader expects it to be a containable brush fire. However, in low trusting cultures, any fire may provide dissidents and resistors with the opportunity to widen it.

Leaders and their staffs inadvertently can set wild fires with off-hand remarks or comments that are insufficiently explained. Sometimes, leaders want to "try out" ideas they have been thinking about. Sometimes, the reaction to these ideas is intense enough to kill further consideration of them. Leaders need to be careful to not to float too many ideas or attempt too many changes at once lest they create more wildfires than thinkers.

Managing Fires

Some leaders inherit perpetual fires that are part of the organization's culture. For example, one 40 year old educational organization was never satisfied with it's name and identity. Every problem or prospect for the future seemed to raise the unresolved issues of name and identity. No amount of discussion about these issues seemed to help, indeed, there were so many different opinions, the fire worsened when attempts to extinguish it were made.

Most of the CEO's interviewed in this study talked about different amounts of time that they, or their staff, spent in putting out fires. Downsizing which is becoming routine for organizations, provides fuel for continuous wildfires. Organizations are comprised of many different personalities with different needs. Some members gain personal satisfaction from setting fires. Often, these are chronically unhappy, distrusting people who resent authority, lack organizational loyalty, and have their own agendas, disenfranchised members who previously have had negative experiences in the organization and seek revenge by being chronic obstacles to progress and change. Every organization has a few such people who usually are the source of gossip, rumors, and fires.

Leaders and their staffs spend a great deal of time managing fires of different scopes. The more the organization is in flux, and the more distrusting it is, the greater the frequency of fires. Fires sometimes are deliberately set to test new leadership to see how it will react. In one organization, some members delighted in bringing up issues that previous leaders had not satisfactorily resolved in order to see how their new leader would react.

Organizations that are moderately trusting will have brush fires, wildfires, and only a few forest fires. Leaders need more than themselves and their staff to manage fires. Fire management can consume enormous time and energy and prevent a future-oriented agenda. That is why it is essential that leaders develop the fire-fighting capacity of the whole organization. This can be done by employing frequent, clear, and full communication with the entire organization to dispel rumors and gossip. Also important is the involvement of members in all phases of the organization. Informed and participating members seldom set fires.

Preventing Fires

Organizations of high trust have few fires. Leaders are experts in preventing them. An anonymous author said "Plan ahead. Noah built the ark before it started raining."[25] Leaders cannot anticipate all fires; indeed, unintended consequences may result from actions or inactions that, from the view of the leader, are minor. Fire prevention depends upon knowing your organization, being able to think like and anticipate the reactions of members, and to know how they see things as a result of continuous dialogue and involvement. This reduces the opportunity for unintended consequences of change.

Some fires are good for an organization. They indicate that the organization is a living system; no matter how much planning and anticipation takes place, it's not perfect. Even high trust cultures and leaders misread or slip up. Fires focus and mobilize organizations. While there is always some destruction, fires lead to rebuilding with a different perspective.

DO PEOPLE REALLY CHANGE?

Some authors of organizational dynamics believe that people don't really change. They modify their attitudes and behavior to do what has to be done. They adapt, but fundamentally, they do not change their personal beliefs and values. Most authors believe that people do change, but they do so at different speeds, in different ways, and at times that are meaningful to them (Binney & Williams, 1995). Usually, people who choose not to change, leave the organization if they can. Those who remain usually are acceptors of change.

Kets de Vries and Balazs (1999) described several prerequisites of personal change. One is that some form of discomfort is a catalyst for change. Studies of personal change indicate that a high level of stress is a major inducement to individual change. Individuals who report major change say that they find the status quo increasingly difficult to maintain. Negative emotions lead to a weighing of the pros and cons in an effort to resolve stress.

Accepting the need for change is not enough to get people to change. They needed a "focal event" to move them forward. Often this is an event that leads them to reevaluate their situation. The focal event helps the person take the necessary action to change.

Kets de Vries and Balazs (1999) pointed out that a third prerequisite to personal change is a public declaration of the intent to change. Telling others what one plans to do indicates an acceptance of change.

These prerequisites help people to take the necessary steps to change. These steps evolve as a process, just as they do in organizations. All change involves letting go of the past and getting used to the new. Leaders who recognize that changing people's mind-set, as well as that of the organization, takes support and prodding, understanding, and tolerance of reluctance and backtracking, will be more successful in seeing the results of real change.

No organization or individual is completely protected from change. Organizations and individuals have a history of how they have handled change previously. Some organizations and individuals are better "fits" for each other than others. Potential employees should carefully select organizations to join. Max De Pree, retired Chair and CEO of Herman Miller, Inc. said that "healthy companies are about shared ideals, shared goals, shared respect, and a shared sense of values and mission."[26] Organizations, on the other hand, should select employees who are able to take the stresses and strains of change, who are experienced survivors of change, and who share the organization's values.

SUMMARY

Change is part of the life of all organizations and the individuals within them. We have some choices about change—we can initiate change rather than let it happen; we can accelerate change; we can resist change, but we cannot eliminate change or fully control its effects. Even closed and physically isolated organizations are influenced by changes in the larger world of which they are a part.

One issue regarding change is whether to plan for its consequences or merely to cope with what change brings us. Organizations with histories of trust tend to plan for change; they want to direct their future as much as possible and minimize unintended consequences. The members of distrustful organizations usually do not trust their leaders to plan for them, and leaders, in turn, do not involve members in planning the organization's future. Distrusting organizations seem to adapt to whatever fate or luck brings them. On the other hand, the members of trusting organizations take a great deal of pride in helping to shape their future by participating in it.

It is possible to categorize, for discussion, the relationship between organizational trust and members' degree of involvement in planned change. The epitome of a high trust/high involvement organization is one in which there is mutual support, wide participation, and enthusiasm. The opposite, the apathetic organization, is one in which members do not "buy into" the leader's agenda, and there is much criticism and cynicism about the results of planning—nothing has happened in the past to expect us to believe that spending time and effort in planning will yield positive results. Hence, leaders of apathetic organizations help fulfill the prophesy by doing the planning themselves.

Leaders in these times, especially, are expected to "involve" and "empower" members of their organizations. Most leaders will say that they do this; however, studies have shown that there is reluctance on the part of many leaders to "let go" of the planning process. Members tend to end up with the tasks of implementing ideas or activities that they had no input into and do not believe in.

Every organization experiences typical types of changes such of leadership succession, personnel turnover, and budget planning and allocations. How leaders and organizations handle "routine" change provides insights into how they will cope with major crises, such as mergers, hostile take-overs, and buy-outs, when they arise. Most organizations do not handle major crises well—they usually focus on financial and market outcomes, and leave employees to the skills of

Human Resources Departments. It is not surprising that there is lay-off rage, no employee loyalty to employers, nor employer loyalty to employees. Trust is not a primary virtue in today's workplace.

But the lack of trust extends to organizations beyond the workplace, where there is a lack of interest in commitment and involvement. The societal emphasis on individualism and personal rewards has overshadowed the value of giving of personal time and energy to a variety of organizations. As Putnam noted in his book, it is easier to write a check.

Organizations have established ways of coping with change; some organizations do not cope well and fall by the wayside. Survivors of change usually are organizations that are in touch with their values and their members; and these organizations are proactive and trusting. Trust survives change. Change usually makes an organization stronger.

Change changes relationships between people in organizations; in particular, their boundaries and social networks. These relationships provide the basis for trust. When they are disturbed through major change, members are left without direction and structure. Leaders often assume that following a major change, employees will fall into place once the managerial, financial, and organizational structures are established. Losing one's social network and working in uncertainty, without limits and expectations, is anxiety-producing and demoralizing. This is why the productivity level of employees falls following a major organizational transition.

Some authors question whether individuals in organizations actually change or whether they just learn to adapt to a different survival plan. Most research shows that organizations and individuals do change, but in their own ways, at their own speeds, and in unique timetables that may differ from others' expectations. Trust is always altered by change; organizations and individuals become more or less trusting depending upon how kindly they have been treated by change in the past.

A key characteristic of a trusting organization that copes well with change is the outbreak of fewer organizational fires. This is because the leadership team is proactive; they know their organization, benefit from on-going feedback from members, and involve members in networking to prevent rumors, gossip, fires, and unproductive behavior. Organizations where leaders and their staffs spend the majority of their time putting out fires are low trust organizations in which the majority of time, effort, and resources are used to contain and maintain activity rather than to broaden and create it. Low trust organizations build fires, moderate trusting organizations manage fires, and high trust organizations prevent fires. One of the most effective tools for preventing organizational fires is trust.

Chapter 7

The Culture That Wouldn't Budge: A Case Study

"Organizations that need help most will benefit from it least."[1]

INTRODUCTION

Many organizational experts dream of developing a new organization from scratch, applying all of the existing knowledge there is about what makes an organization "good," "healthy," "effective," and "productive." Most new organizations start out with the intention of becoming models. Despite good intentions new organizations soon learn the realities of culture. Two common myths are soon dispelled: (1) culture is strong enough to resist all change—the fantasy that the new organization always will remain vigorous and fresh; and (2) culture change can be managed—the fantasy that the leaders of organizations will be able to successfully manage change so that the craftsmanship, and original mission, and tenets of the founders are not altered (Deal & Kennedy, 1999). As we learned earlier, once a new organization begins its lifecycle it changes continuously. Leaders and members of organizations come and go and leave their marks on the organization, but the forces of change and processes of growth or decline continually shape the organization's future.

Following is a case study of an educational institution that wanted to change, but as one member said, "We just can't seem to get it together so that things happen for the good—our culture always seems to get in the way of constructive change." The organization has changed by inches, indeed, it had to because of changes imposed on it by its parent institution, but for one step forward it always seemed to take two steps backward. Over its 35 year history, a succession of eight CEO's were unable to move the organization forward significantly. The author had the opportunity to be a consultant to this organization for several years. The account and analysis that follow are an attempt to unravel and understand what went wrong and what went right over a period of years. Participant observers are never free from their biases, yet it is hoped that this in-depth case analysis can help the reader to understand why, and how, distrust develops in organizations.[2]

TEN THEMES

This case study is structured around ten themes that have dominated this educational institution's life history. The case study is labeled, "The culture that wouldn't budge" because the mission, goals, and objectives of the organization remain as they were outlined at its founding; only words have been rearranged in the course of many strategic plans. Deal and Jenkins (1994) use the image of the theater to help understand organizations, especially the hidden side of organizations (their backstage). The front-of-the house, more visible aspects of organizations change with the least effort and controversy. Most of the work in organizations is carried out backstage. The hidden aspects of organizations are powerful. In this case study, the backstage kept the organization from progressing to its potential.

A Love-Hate Relationship with the Past

This educational organization was created because of an opportunity—the closing of a military base near a large city. The governor of the state, in conjunction with a university president, was able to acquire the land and buildings, to be converted into a branch campus. The stark military buildings were not as welcoming as the older, rustic ivy-covered buildings in nearby private colleges, but the state university saw this as an opportunity to have a presence near the state legislature and offer educational opportunities to working adults who wished to complete their baccalaureate degree or who sought a graduate degree.

The culture of the college was rooted in this mission. The university had the hope of serving and influencing state government, which provided the majority of its budget. The community, in turn, saw the upper division and graduate institution as an opportunity to obtain associate, baccalaureate, and graduate degrees without having to leave the immediate area.

Dorms were provided for full-time students; classes were available nights and weekends to accommodate working adults. Faculty members were dedicated teachers who personalized their relationships with students by serving as coaches for sports teams, advisors, and mentors. The presence of the college was extended downtown to include an outreach center in a building which had been purchased by the university directly across from the capital. This center provided noon seminars and other opportunities for policy makers to mix with educators and community leaders to dialogue about pending legislation. A benefactor donated another building also near the capitol where classes could be held during the lunch hour and after work to accommodate state workers. The city saw this downtown extension of the branch campus as an attraction to draw business to the city and create opportunities for students and faculty members to participate in research, policy development, internships, and the evaluation of state funded programs.

In the early years of its lifecycle the branch campus was small, intimate, and grew slowly. The campus and its leadership was given a great deal of autonomy in curriculum and policy matters by the university. Many of the first faculty were primarily teachers without research agendas. The first students had earned Associate degrees at a local community college and were eager to complete their bachelor's degree. Following the Vietnam War, the campus burgeoned with students. While faculty liked the way the college had evolved, they soon faced problems of growth. There was a need for graduate degrees and hence a need to recruit doctoral level faculty. There was a decreased need for campus resources for full-time students since most were older, working adults, many with families who did not need to live on campus. As the student body grew, so did the a need to update and expand teaching facilities. Administrators saw this as an opportunity to ask for new funds to transform the military appearance of the campus. However, for a variety of reasons the university did not support this request. Faculty members continuously complained that the "look" of the campus was a deterrent to recruiting students and faculty. Nearby public and private colleges and universities heightened their recruitment of students and offered competing degree programs. The faculty at the campus had pride in the small, personal atmosphere of their college and its quality, but believed "that we can be better than we are now." Yet, they resented attempts by the larger university to make the campus conform to the policies of the parent university. Later in its lifecycle, the university would experience a large reorganization that caused the campus to reluctantly merge with a nearby lower division campus creating a four-year college in the same university system. Faculty at the upper division and graduate campus who resented not having a vote in the merger, asserted, "we were better than we are now."

The upper-division and graduate campus had formed a small, cohesive culture of teachers and researchers who wanted to become a four year college and graduate center on its own merits. The forced merger with a lower division campus, even within the same university system, was felt to be "degrading"—"they don't do research like we do," "they are like a community college," "what will they do for us?" A great deal of distrust developed toward administrators at the parent university. The campus faculty and staff believed that they were being treated like "stepchildren" and that university administrators wanted to spend money on the parent campus instead of improving the branch campuses. Over the years, a love-hate relationship with its past and future developed at the branch campus—potential was seen as where the campus had been, and that was always better than where it currently was.

We've Had Poor CEO's

Other nearby universities and colleges offered new degrees and curricula, formed consortia and coalitions, and developed incentives to attract students. They also acquired space downtown in the capital city where they instituted many competing programs. Faculty bemoaned these expansionary efforts as opportunities missed by their college leadership. To encourage faculty to use these facilities, one CEO held many meetings at the college's two downtown locations, taught a course downtown and strongly encouraged the faculty to offer courses downtown. The faculty complained of difficulties in parking, of the 20 minute drive, of the lack of food in the buildings, and insufficient security. As competitors became more innovative and captured more of the market, the college faculty complained that the college was not moving forward; yet faculty were unwilling to extend their efforts beyond the security of their offices, classrooms, and parking spaces that they had held for years.

Faculty placed the blame on "poor CEO's." As noted earlier, the college had a succession of leaders over it's history with an average tenure of four years. The more the CEO's did to connect the college with peers and colleagues, the more the college faculty resisted. CEO's planned artistic, musical and social events to draw the community to the campus, but faculty members, because they usually left the campus after teaching their courses, did not attend. They would not return to the campus for evening or weekend events. All college meetings and forums were poorly attended. CEO's developed opportunities for colleagues in nearby colleges and universities to meet with college faculty to explore joint teaching and research efforts but to no avail. One CEO sponsored lunches, inviting colleagues with similar interests to the college campus, but there was no follow-up by college faculty. The attitude that "we are not as good as we have been, or could be, because of poor leadership," was a common response to any leadership effort within the college to reach out to its larger community.

Too Good to be True

The more CEO's pointed out the potential for the college, the more the faculty responded with "it's too good to be true—we've heard that before." The culture of the college had become fixated on what it offered and faculty made minimal efforts to change their teaching place or time to help meet changing needs in the larger community. As faculty learned not to believe what their leaders told them, leaders, in turn, learned that they shouldn't expect much from faculty beyond the limits of their contracts. No one seemed willing to work for the benefit of the college as a community.

In one educational unit of the college, a faculty member, who had been disenfranchised by previous CEO's, criticized the administrators in his classes, and organized meetings to which he invited administrators to meet with students to discuss concerns. The students had been coached to make the meeting confrontive and adversarial. Administrators later learned that this faculty member had gone on recruiting trips in the state, discouraging prospective students from coming to his college. This faculty member posted criticisms of his colleagues on bulletin boards and organized subversive efforts to discredit the application of an African-American colleague for tenure and promotion. He rallied support from other disenfranchised faculty who had been unsuccessful in their bids for tenure and promotion, and who were poor teachers, conducted no research, engaged in little professional service, and were generally unproductive. Through letter writing to alumni and other efforts, this faculty member and his supporters perpetuated the idea that whatever was wrong with the college was because "we have had poor CEO's."

We've Done That and It Didn't Work

The goal of successive CEO's was to break the cynicism, negativism, and apathy of the culture by offering numerous positive alternatives. One idea was to develop an Honors Program. There was interest in this idea on the part of a minority of faculty who saw this as a way of recruiting excellent students from two year colleges with Honors Programs and for retaining baccalaureate students for graduate programs. A faculty meeting was held with much debate; many faculty members viewed an Honors Program as more work for them and wanted the assurance of course releases. They criticized Honors Programs as fostering elitism among students and the faculty who taught Honors courses. After much debate the decision was made to develop an Honors Program on a trial basis because the idea had been suggested and tried previously, but failed. The second attempt failed also, despite generous administrative financial support for faculty and students, new resources, and space. Faculty members who did not support the program, and were not asked to teach in it, disparaged it in their informal comments with students—"why do all that extra work to be recognized as an Honors student?"

Officials from city government approached the college with a unique opportunity to partner with them in working with a city in Mexico. The venture provided business opportunities for the U.S. and Mexican cities as well as a partnership between a university in the Mexican city and the college campus. The two cities became sister cities and the university and college became partners in a series of planned exchanges of faculty and students. There was little interest among faculty in the U.S.-Mexico opportunity. Students who heard of the program asked why more people weren't taking advantage of it. Only one educational unit in the college was actively involved in this multi-national opportunity. Little interest and no energy seemed to be expended to make this opportunity work. Eventually, the educational partnership dissipated. Programs that failed because of the lack of involvement and support were used as an example to support the attitude, "we've done that and it didn't work." It seemed that no spark that would ignite a sufficient number of faculty to create and sustain innovation and positive change.

Staff often are overlooked as a barometer of spirit in organizations, primarily because they lack power. But the staff of this college consisted of extremely hard-working, loyal, long-term employees who were also astute observers. Some staff members had worked for a number of CEO's and affirmed, with shaking heads, that changes in the culture were needed, but no one had been successful in creating long-term behavioral change. The staff had a great deal of esprit de corps and pride in their work. The physical plant and grounds of the college were kept immaculate, floors shone, walls were freshly painted, and it was rare to find a burned out light bulb. Staff provided warmth to the ordinarily unfriendly, sterile, class-like atmosphere, with greetings, smiles, and hallway conversations. Ironically, staff members would talk about the opportunities they saw for the college, and the repeated failures of administrators to garner support for them. Staff members witnessed the realities of "we've done that and it didn't work".

What's in it for Us

Perhaps the most common and destructive theme of this organization was "what's in it for us?" Faculty members excused themselves for not taking on new challenges claiming that they were overworked and underpaid, or that they were busy focusing on getting tenure and had to attend to scholarly pursuits, or that they were already doing more than what they perceived to be a fair share of work. The bottom line of most organizational change is usually an assessment of how the charge will affect the individual. Self-interest is the enemy of organizational interest. Perhaps this is why change needs to be imposed to move organizations ahead. Yet, imposed change is usually resented and resisted unless there is a great deal of trust in the leaders and a risk-taking attitude among members. Imposed change is more acceptable when it is perceived as not interfering with one's personal security or integrity.

"What's in it for us" is another way of saying, "what additional responsibilities will we acquire and how will that help us without disturbing our current way of doing things?" Opportunities in this college culture always were viewed as being more self-serving than mutually beneficial. The Dean of Students told one new CEO, "I won't play in your sandbox if you don't play in mine." Problems were not discussed to try to find solutions; rather, great amounts of time were spent defending the solutions after they were determined and implemented. Because problems were not discussed there always was a question about whether the implemented solution was the best one. Leaders of the organization inherited the effects of the poor solutions of previous leaders, which members of the organization remembered and revived periodically to show that the organization had not solved problems in the appropriate ways. Attempts were made to create a leadership team which would take a proactive stance regarding perceived or impending problems, discuss the problems, options for solution, and how to prevent further iterations of the problems. The preventive approach to management was foreign to most members of the leadership team; unfortunately, managers seemed to be most comfortable with, yet criticized, the crisis approach to problem-solving.

Leaders and managers did not want to take responsibility for what they viewed as boundary problems. Leaders and managers handled problems that occurred on their own turf, but they felt uncomfortable about discussing solutions for problems that crossed boundaries. This, of course, requires a great deal of teamwork and trust, which leaders and managers espoused, but lacked.

"What's in it for us?" is commonly asked in distrusting organizations, where members shy away from accountability and responsibility. One example in this college culture was the reluctance of the deans of the schools to formulate standard degree plans for students. One complaint of some students was that some courses were only offered once a year and being part-time students they wanted to know when these courses would be offered so they could better target their graduation. Some students complained that, as part-time students they took longer to graduate, having had a succession of advisors who assessed their need for certain courses differently, often delaying their graduation. But, while the school leaders, acknowledgd these points as valid they felt that standard degree plans reduced their curricular flexibility (translated, this means that some faculty would not commit to when they might teach a course, and therefore the amount of funds available to hire part-time faculty to teach courses varied). To develop standard degree plans so that students would know what courses were required for graduation and when they would be offered required cooperation from faculty, who valued their flexibility and independence regarding teaching. Faculty often chided administrators that "the faculty, not the administration, owned the curriculum."

We Aren't Appreciated

There was a general feeling that individuals were unappreciated in this college. This feeling was the basis of some anger regarding insufficient rewards or public recognition for individual accomplishments, and some resentment and jealousy over some individuals getting more that their share of rewards, e.g., raises, promotions, computers and software, than others. The feeling of being unappreciated also related to the climate of incivility and political correctness that pervaded the college. Factions of feminists, Black-Americans, Hispanics, Gays and Lesbians and other groups focused on their own agendas, often to the detriment of each other and the college. While the college was multi-ethnic, having about 27 different groups represented among its students, faculty, and staff, strong undercurrents of discrimination and intolerance existed. Often, faculty members who were not successful in receiving tenure or a promotion proposed that their ethnicity or religion was the real culprit. Continuous grievances were filed with Human Resources that focused around gender, ethnicity, and religion. Many of these "wars," involving the same individuals were periodically revived to be reinvestigated and mediated. The college administration was continuously distracted and consumed by internal disputes, which had long histories and were fueled by long memories.

In addition to the general feeling of being unappreciated, some individuals in the college were disenfranchised, usually because of their own actions or inactions. Substantial efforts, which included outside mediators, the affirmative action and human resources offices of the university, and administrators at the college taking conflict resolution workshops, did not help to resolve the deep anger and resentment that pervaded sections of the college.

Some angry faculty members chose to write letters to community leaders and anti-defamation organizations, taking their complaints outside the organization, despite vigorous attempts and enormous time and energy expended by college leaders to resolve these disputes. The level of productivity in the college suffered, distrust accelerated, and everyone began to feel unappreciated because of the time and energy devoted to a few dissidents. The university expended substantial, and some felt, an unrealistic amount of resources on these few individuals who continued to test each succession of new CEO's at the college.

Planning Ahead and Looking Backward

A great deal of time and energy were spent in fighting old battles, reliving the past, and feelings of anger, resentment, and unappreciation. Therefore, there was little time for strategic planning for the college, which was required by the university as part of the annual budget process, and viewed by faculty as a bureaucratic exercise, despite attempts by the CEO's to make planning a serious opportunity to plan the college's future. Dialogues about the college's future was held at the department and school levels and in campus-wide meetings in attempts to broaden participation. Planning extended over an entire year to insure total involvement, synergy of opinions, and the development of relevant goals and objectives on a projected timetable. Many of these sessions were poorly attended and only perfunctory, last minute attempts were made by school deans to engage their faculty.

Therefore, it was not surprising, as a draft of the college's five year strategic plan was being critiqued throughout the college, that a small group of faculty members should visit the CEO complaining that they had no input into the plan and that it was not written as it should be. They felt the plan presented an opportunity to market the campus to the larger university administration in order to win more resources. This small vocal group of faculty offered their own rewrite of sections of the strategic plan. Some accommodation was made, but the strategic plan, despite the considerable time and energy devoted to making it democratic, visionary, and strategic, never won the enthusiasm and support of the college.

Many faculty members in the college saw annual evaluations of personnel, the annual budget request, and the annual update of the strategic plan as ways to "right past wrongs," such as inequities in salaries, inadequate resources, and a lack of improvements to the physical facilities. Of course, they were always disappointed in whatever resulted, which confirmed for them that they were being treated as stepchildren by the university system. They blamed the campus CEO because he did not present a strong enough case for the campus. Therefore, there was continuous fodder for feeling unappreciated and the reluctance to do more than the minimum for the institution and campus.

Most members of the college had visions of what their military looking campus could look like. Physical improvements were made to the campus, including a new $15M library, new student housing, remodeled and expanded exercise facilities, including a natatorium, cafeteria, offices for student organizations, parking, and new campus landscaping. Despite these successes there continued to be a lack of pride and a lack of community spirit. In an effort to unite the college with the community in which it resides, an annual Arts and Crafts Festival was proposed by one CEO and the Mayor. The event attracted people to the campus so that they could become better acquainted with the college and its activities. It also created good will between the college and the community. This marketing effort was one of many venues developed to recruit students for the college and generate favorable public relations with the community. The community and college adopted each other as partners and college flags became permanent additions to light fixtures in the downtown area. Students, staff members and the community attended this weekend event, which grew over a period of years. Most faculty members did not attend; some were not even aware of the event. The event continued because of a determined Mayor and an enthusiastic planning committee. Planning ahead takes more than vision, ideas, and resources, it takes a community of members who collectively believe that they can shape their future and are willing to spend the time and energy to make it a reality. To date, there is not that momentum at this college.

Looking for Greener Pastures

"If things don't change, I'll leave," is a common phrase heard in cliques and hallway conversations at the college. This illustrates the lack of loyalty and commitment to the college and the attitude that others are responsible for creating change, but "I" will evaluate whether or not it is the right change. Certainly, one way to deal with one's unhappiness in an organization is to leave. Others choose to stay but withdraw. Still others are critics no matter what happens. Only a few seem willing to help to make the organization more healthy. With downsizing and other organizational transformations occurring as part of "business as usual" for organizations, neither employers or employees are loyal to each other; both can be replaced. Looking for greener pastures is often an ongoing option for organizational members who seek the benefits, but are unwilling to put in the effort to be participating members of the organizations they join. Organizations are used by members and members use organizations to meet respective needs, but for organizations to be positive, innovative, and vibrant there must be reciprocity. This college's culture lacks reciprocity.

In order for organizations and their members to benefit from each other there must be a readiness to be flexible, to make trade-offs, to play win/win games and to give and not always take. Organizations and members that cannot do these things will abandon each other at their own convenience. The attitude that members of organizations and CEO's are dispensable does not create organizational trust, nor does it encourage people to be trustful individuals.

We Can't Recruit Our First Choices

Distrustful organizations never seem to be able to recruit top candidates. In this college they were fortunate to attract their third or fourth choices; sometimes faculty lines were left vacant and monies were used to pay part-time faculty to teach courses. Usually, when senior faculty resigned or retired, they were replaced by lower ranking, less expensive faculty. This watering down of organizational expertise did not help to maintain the quality of graduate programs.

Candidates for faculty and CEO positions are not always fully aware of the history and dynamics of the organization they are considering joining. Organizations that try to fill positions put their best foot forward. Candidates may not fully disclose their professional histories and experiences. Faculty in this college often attributed their failures in recruitment to the unattractive physical plant and environment of the campus. The culture of externalizing or projecting blame when things went wrong was so strong that there was an unawareness that there was anything wrong with such thinking, but distrust was palpable to those outside the college. Some distrustful organizations seem to draw distrusting members or reformist CEO's who believe that they can change the organization. The challenge is to change the culture as well as the attitudes and behavior of individual members.

The Way We Were Meant To Be

There is a pervasive attitude in the college that maybe this is as good as things get—an attitude of acceptance or resignation. Nothing has seemed to work, no leader has been successful in turning it around, the university is not going to invest more money in our campus, we don't seem to be growing, and our public image maintains itself through the performance of our graduates. There is a general belief that "our culture is our problem, and not enough people see it as a problem to do something about, so we should accept ourselves and our college as we are." This carries us full cycle to the love-hate relationship with the college's history. "We were better and we can be even better, but there is no agreement on what better is." So the culture remains the same except for the occasional push from the parent university to fine-tune certain policies or procedures. As the college reaches its chronological age of 40, it still searches for other identities and names, and has visions of being something other than what it was meant to be.

ANALYSIS

Not All Distrusting Organizations Are Dysfunctional

This organization, while distrustful for the majority of its lifecycle has never been dysfunctional to the point of being unproductive. But it was not healthy. This case history has illustrated how irrational acts and behavior affect the life of an organization. Whatever issues or problems arose, members of the organization seemed to look back instead of forward for answers. Members yearned to be more than they were, but the past always seemed to present safer choices, and regretting and reliving passed up opportunities was less threatening than facing the reasons for failing to take advantage of current opportunities. Opportunities were questioned and bludgeoned to death by questions, "what ifs," and the enumerating of the possible consequences of various options and approaches. There were always more reasons not to do something than to do it.

Distrust of each other and the current leader made taking advantage of current opportunities too risky. Decisions were frequently left to the CEO, who, whatever decision was made, was considered wrong. The blaming and finger pointing made everyone a possible victim or scapegoat, there were never any heroes. Any who emerged, even briefly, were beaten down.

However, the organization continued to attract quality students, and some quality faculty. Staff members seemed to provide the greatest stability and loyalty; staff members could be compared to observers of a play in which different players entered and exited and acted out their own plots with common themes of collective inadequacy, insecurity, and distrust. The various CEO's could not convince organizational members of their talents and abilities, or persuade them to be more proactive and put aside grievances. Because everyone acted as if they were temporary members of the college, and were unwilling to "buy into" the future of the organization, a foundation of trust could not be established.

The college acquired some external funding, faculty were engaged in research, scholarship, and outreach. The college held social events and functions, conducted a successful capital campaign and strengthened alumni relations. But, there was rarely widespread enthusiasm for becoming involved in these events. Only about a quarter of the college population were involved citizens who were committed to realizing the college's potential. The organization "got by" and rarely, if ever, received accolades. It was a distrusting, but functioning organization.

Culture Can't Be Changed Unless Organizational Members Want To Change It

Culture is sometimes viewed as "something" that can be changed or managed just as a policy or procedure can be changed or managed. People form a culture, it is a human phenomenon; therefore, it cannot be changed unless organizational members want it to change. Culture is not something to be added to or subtracted from, it is a matrix of beliefs, values, customs, and principles which guide the attitudes and behavior of a group.

Kets de Vries and Miller (1991) point out that organizations have styles of behavior that permeate culture. Some of these styles are "neurotic" in organizations just as they are in individuals. There are organizations which are stagnant because depression permeates the culture, or impulsive organizations that are consumed with acquiring power and risk-taking, especially the urge to grow and expand. Neurotic organizational styles do not necessarily require that the CEO exhibit them; the styles evolve and become firmly established over the lifetime of the organization in spite of the various leadership styles of different CEO's.

Kets de Vries and Miller discuss the characteristics of five "pure" neurotic styles that predominate in dysfunctional organizations, i.e., paranoia, depression, compulsiveness, detachment, and grandiosity, but mixtures of these features also are common as the case study illustrates. Members of organizations grow to be comfortable with their "fit" within their organizational culture and resist changing it, especially if their needs are being met. Organizations recruit new members and leaders who will "fit" into the organization's cultural style. Members who do not "fit" leave or are forced out.

Comfort with the neurotic styles in organizations is a key reason why individuals, and in turn, organizations, resist change. Most organizations spend time coping with changes that happen to them rather than changes they create. Organizations accept more easily those changes that fit their culture and neurotic style, and thereby perpetuate their style.

Kets de Vries and Miller note that, although the personality of the CEO can vitally influence an organization, a reverse relationship also exists. In the case study described here, the culture of the organization was a more powerful force than any of its eight CEO's. A dysfunctional organization can cause its leader to become depressed and hopeless because of the apathy and recalcitrance of its members. CEO's leave the organization, but the culture and those who support its style remain.

The college in our case study illustrated a mix of neurotic styles. It was a paranoid culture pervaded by distrust and the need to find someone or something to blame. Members of the organization were unwilling to accept responsibility for their own actions and lacked insight into their weaknesses. They distrusted each other; everyone was a competitor, and so, great efforts were made to protect oneself. The organization was also pervaded by a sense of helplessness. Members saw glimpses of opportunities and possibilities, but felt no need to expend the effort to take advantage of them. While they believed, as individuals, that they had various skills and expertise, collectively they could not coalesce to mesh these talents for the benefit of all. Members believed that they were stepchildren of the larger university which ultimately called the shots because it controlled budget allocations. There was a pervasive sense of futility, so people did the minimum. Another neurotic style was detachment. Members regarded the college as highly politicized and therefore the leader could do little to effect changes that the university did not want. The college was schizoid; the actions of one group worked against those of other groups—there was little loyalty toward the college or to the university. The focus of the college was internal, and therefore, external opportunities were missed or dismissed with the excuse that the members already had too much to do.

This mix of styles shifted and changed in the college with events and changes in personnel and leaders, but the styles could readily be identified by visitors and outsiders. However, no one in the college thought that the college needed help—the idea of bringing in consultants was scoffed at by members who believed that all the expertise that was needed resided in the members. Kets de Vries and Miller stress that styles of behavior are deeply rooted. To naive, but optimistic new CEO's, it would seem only a matter of patience, creating opportunities, providing support and resources, and giving consistent encouragement and positive leadership to turn this culture around. But the culture never moved.

Change Was Never Part of the Plan

Drucker (1995) said that every organization has to build change into its structure. Organizations must constantly upset, disorganize, and destabilize themselves in an effort to improve and become more responsive to the external environment. In the case example described here people in the college did not expect or want great changes, and the changes that they expected, they thought they could manage. Drucker (1999) pointed out that change cannot be managed, organizations and their leaders need to anticipate and plan for change, not simply react to it. Furthermore, learning organizations create and encourage change.

The personnel in the college in this case study never dreamed that they would be merged with personnel in another campus, especially a campus which they would never have selected as a partner. The only thing the college and the two year campus had in common was that each was part of the same university system. Five years later the merger has not been completed. The best the college hoped for is that it would become the dominant partner in a coalition with a local community college. Massive change was never part of the plan for the college. As a result, many of the faculty who opposed the merger continue to express their anger about it, doing nothing to facilitate the integration of the two campuses, and talking openly about their retirement or another job opportunity.

The Future Is The Present

This case study illustrates that organizations that do not plan their own future are destined to live out futures that are not of their own making. Organizations whose futures are the present become so internally focused that they seem numb to external forces of change. Such organizations lack strategies to deal with the new certainties of the world in the 21st century (Drucker, 1999). Strategy enables an organization to achieve its desired results in an unpredictable environment. Strategy allows an organization to be purposefully opportunistic (Drucker, 1999).

In the case study presented here, the college had no strategies for change upon which its faculty could agree. Schein (1992) concluded, in his case analysis of MultiCompany that the cultural paradigm of the company had not really changed at all. Certainly changes had occurred in both case examples, changes that members labeled as cultural; however, the basic, deep beliefs of the organizations did not change. Cultures can change superficially and get by, but unless organizational members and their leaders are willing periodically to examine the relevance of the beliefs and values of their organization, and be willing to modify them, organizations will function below their potential.

SUMMARY

Culture can be used as a weapon to protect itself or it can provide the basis for innovation, growth, and the sharing of prized beliefs and principles. Cultures do not just happen; they are created and sustained by people. People come and go, but if a culture is strongly grounded, it will prevail. Culture takes the shape and form that its founders wish it to. Some cultures are closed and relatively fixed, others are open and feed on change. Organizations have a variety of cultural shapes and forms, depending upon their original purpose. Successions of leaders and members of organizations make changes to culture, usually superficial ones, but some organizational cultures are distorted or destroyed in great upheavals, such as mergers, acquisitions, and take-overs, where one culture is a winner and another the loser.

The case analysis presented in this chapter offers an abbreviated look at selected aspects of a culture that became its own enemy. This college culture valued the teaching and discovery of knowledge and rewarded individual achievement toward these ends, but members of the college, as it traveled down its life-cycle, neglected their culture—they took more from it than they put in. They nourished their careers and ambitions and failed to plan for change. Change happened, members of the college reacted, proaction was feared, and so everyone looked back for better days. The college had a succession of CEO's who attempted to rekindle spirit and enthusiasm for new goals, talked of new challenges, and created opportunities, but there was never enough inertia for the college to make great strides. Change was never part of the cultural plan for the college. As the college grew in size, many taught in the same way they had for decades and did little to enhance their own knowledge base or acquire new skills. Attrition by retirement permitted some changes, but the culture welcomed newcomers who liked the security of a status quo environment.

The college was not dysfunctional, but it was a distrusting place. The larger university of which it was a part was distrusted because there always was inadequate funding for branch campuses and pressure to conform to the way in which the main campus of the university did things. As in so many organizations, units away from headquarters were often taken for granted. The fact that this college was created on the site of a former military base gave it the physical environment of a highly structured, sterile place. Over the years, only minimal efforts were made by the university to improve its physical appearance; hence, the campus was thought of as a stepchild by faculty members. There was not a careful selection of recruits to the college over the years, resulting in many faculty members who were not loyal team members and were critics of the culture. There was little interest on the part of members of the college in making it a better place. Administrators were seen as instruments of the larger university who had no long-term commitment to the college and did not have to live with the effects of their decisions as they passed through the college to other higher level jobs. Members of the college were quick to file grievances and lawsuits, demand their rights, and establish limits for what they would or wouldn't do. The result was a fortress where people protected themselves, contributed the minimum, volunteered for nothing, and kept to themselves or their cliques.

Efforts by leaders of the college to create an open, safe, interactive, civil atmosphere were unsuccessful. There were always wild fires to be fought which diverted attention away from strategic planning, goal-setting, and envisioning of the future. There were pockets of healthiness in the college, but collectively it was marginally productive and not a leader among peers in the region.

An analysis of the reasons for this seemingly immobile culture is that the majority of members despite their verbal claims to the contrary, were comfortable and did not want change. By minimizing change that is created internally, it is possible to control stress and promote feelings of comfort and safety. Drucker said, change must be built into the structure of every organization if it is to remain vital, growing, and productive. And change must be proactive, not reactive. Change was never part of the plan for the majority of members of this college. The future was, and continues to be, the present.

Chapter 8

The Health of Organizations

"The best managers increase the health of the workers they manage."[1]

"... Accountants must try to figure out some way of turning into balance sheet terms the intangible personnel values that come from improving the people of the organization ..."[2]

INTRODUCTION

Organizations are living systems with their own needs and life cycles. Like other living things, they experience change and conflict as they grow and develop. Sometime during their lifecycles, most organizations become ill and need treatment and rehabilitation.[3] Some organizations, like people become chronically ill but continue to function until their eventual demise, other organizations successfully conquer acute episodes of illness, and still others appear to be "genetically" favored and rarely experience illness.

Most of us work in organizations that are relatively healthy. However, the concept of a healthy organization is idealistic. Organizations are never fully stable, they never maximize their potential, and they never achieve complete harmony. Yet, most managers and leaders want to make their organizations more healthy and, therefore, successful in their mission.

WHAT IS A HEALTHY ORGANIZATION?

What is a healthy organization? To many it means financial success, productivity, size and power. Jack Welch recounted the presentation of his vision for the "new GE" to Wall Street analysts in 1981. He talked of melding the "hard" aspect of the corporation with "soft" issues like reality, quality, excellence, and the human element. Welch said that he wanted to foster an environment where people would dare to try new things, where they would feel assured in knowing that only the limits of their creativity and drive would be the ceiling on how far and how fast they could move. By melding hard and soft messages, GE would become a place that was more high-spirited, more adaptable, and more agile than other companies a fraction of its size. Welch says "... the reaction in the room made it clear that this crowd thought they were getting more hot air than substance." One of our staffers overheard one analyst moan, "We don't know what the hell he is talking about."[4]

Rosen and Berger (1991) offered a sketch of a healthy company. They concluded "perhaps the most remarkable aspect of this ... atmosphere is a feeling of respect. From the flexible schedules to the fair salaries and benefits to the sharing of vital information, the company shows that it truly cares about people, and employees reciprocate this trust with loyalty."[5] Lewis (1985) talked about developing and managing "excellent" organizations that are characterized by four features:

- a unity of purpose (strong culture)
- responsive components (components respond to each other)
- reacts to environment (exchange ideas)
- interrelationships on individual, team, and organizational levels.

Beckhard (1997) provided a profile of some 15 characteristics of a healthy organization which included:

- a strong sense of purpose
- keeps communication open
- congruent reward systems
- high tolerance for innovation and creativity
- identifies and manages change
- makes decisions closest to the customer
- respects customer service
- uses team management
- management is information driven.

What then is the definition of a healthy organization or company? It is the combination and coordination of people and practices that produce exceptional performance.[6]

What is meant by the health of an organization? Health is the body, mind, and spirit of an organization. Body refers to the structure of the organization, how it is organized, how power and authority are exercised, how information and communication are accessed, and how work is distributed, carried out, and rewarded. Mind refers to how the organization functions, how beliefs, goals, policies and procedures are implemented, how conflict is handled, how change is managed, how members are treated, and how the organization learns. Spirit is the soul of the organization—invisible, but palpable. Spirit is more than high morale and an *esprit de corps*. Spirit is the core or heart of an organization, it is what moves an organization, what makes it vibrant, and gives it vigor. It is measurable by observation. Robert W. Reed, Vice-President of Intel Corporation said, “A healthy company is immediately noticeable. Employees bounce into work, they are interested in their jobs, they speak in the first person rather than the third person, and they go home feeling good about themselves and their accomplishments.”[7]

It is a common myth that the leader determines an organization’s health and success.[8] Kelley (1992) pointed out that a leader’s effect on organizational success is only 10 to 20 percent; followership is the factor that makes for success. Bolman and Deal (1991) stressed that neither the leader nor the followers, but the interaction between the two, makes a workplace healthy. It is how the psychodynamics of an organization are managed, and the capacity of its leaders and followers to repair broken relationships, that influence an organization’s health (Hirschhorn, 1988).

Numerous authors use the metaphor of health or sickness to describe organizations. This metaphor for understanding organizations offers at least three advantages; first, we know from the World Health Organization’s (WHO) definition of health that it is not simply the absence of disease. WHO defines health as a state of complete physical, mental, and social well-being and not merely the absence of disease or infirmity.[9] The second advantage is that it focuses on processes not products. The literature on health, and particularly health promotion, identifies biological, psychological, and social processes by which a person may become sick or healthy. Third, the health paradigm has a strong behavioral component. Behaviors such as smoking cessation, exercise, diet modification, and stress management improve our chances of remaining healthy. It is the author’s premise that examining the health of an organization will provide valuable insights into how an organization becomes dysfunctional.

An organization may be sick or dysfunctional and yet productive. In many organizations there is a time lag that allows organizations to continue to be productive while they are in declining health. However, eventually sick organizations become unproductive. The advantage of examining the health of an organization is that health predicts productivity. If the illness is acute, productivity may not suffer at all. However, when the illness is chronic and untreated, productivity is threatened.

It might be argued that it is essential for only insiders or members of an organization to decipher their organization’s health, it usually takes an outsider’s inquiries to stimulate insiders’ awareness of their organization’s behavior (Schein,

1992). Usually the assistance of an outsider's analysis is solicited when leaders experience their organization's declining health. Unfortunately, when leaders are part of the reason for their organization's declining health, and do not recognize it, organizational members may seek the advice of outsiders without the leaders' knowledge. Informal feedback about an organization's culture can be used for constructive change instigated by insiders. This can involve pressure from organizational members for a change in leadership.

It is the author's experience that members of organizations that are experiencing a period of dysfunction, especially when the leader is part of the problem, often reach a state of helplessness and seek informal advice and guidance from sources outside their organization. Informal advice from outsiders is used by members of sick organizations to make decisions, whether the advice assists individuals to leave for other jobs or work for change within the organization. It is also the author's experience that sick organizations more often meet an early demise rather than experience rehabilitation and revitalization because symptoms of unhealthiness are not recognized or are denied by leaders.

This chapter describes an approach whereby an objective assessment can be made of an organization's health without a formal request for consultation from an organization's leader. The approach proposed involves observing the behavior of organizational members in a variety of work situations, obtaining information on the organization's leadership history and performance, eliciting the organization's mission and goals as perceived by members at different levels of the organization, and inquiring about the satisfaction, accomplishments, and morale of members at different levels of the organization. Such a cursory assessment of organizational health can be of benefit to persons who are considering accepting a job or making other contractual relationships with an organization. As assessment is also necessary if one is to diagnose and prescribe a remedy for a "sick" organization.

SIMILARITIES AND DIFFERENCES BETWEEN INDIVIDUALS AND ORGANIZATIONS

The major difference between individuals and organizations is that an organization has the potential for being immortal. People grow old and die of natural causes. Organizations die, but for different reasons. More important, individuals are more or less coherent beings. They function because of the smooth integration of numerous organs, but these organs are coordinated by unconscious means. Organizations consist of many independent organisms that are coordinated by sets of similar needs, but they consist of autonomous individual consciousnesses.

The similarity between organizations and individuals is that they are both influenced greatly by internal and external events. We use words like morale and pride to describe both individuals and organizations because they define these entities' approaches to existence. These words describe a real but intangible aspect of both individuals and organizations that is connected with their ability to survive and flourish.

Human spirit may be broken by adversity, by a lack of nourishment, and even by punishment for the possession of admirable qualities such as creativity, enthusiasm, honesty, directness, self-confidence, and initiative. Organizations and individuals can be broken by adversity. The business climate changes, the government cuts funding, a highway blocks a restaurant entrance, a war starts, a hurricane sweeps in, a loved one is taken by accident or disease. Often, however, in the case of both individuals and organizations, something damages the spirit. An organization, because of faulty leadership, can destroy the internal climate, that is, office politics determines who gets promoted, honesty is punished and sycophancy encouraged, new ideas are devalued, and the tried and true are elevated to immutable law. However, organizations do not always respond to adversity by becoming sick. Some organizations are able to increase their resistance to disease, to adapt to changes in the environment, and to become more healthy as a result of coping with adversity. Changes toward total quality management made by Ford, General Motors, and Chrysler serve as examples of organizations that have survived adversity. Each may survive as a healthier organization by virtue of its response to adversity.

CHARACTERISTICS OF HEALTHY ORGANIZATIONS

A healthy organization has been defined as one in which the individuals and groups that comprise it reach homeostasis or equilibrium in their capacity for growth.[10] Albrecht and Albrecht (1987) have said that a healthy organization is one in which the authority structure, value systems, norms, reward systems, and sanctions operate to support the success of the organization, its environment, and the well-being of its personnel. Health may be defined differently by members of an organization and those outside it because health is a value-laden term; values are reflected in how we perceive and interpret behavior. The state of an organization's health, therefore, is, to some extent, perceptual. However, people act on their perceptions, and the resultant behavior can be constructive or destructive. We can learn a lot about beliefs and values in an organization by examining its employees' behavior.

Certain key characteristics, collectively, make an organization healthy (Figure 8.1). The culture or environment of an organization provides the context for organizational behavior. The tone set by the culture influences employee behavior. Organizational culture is established largely by the leaders of an organization. When leaders change, the culture also changes; even when new leaders

Figure 8.1. Characteristics of Healthy Organizations

attempt to maintain the same culture, it never is exactly the same. Changes in employees also modify an organization's culture.

Lyth (1991) outlines some measures of organizational health such as productivity, morale, and loyalty. She notes that task-effective organizations tend to be healthy for their members. Efficient task performance is rewarding and increases confidence and self-esteem. Healthy organizations provide the opportunity to confront and work through problems, deploy people's capacities to the fullest, provide independence without undue supervision, demonstrate visible relationships between effort and rewards, avoid using repressed defenses to deal with anxiety, and permit members to exert realistic control over their life in the organization.

A healthy organization has a clear mission and a set of consistent principles that frame it and distinguish it from other organizations, but it is its values that provide the how and why for people in the organization to behave as they do. An organization that values democracy, autonomy, and entrepreneurship empowers individual employees to share their talents, skills, and ideas in helping the organization achieve its goals and stay focused on its mission. An environment of open communication and sharing of information conveys to all employees that the leaders are not the only persons in the organization who have good ideas. This provides for a work environment of trust and encourages creativity and innovation.

A healthy culture is more team-oriented than territorial. This does not mean that healthy organizations are not competitive; they are, but they provide freedom to negotiate boundaries in order to accomplish organizational as opposed to individual goals. Every employee in a healthy organization is an investment and, as such, when permitted to grow and develop, helps strengthen the entire organization.

Finally, healthy organizations plan for, rather than wait for, change. Healthy organizations initiate change, encourage change and renewal, and, as a result, change usually can be directed and the effects of change can be controlled.

Hewlett-Packard built its philosophy around trust. Hewlett-Packard uses three methods for remaining innovative and healthy. First, managers are reviewed on their ability to manage people. Second, employee input is obtained through communication sessions. Third, employees are encouraged to speak up when they feel that things aren't right. Hewlett-Packard puts these words into action by operating on "guidelines" rather than on rules and regulations.

Another example of a healthy organization is Aetna, which strives to create an environment that is conducive to people wanting to work there. Aetna is proactive on workplace issues. They have developed elder care programs, a management advisory council, alternative staffing programs, and hiring and training programs for the historically unemployed. Aetna pays its employees well, which is a necessary, but not sufficient condition to bring a healthy organization. It is its additional programs that help Aetna remain healthy.

De Pree (1989) said that chief executive officers should create an organizational environment that is kind to the user. Organizational leaders should make their values and expectations explicit. Employees in a healthy organization know what is expected of them and know how they can contribute to the organization's goals. It is important that leaders share their vision with employees. Visions can only become realities if they are adopted by all the employees in an organization. Consistency and congruency in a leader's values convey feelings of both stability and direction in an organization. Much is written about management style as an essential factor in shaping the environment of the workplace. Collaborative decision making, participative management, delegation of authority and responsibility, and the encouragement of feedback by the leadership sends employees the message that they are valued, trusted, and empowered. Good leaders also permit failure and the chance to try again.

The leaders of a healthy organization plan, set priorities, and monitor their progress toward achieving goals. They are proactive problem-solvers who consistently manage boundaries and paradoxes, thereby preventing the need to resolve conflicts that divert managers and others from their primary tasks. A healthy organization has few "fires" to put out because the leadership ethos has an effective fire prevention program.

The measure of leadership is in action, not in words. There are many leaders who can speak eloquently about participative management, visions, delegation of authority and responsibility, and proactive problem solving. However, there may be large gaps between words and deeds. Leaders who surround themselves with only a few "trusted" associates (many of whom have more than one title), who are constantly focusing on the failures or failings of individual employees, who begin discussions by accusing rather than questioning, and who make decisions on the basis of incomplete or incorrect information, are leaders of sick organizations regardless of what they profess.

Employees directly contribute to maintaining a healthy organization when they are valued and feel in control and effective at their jobs. Employees feel invested in an organization when they feel free to take risks and can contribute ideas for the organization's improvement. Employees in a healthy organization are encouraged to be creative, to learn new skills, and to assume greater responsibilities. This is reinforced when employees are given feedback on their performance and employee rewards are made explicit. Employees want to continue to work in a healthy organization where they are happy, productive, and receive rewards.

The reward system in healthy organizations starts with compensation and benefits, but it does not stop there. Organizations reward employees by valuing their input and by developing programs that are designed to meet both personal and organizational needs. Programs such as employee assistance, child care, elder care, flex time, and personal leave are examples of how healthy organizations reward employees.

HOW ORGANIZATIONS BECOME UNHEALTHY

Organizations can become sick quickly or slowly for a number of reasons. First, organizations can become sick very quickly. For example, a married, male CEO of a large corporation had an affair with a female employee, who quickly rose through the ranks of the organization. Confronted with these circumstances he had two choices, either face a sexual harassment suit by his lover (and possibly a divorce from his wife) or resign as President, he chose the latter. In a few months as the rumors, and gossip made its way throughout the organization and community, the CEO compromised his integrity and any of his pronouncements regarding personal or organizational values were scoffed at. The organization waited to see what would happen. This organization lost momentum for almost two years while it searched for another CEO. A new CEO, no matter how impeccable morally, begins with a tainted reputation about administrators.

Secondly, organizations can become sick gradually. A succession of poor leaders, repeated economic setbacks, the lack of, or too rapid a response to, external pressures or requests, usually establish a fatalistic climate within the organization of "we aren't going anywhere" and a reputation outside as nonresponsive and passive, tentative and safe. The case study discussed in Chapter 7 is an example of an organization that became increasingly sick over time. In that case, a succession of short-term CEO's reinforced unhealthy expectations inside and outside of the organization. The philosophy of the university was to change CEO's rather than address the sick culture. The causes of chronic illness in organizations is like chronic illness among individuals, usually caused by lifestyle, that is, unhealthy patterns and behaviors. On the other hand, the sudden acute illness in organizations is usually precipitated by an unexpected event often internal to the organization.

Kets de Vries and Miller (1984) point out that troubled organizations have symptoms and dysfunctions that combine to form an integrated syndrome of pathology. Pathology may be a mixture of neurotic styles. These authors note that parallels can be drawn between individual pathology, that is, the excessive use of one neurotic style, and organizational pathology, resulting in poorly functioning organizations. The personality of the leader can influence the structure, strategy, and culture of an organization. Not all unhealthy organizations are run by neurotic leaders. However, the personality of the leader, especially if the leader is concerned with the centralization of power, can create a gestalt that reflects throughout the organization. Organizations can recruit leaders and managers with similar styles; therefore, there will always be a danger that the lack of diversity may give rise to organizational pathology.

Organizations become sick through neglect and lack of preventive maintenance, through inflexibility and intolerance of change, and through the arrogance of power and insensitivity of the leaders to the needs of employees. Organizations rarely become sick suddenly; symptoms, if neglected, accumulate over time until the organization becomes incapacitated. Symptoms of dysfunction are often more observable to people outside an organization than to those within. Figure 8.2 lists some symptoms of unhealthiness in organizations.

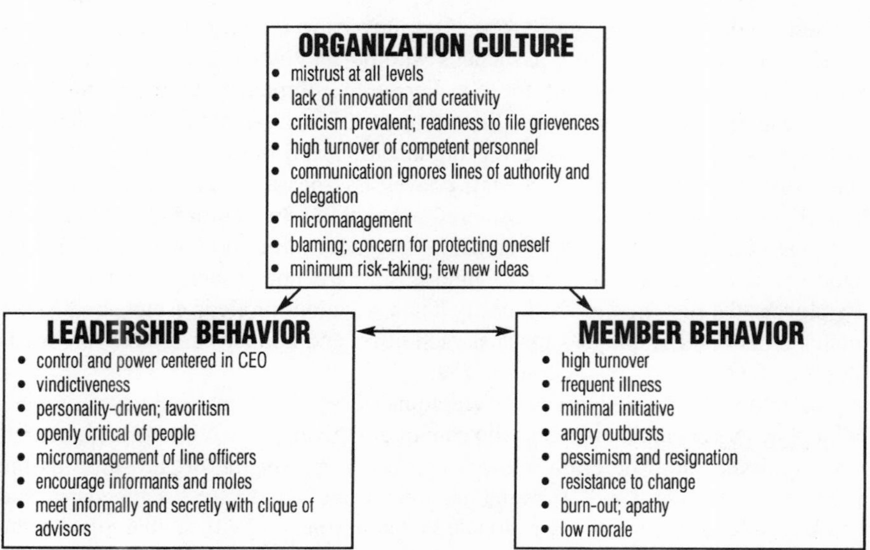

Figure 8.2. Symptons of Unhealthiness in Organizations.

A culture of mistrust in an organization and evidence that the CEO and top management check up on people produce an atmosphere in which employees cover themselves, take minimal risks, and do only what is necessary to do their jobs. This kind of atmosphere puts people on guard to protect their turf and creates a defensive climate. Criticisms and grievances are common, because people lack loyalty to others or to the organization. Employee comments about the organization, their jobs, and the leadership may be the best clue that the organization is sick. When many employees take the role of a victim, then the organization is unhealthy. Comments such as: "I'm stuck here," "It's just a job," "That new guy with good ideas won't last long," "We will never get a raise," "It's not my job to think," "The CEO won't give up control," and "It's no use trying to change things here" are examples of comments that have an underlying theme of victimization. Whether these comments are a product of experience or simply self-fulfilling prophecies is not a critical issue; in either case, the organization is sick.

Other clues to an unhealthy organization include: frequent turnover of managers and administrators; the reputation of the CEO as a micromanager; communication patterns that ignore the organization chart; a lack of innovation and creativity; and strong resistance to change and upholding of traditional patterns of authority that are based on centralized control at the top of the organization.

Organizations become sick when they serve the psychological needs of the leader. Some leaders become blinded by power and the need to satisfy their own egos and ignore the realities of an organization.[11] These leaders fashion a personality-driven organization where they reward and favor employees who cater to their needs and are vindictive toward employees who do not. Other leaders cultivate a small group of close associates who do only what they know the leader wants and expects. As a result, these leaders are reinforced by their own thinking.

Leaders who do not permit line officers in an organization to do their job without close supervision stifle the organization and the line officers. Leaders who treat their line officers like staff convey the message to all in the organization that control and power are centered in the CEO. In sick organizations, leaders may continue to exert tight control while advocating empowerment or total quality management. Since these innovations are not modeled by the leader, employees distrust the CEO's sincerity. Thus, a vicious circle is established where management and employees distrust each other and neither party will risk trusting the other.

Perhaps the most significant symptoms of organizational sickness are manifested by leaders and managers who cannot effectively cope with difficult boundaries or issues and therefore identify certain people in the organization as the problem. The "identified" persons are treated as "devils" or "scapegoats" and marked for dismissal with the rationale that a new person will be able to solve the existing problem. A second symptom is leaders and managers rewarding good work with more work. An organization that only lets employees know they are valued by giving them additional jobs is indicating that its reward system is unhealthy. The message sent to employees is, don't do an outstanding job; you will only be rewarded with more work. Overworked people do not and cannot perform at their peak. Over a sustained period overworked people put themselves at risk for personal health problems. This further illustrates the insensitivity of unhealthy organizations to the social and psychological needs of its employees.

Employee behavior is often the most obvious way to diagnose an unhealthy organization; it is not difficult to ascertain employee attitudes of anger, apathy, low morale, pessimism, and passive-aggressiveness. Organizations that have high absenteeism and turnover rates are unhealthy. Employees in unhealthy organizations show little loyalty toward the organization, little enthusiasm for their work, or little optimism about their jobs. If the atmosphere at work is grossly vindictive, there may be a reluctance to communicate in order to protect their jobs.

CYCLES OF SICKNESS AND HEALTH

Sick organizations do not necessarily decay, decline, and die. Some organizations live protracted yet sick lives. Sick organizations have an impact on the people who work in them. Some sick organizations may attract and retain sick employees; needs may become enmeshed and reinforced. In fact, in some family businesses, family dynamics in the form of rivalries and jealousies are played out to the point where family members leave the business or open directly competing ventures.

We spend the bulk of our daily lives at work. Work becomes a place where we play out many of our goals and aspirations as well as problems. Organizations, like people, can become addictive and foster addictive (dysfunctional) behavior.[12] For example, in dysfunctional organizations communication is often indirect, vague, confused, and ineffective. Gossip, triangulation, secrets, and extensive written memos help avoid face-to-face interaction, confrontation, and intimacy. Such a culture fosters dishonesty, creating "in" groups, tension, defensiveness, and controlled feelings.

Healthy organizations, on the other hand, tend to remain more or less healthy with occasional crises. Healthy organizations tend to select their employees with careful attention to philosophy, past work records, and personal goals. Since healthy organizations are team-oriented, their employees usually have good interpersonal skills. Healthy organizations tend to stress group goals and successes; it is unlikely that an employee who is highly competitive and in need of constant individual recognition and rewards would be selected to be part of a healthy organization. Open, direct, and honest communication fosters a group spirit, and destructive behavior is usually prevented by positive group pressure or early intervention.

Healthy and unhealthy organizations are influenced by their leaders. Both types of organizations look for leaders who will promote the organization as it is.

Healthy organizations usually attract healthy leaders, and unhealthy organizations usually attract unhealthy leaders. However, mismatches occur when a healthy leader becomes the head of an organization that he/she discovers is unhealthy. The leader who attempts to change an unhealthy organization is likely to be met by strong resistance. It is unlikely that a healthy leader would stay long in an unhealthy organization. Unhealthy leaders may not be known until they have been in a leadership position for awhile. Unhealthy leaders who have been unsuccessful in a prior job may have been given good references by supervisors who wished to get rid of them. However, when unhealthy leaders are detected, it does not usually take long for a healthy organization to close ranks against them. Votes of "no confidence," petitions, and pressure from board members, politicians, or the public can lead to their termination.

The leader is not always the problem in an unhealthy organization, or if the leader is a problem, it is not always feasible to change leaders or to change their behaviors. Howell and colleagues (1990) suggested ways to "neutralize" the negative impact of a leader, such as peer support groups. It is difficult for members of an organization to provide substitutes for negative leadership, because leaders who are concerned with control will doubtlessly prevent innovations that would circumvent or inhibit their ability to control. Unfortunately, members often find it easier to leave an organization than to try to modify it.

DEGREES OF ORGANIZATIONAL HEALTH

The health of organizations is relative and is subject to change by the internal and external forces that act upon it. Figure 8.3 shows the key elements in the process of maintaining organizational health. The interaction between leadership styles and organizational culture is more obvious in organizations where decision-making power is centralized. Kets de Vries (1991) described five constellations of how the personality or management style of the leader can impact an organization's culture. A suspicious style can lead to a paranoid culture and organization. A depressive, dependent style can result in an avoidant culture and depressive organization. A dramatic, narcissistic leader can create a charismatic culture and an impulsive, venturesome organization. A compulsive leader can create a bureaucratic culture and a controlling organization. Finally, a detached leader can create a politicized culture and schizoid organization. While these are pure prototypes, they exemplify how the structure of an organization can be influenced by the personality of its top manager.

The more centralized an organization, and the more power given its leaders, the greater the impact of their personality on the culture and structure of the organization (Kets de Vries, 1989). Healthy organizations have a mixture of personality types; unhealthy organizations are more likely to be described by one of

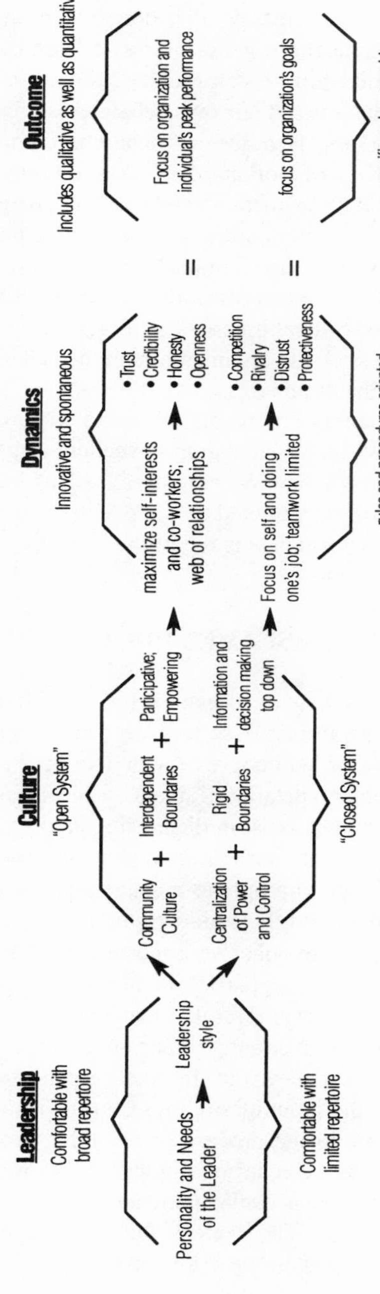

Figure 8.3. Effects of Interaction Between Organizational Culture and Leadership Style on Organizational Health.

the five prototypes. In healthy organizations employees know how to get along with their coworkers and leaders in ways that benefit the organization (Kelley, 1992). The best followers treat the organization as a "commons." This attitude helps in organizational relationships. A community culture is established in which employees not only try to maximize their own self-interest but also help to facilitate the interests of coworkers. Healthy organizations demonstrate "a web of relationships" among all levels of workers that is based on trust, credibility, and honesty. In Hirschhorn's (1988) terms this would be an "open system." To maintain a healthy organization, leaders must develop strategies of management that are neither too open nor too closed. In healthy organizations, boundaries are interdependent; they must be managed carefully to allow negotiations yet not create distrust. Thus, the degree of healthiness of an organization is fluid. The challenge to the leadership is to keep the organization on the side of healthiness more often than on the side of unhealthiness.

While organizational environment or culture is a powerful variable that affects the performance of an organization, excellent organizations become "peak-performers" largely because they employ excellent individuals.[13] People who are peak performers will be attracted to work with other peak performers in organizations where peak performance is the norm.

HOW AN ORGANIZATION SOLVES PROBLEMS

One approach in diagnosing an organization's health is to ascertain the process by which the organization solves problems and resolves conflicts. The process or method of resolution will convey much about the leadership style and organizational climate of the organization. Table 8.1 shows six aspects of problem solving or conflict resolution that assist in diagnosing an organization's health. In healthy organizations, problems or conflicts are openly discussed and identified so that they can be brought to the appropriate manager for resolution. There is no motivation to keep problems or conflicts hidden in a healthy organization, as this would undermine morale and the cohesive atmosphere of the working environment. In healthy organizations, the parties involved in a problem or conflict actively work to resolve it rather than refer it to management for solution. It is rare that the CEO becomes involved in solving minor problems in a healthy organization unless the issue is one of concern to the total organization. Even then, it is likely the CEO will ask for the input of employees in the resolution. Perhaps one of the most important points in the process of resolving problems in a healthy organization is the attitude and behavior of employees following the resolution of a problem. A healthy organization is resilient and adaptive; it is not concerned with personalities or holding grudges. The work of the entire organization transcends the problems of individuals and groups. Organizations that repair themselves

Table 8.1. Approaches to Conflict Resolution in Healthy and Unhealthy Organizations

Approach	*Healthy Organizations*	*Unhealthy Organizations*
Identification of problem	Open discussion, dialogue	Attempt to hide or minimize the problem, or expand and generalize it
Behavior of parties involved	Bring to the attention of management, confrontive	Blaming, scapegoating, gossip
Parties' motivation for solving problems	Improve morale and working environment	Fear, retribution
Degree to which parties are involved in resolution	Participative	Reluctant, cautious, protective
Type of dialogue of parties	Problem-solving, mediative	Threatening, litigious
Involvement of CEO in resolution	Rare	Often
Working climate after resolution	Adaptive	Resentment, grudges
Style of dealing with problems	Preventive	Crisis intervention

acknowledge good and bad experiences openly and directly, and employees have the attitude that they can learn from both failures and successes.

An observer of an organization can readily elicit the process by which problems and conflicts are resolved and will be able to diagnose the relative health of an organization. Since "health" is an ideal, it is rare that one would find a completely healthy organization; it is likely, however, that a "sick" organization would be detected. The purpose in diagnosing an organization is to determine its usual patterns of behavior. Healthy organizations have the ability to adapt to fluctuation and change and return to their usual, stable pattern of functioning. Sick organizations, on the other hand, become sick because they are not flexible and adaptive (Stacey, 1992). Leaders and managers in a flexible, adaptive, or healthy organization need to let the type of problem or conflict determine the resources they will use to correct it rather than use a common approach or common set of problem-solving tools to solve all problems or conflicts.

Healthy organizations respond quickly to resolve problems and conflicts. The openness of the organization and the emphasis on preventing problems through on-going problem-solving, minimizes large or cumulative conflicts. When there are problems members of healthy organizations are eager to participate in solving them through established procedures in the organization. There is concern for individual members as well as for the organization as a whole.

Healthy organizations are learning organizations and, as such, learning how to solve problems more effectively is part of the ongoing process of learning how to improve the total organization. An organization that learns benefits from its mistakes and failures. Learning organizations are skilled in five major activities: systematic problem solving, experimentation with new approaches, learning from their own experience and past history, learning from the experiences and best practices of others, and transferring knowledge quickly and efficiently throughout the organization (Garvin, 1993). Garvin states that many organizations do these things to some extent, but few are consistently successful because the entire organization is not involved, hence there may only be isolated units that learn. This is because organizational leaders do not continuously support on-going learning by integrating learning into daily operations and provide training and resources to integrate new members in the organization. Learning organizations, for those that are successful, is not a fad, not a sporadic exercise, and once instituted will carry itself.

Unhealthy organizations become unhealthy when the majority of time is spent in solving-problems. Leaders become consumed with grievances, lawsuits, and dissension. The focus is not on learning, but getting through each day. When problems arise they are usually long-standing, systemic problems that have had band-aids applied to them. Members of unhealthy organizations become disloyal to their organization and seek protection from administrative abuse. Often members have consulted with attorneys and made their points of view known outside the organization. From their viewpoint, there are no trustworthy resources within the organization to help them. Enormous time and energy is spent in solving problems which involve only a few members. Therefore, the majority of members are unhappy because the organization is not moving ahead. Leaders have visions and plans that are often shelved because organizational members are not receptive to hearing about them. When problems are "solved" in unhealthy organizations they never seem to go away. Involved parties have long memories and use the past to distract fellow members' attention from the future. Unhealthy organizations and their members tend to victimize each other. Distrust reinforces this relationship and it becomes cyclical.

PREPARING FOR UNCERTAIN CHANGE

Trust is not an entity to be captured, guarded and cultivated. Trust is the result of a process influenced by the characteristics of a person, such as a leader, and the knowns and unknowns of the situation. Thus, there are degrees or limits to trust. The more certainties there are regarding the object and situation of trust, the greater the chance that trust will happen. However, in the current societal environment of turbulent change regarding people and situations trust often becomes a moving target. People and situations thought to be trustful can suddenly become distrustful. Distrust can widen and deepen. Distrust cannot be turned around. The trust process must begin anew.

Despite uncertainties, trust must exist for individuals and organizations to function optimally. There are ways for individuals and organizations to cope with uncertainty. One such way is through *preparation and prevention*. Change is going to occur and, based on how we previously prepared for the changes we experienced, we can learn what worked and what did not work in preventing harmful impacts from the change. Thus, we can prepare for uncertainties by strategizing about certainties, as Drucker (1999) has discussed. For example, we know that the world has become smaller due to technological advances in communication and transportation, and economically more interdependent. Therefore, any organization planning for the future must become more multiculturally sensitive and inclusive. Organizations that prepare accordingly can prevent interpersonal and intergroup conflict by broadening its tolerance of a multicultural workforce. A second way to cope with uncertainty is for an organization to examine the way it *responds to surprises*. How has the organization responded to certain unexpected changes in the past? Is this the best way to respond to new unexpected change? Organizations that delegate decision-making help to ensure that responses can be more immediate and relevant. The organization could prepare itself by considering various options by different levels or units in the organization for responding to different scenarios of unexpected change. Brainstorming options can often psychologically soften the impact of sudden change. A third way to cope with uncertainty is to use *diverse resources or mixed strategies*. Organizations that are flexible, less bureaucratic, and used to involving its members will have more diverse repertoires to help in coping with uncertainties. In other words, use the connectedness of the organization to broaden resources and heighten the response level to surprises.

Being prepared for and preventing the uncertainties of change, broadening responses to unplanned change, and using diverse resources and mixed strategies can help organizations cope with their changing world. Not all strategies will work all the time even for previously experienced change. How an organization copes with change will directly effect how well it can maintain trust.

TRUST AND THE HEALTH OF ORGANIZATIONS

How trust is used in organizations is key to an organization's health. Trust and health are interdependent. Health is the global assessment of an organization's environment and how members interact with that environment. Trust is the core of an organization. It influences how members interact with the environment in an organization and how the total organization functions and interacts with its larger environment, e.g. other organizations.

The level of trust and the healthiness of an organization is inherited by a leader. A leader and his team through their actions and inactions, strengthen or weaken existing trust and thereby influence the existing degree of health of an organization. A new leader cannot ride on the laurels of the trustfulness of his predecessor, but the *expectations* of a leader's trustfulness is embedded in the position. Leaders must establish their own trust credibility. Members of the organization will compare each new leader's behavior with that of his predecessor and arrive at their own determination of how trustful the leader is. Healthy organizations have experienced a high level of trust and have leaders who are trusting and trustworthy. Organizations that are unhealthy have experienced a high level of distrust and leaders who are distrusted and distrustful. Thus, the culture of an organization (through its members) carries expectations about trust from leader to leader. The organization at each succession of leadership is either more healthy or unhealthy. The culture of an organization (through its members) has expectations about its degree of health based on its past.

Therefore, it is erroneous to believe that an organization's culture or its health can be "managed", that is, altered by manipulation, made or kept submissive, or contrived. People can be managed; it is their beliefs, values, and attitudes, that form an organization's culture. Organizational culture and health can be influenced and changed by members. Leaders alone cannot alter the culture or health of an organization.

Trust is a barometer of the health of an organization at any point in time. Trust is an essential value in organizations, but may be more prized in some organizations than others. Trust is an assessment made based on "feelings" and "impressions" from observations and interactions with a person, group, organization or larger entity. Therefore, we make judgments about the trust of organizations based on our encounters with its members over time and its reputation. A new leader may attempt to convince others of the trustfulness and the healthiness of his organization which may or may not match the experience or expectations that others have had with the organization.

An organization's experience with and reputation regarding trust can outlast a leader. An organization's experience with trust or distrust can profoundly influence the kind of effects a leader can have on an organization. Healthy organizations can remain healthy or become unhealthy, and unhealthy organizations can remain unhealthy or become healthy, but these efforts require more than a trusting or distrusting leader. Turnarounds require substantial cultural shifts which must have the support of members and which usually take time to achieve.

CAN TRUST BE TRUSTED? FAMILY BUSINESSES: TWO SIDES OF THE SAME COIN

Over 95 percent of all businesses in the U.S. are family owned. Family businesses produce almost half of the gross national product and generate about

50 percent of the total wages paid in the U.S. The culture of the family firm largely determines its ability to survive. Family businesses tend to have relatively short life spans, averaging 24 years (Dyer, 1986).

Family businesses provide a good example of how kinship ties facilitate the production of trust, yet only 13 percent of successful family businesses last through the third generation due to a significant decrease in trust among the top managers and a significant increase in family discord between first and second generation families (Raskas, 1998).

The founders of family businesses often create a culture that leads to a stagnant organization and its ultimate failure because the founders distrust others in the family. Ward (1987) described a stagnant organization as one:

- that has the structure of an inverted pyramid with the founders at the top
- centralized control where the founders have many people reporting to them
- little or no delegation of authority where subordinates get little management experience
- an attitude of indispensability where the founders have not developed people who can replace them
- stagnation creates low turnover and vice versa

This is referred to as a *paternalistic culture* where people are basically considered untrustworthy. Dyer describes how DuPont and the A.T. Cross Co. created a climate of distrust when a few family members attempted to gain control of their companies by a secret stock purchase. When the other family members found out about it the battle lines were drawn and prolonged conflicts ensued.

On the other hand, firms that had a *laissez faire culture* or a *participative culture* (people are good and trustworthy), tended to have successful firms. A collaborative family culture and an advisory board created an openness to ideas and opinions from others. This configuration produced an organization that fostered trust, collaboration, and teamwork. Successful family firms were future-oriented and had planned for succession and unexpected contingencies, developed mechanisms to handle conflict, and had shared goals and values. Family firms that are successful are generally aware of the problems that confront them. When nothing is important except business success, family relations suffer (Dyer, 1986).

These findings were also confirmed in an intensive study of seven family businesses that had survived five generations (La Chapelle, 1997). There were four key elements that fostered and strengthened trust in these firms: (1) effective communication; (2) the attitudes and practices associated with leadership; (3) trust was a proactive process; and (4) a family history of strongly shared values and strong role models. The four elements associated with mistrust were: (1) family members competed among themselves; (2) long-standing problems between members dated from their early childhood; (3) avoidance of communication;

unable to confront each other or to reach agreement; and (4) a high need for individual control.

Family businesses illustrate the interrelationships between organizational culture and management style in creating an environment of trust or distrust. Organizations in general can learn several important lessons about trust from the successes and failures of family businesses, such as:

- the importance of ideas from outsiders through advisory boards, partnerships, or consultants helps to prevent organizational myopia (Kets de Vries, 1993)
- periodic reviews of the organization involving both insiders and outsiders helps to identify problems before they become crises.
- information and communication flow patterns should be continually monitored and enhanced; there is always a need for better information in organizations, when it is lacking information is created
- linkages and ties to other organizations need to be continually developed and nurtured; no organization can exist in isolation and be responsive, competitive or contributive
- organizational secrets eventually became known and at a significant price
- trust is not automatic, even among blood relatives
- when business outcomes matter most, trust and loyalty can become dispensable
- trust, loyalty and related virtues cannot be demanded, they are reciprocal, earned, and situation-specific
- healthy, trusting organizations create a family-like atmosphere, but not all family organizations are healthy and trusting
- CEO's and organizational leaders need to be screened and selected on their track records with human relations, their current place of employment needs to be visited and people interviewed about the CEO on site. Too often the human side of leadership is overlooked or purposely ignored by Boards and search committees which focus on resumés, connections, recommendations, and theater-type interviews.

Can trust be trusted? Trust as an attribute of character is stable, that is, trustful people usually remain trustful and distrustful ones distrustful. However, trust relationships are changeable. To keep relationships trusting requires work because many factors can alter relationships and hence, alter trust. Trust relationships must be nourished, reinforced, and tested. Situations change and so can trust.

Some leaders cannot trust. They fear failure if they do not maintain control. They cannot trust trust. In their position as CEO leaders play out how they experienced trust in their family and early life. If they were not trusted, they will not have learned the goodness of trust. No list of things to do to create trust will work for them. They need to learn to trust by learning to trust themselves. Kouzes and Posner (1993) discussed the steps toward discovering oneself, and developing a leadership credo. Trust is learnable and is essential in building and maintaining healthy organizations. Max De Pree expressed this clearly when he said, "We must trust one another to be accountable for our own assignments. When that kind of trust is present, it is a beautiful, liberating thing."[14]

Just as the health of organizations is relative, what constitutes a healthy organization is also relative. Drucker (1993) pointed out that a new type of organization is emerging; we are entering a period of change from command-and-control organizations (the organization of departments and divisions) to information-based organizations (the organization of knowledge specialists). The organizational chart of the information-based organization will be flatter, with decentralization into autonomous units; task forces will be assembled to solve specific problems. The entire organization, to accomplish such a restructuring, will have a cohesive and common vision, bonding the decentralized units together. The health of an organization will be determined by the health of its various units and their ability to contribute to the mission and goal of the entire organization. The information-based organization will need to adopt a new set of values, structure, and behavior. Schein (1992) said, "My sense is that the various predictions about globalism, knowledge-based organizations, the information age, the biotech age, the loosening of organizational boundaries, and so on have one theme in common—we basically do not know what the world of tomorrow will really be like except that it will be different. That means that organizations and their leaders will have to become perpetual learners."

SUMMARY

Organizations are living systems with their own needs and lifecycles. Like other living things, they experience change and conflict as they grow and develop. Sometime during their lifecycles, most organizations become ill and need treatment and rehabilitation. Some organizations become chronically ill but continue to function until their eventual demise, other organizations successfully conquer acute episodes of illness, and still others rarely experience illness.

Most of us work in organizations that are relatively healthy. However, the concept of a healthy organization is idealistic. Organizations are never fully stable, they never maximize their potential, and they never achieve complete harmony.

It is a common myth that the leader determines an organization's health and success. Yet it is the interaction between followers and leaders that makes an organization healthy. It is how the psychodynamics of an organization are managed, and the capacity of its leaders and followers to repair broken relationships, that influence an organization's health.

An organization may be sick or dysfunctional and yet be productive. However, eventually sick organizations become unproductive and often meet an early demise because symptoms of unhealthiness are not recognized or are denied by leaders. Indeed, the leader may be a large part of the problem.

Organizations become sick for many reasons which include: egotism and the personal indiscretions of leaders; the failure to adapt to change; pockets of ongoing dissent that drain morale and sap the organization's spirit; when members of the organization feel victimized by change; when the organization needs a future, but can't agree what it should be; mean-spirited managers and leaders; distrust; frequent turnover; over or underbounded cultures; and a tough culture. Not all organizations are introspective enough to identify the causes of their problems; they only know they are experiencing more problems, which are consuming more time and energy, and resolving few, if any, of them.

Trusting organizations have problems too, but they have plans to prepare how to cope with them and minimize their reoccurrence when possible. Organizations, like individuals, can be surprised by unplanned change, and stymied by it. Yet, a healthy organization which involves its members in its operation is more likely to use its flexibility and diverse resources to help it cope with uncertainties. Unhealthy organizations, on the other hand, are not connected enough to rally themselves to the challenge of surprises, especially those that need quick responses.

How trust is used in organizations is key to an organization's health. Trust and health are interdependent. An organization's experience with and reputation regarding trust can outlast a leader. An organization's experience with trust or distrust can profoundly influence the kind of effects a leader can have on an organization. Leaders can only partially contribute to an organization's health. Turnarounds from sickness to health require substantial cultural shifts which must have the support of members and which usually take substantial time to achieve. The ultimate managers of the trust and health of organizations are the members.

Family businesses provide an opportunity to look at two sides of trust. While 95 percent of all businesses in the U.S. are family owned, only 13 percent of successful family businesses last through the third generation due to a significant decrease in trust among the top leaders and a significant increase in family discord between first and second generation families. A paternalistic organization where family members who are the leaders do not trust other family members can lead to a stagnant organization that is certain to fail. On the other hand, an organization with a collaborative family culture which is open to ideas and feedback from others, has mechanisms to handle conflict, has shared goals and values, is future-oriented, and has a succession plan, is more likely to succeed. Family businesses illustrate the interrelationships between culture and management style in creating a trusting organization. We can learn much about how to build trust into organizations in general by studying family businesses that have succeeded and failed.

Some leaders cannot trust. They have a fear of losing control and of failure. Leaders play out their early childhood experiences with trust and distrust as CEO's. No list of things to do to create a healthy and trusting organization will help a CEO who has never experienced trust. They first need to learn to trust themselves. Self-trust is learnable and essential in building and maintaining healthy organizations.

Chapter 9

The Ethical Organization

"Bureaucracy is explicitly unfriendly to the idea of trust."[1]

WHAT IS AN ETHICAL ORGANIZATION?

Organizations are ethical in their own ways; there is no ethics of organizations as there is for individuals (Phillips & Margolis, 1999). Individuals develop morally in stages and sequentially, progressing from reasoning governed by fear of punishment to concern for others and concern for universal rights and humanity as a whole (Kohlberg, 1981). Within this progression there are three types of ethical standards namely self-interest, caring, and principle, which reflect three major categories of ethical theory, i.e., egoism, utilitarianism, and deontology (Fritzche & Becker, 1984; Williams, 1985). There is no comparable process of moral development for organizations. Several authors have suggested that there needs to be an ethics of organizations (Hartman, 1996; Phillips & Margolis, 1999).

Why should organizations be moral? Hartman (1996) agrees that any good community, any good organization requires not only good rules, but also people of civic virtue. Moral persons are necessary in order to have good organizations and good organizations help make people moral.[2] Organizations influence the conduct and lives of those who belong to them. People spend a great deal of time in organizations, which become a formative social environment akin to the family (Okin, 1989). Organizations shape, influence, and support virtually every aspect of our lives, directly or indirectly. Therefore, organizations provide a mechanism by which we institutionalize ethics and establish cultures based on ethical values. The degree to which an organization contributes to, and benefits from, the public good is what organizational morality is all about. While organizations do not progress through identifiable, sequential, and progressive stages of moral development, they can be judged against the moral frameworks of self-interest, caring, and principle.

Theoretical Ideas of an Ethical Organization

One of the key elements which is thought by many scholars to promote better decisions and more effective and higher performance in an ethical organization, is participation. Most moral theorists would posit that participation is a fundamental obligation, if not a right, on the part of an organization. How participation is allowed, facilitated, encouraged and its expected outcomes, depends on one's theoretical perspective. Four such perspectives are offered here (Zajac & Bruhn, 1999).

1. *Deontology*. The deontologist sees participation as a good in and of itself. The organization owes its members the opportunity to fully participate in organizational decisions that affect their lives. Members have such special claims because of their connection with the organization, where they spend a majority of their time and are part of social networks. Members of organizations are touted as their most important asset and have much to gain, or lose, through participation. Decisions, particularly those which result in changes to policies, practices, rules, operations, and conditions of employment fall within the boundaries of members' participatory rights in organizations. An organization also has an obligation to ascertain what forms of participation are meaningful and desirable for members.
2. *Utilitarian*. The utilitarian sees participation as a means to an end rather than a good in itself. The utilitarian advocates that participation benefits the majority interests of the organization. Participation enhances members' morale. There is no generalized right to participate in decision-making; participation is considered a management tool rather than a moral imperative. Concerns for the larger social and organizational good take precedence over concerns for individual rights, autonomy, or self-actualization.
3. *Rawlsian*. The Rawlsian theorist (justice-based) proposes that organizations should provide the greatest possible benefit to the least advantaged members. Thus, organizations need to make special efforts to include the least advantaged, making sure that their contributions are especially valued. Justice-based participation encourages the full participation of organizational members to the best of their abilities. The Rawlsian theorist takes participation seriously even under trying circumstances.
4. *Virtue*. Virtue-based ethics has a greater focus on the individual than any of the other three moral schools of thought. The notion is that the organization should help develop excellence in, and make better persons of all of its members.

There are many ways of conceptualizing an ethical organization, but it is not possible to please all members of an organization by offering all forms and variations of participation. Yet, participation which makes members feel validated because they can have an impact on others is essential in creating a humane workplace and providing opportunities employees to work toward their potential.

Other Characteristics of an Ethical Organization

First, an ethical organization, in addition to insuring participation by its members, creates good citizens. Good citizenship is a product of organizational culture. Every organization has a "shared reality" which sets certain patterns of behavior and influences members' beliefs about expected behavior. Citizenship has two dimensions, legal and ethical. Legal citizenship is prescribed and defined in terms of qualifications, rights, and obligations. Ethical citizenship is broader and is concerned with membership in a community. Good citizenship behavior in organizations is a blend of rights and responsibilities which results in members engaging in behavior that is discretionary, beyond the call of duty, and that is not tied to any formal organizational reward structure. Good citizenship means more than going to work every day and fulfilling contractual obligations. It means exhibiting what has been termed "the good soldier syndrome," that is, altruism, helping, conscientiousness, neighborliness, sportsmanship, and civic virtue. The standards of moral behavior and good citizenship involve the interaction between an organization and its members (Bruhn, et al., 2002).

A second characteristic of an ethical organization is that leaders and members are never satisfied with their level of excellence; they strive to become even better. They accomplish this through self-scrutiny, feedback, honest evaluations and striving to meet goals, which are escalated as they are achieved. While ethical organizations are competitive and strive to "win" over other competitors, they also compete with themselves. Therefore, ethical organizations are allies rather than foes of change, and they are willing to make changes in their culture to become a more ethical and effective organization.

A third characteristic of an ethical organization is there is little or no defending "I", but rather advocating "we." Participation, good citizenship, and working toward greater excellence, are values which are emphasized, reemphasized, and rewarded from the top. Ethical organizations have members who excel as good citizens.

Finally, every leader leaves an ethical culture for their successor. Ethics needs to be part of every leader's daily agenda, as the organization and its members are undergoing continuous change. Ethics need to lead rather than follow, organizational change. An organization that frames change around its ethical standards and expectations always asks, "to what extent are our practices consistent with the values we espouse?"

If CEO's and members of their organizations were asked to rate how ethical their organizations were on a scale of 1 to 10 there would be a range of responses. There are differences in opinions of what constitutes ethical behavior within organizations. However, there should be general agreement among leaders and members of organizations that morality is not just an evaluation of certain acts, but about the total character of an organization. An ethical organization is one in which the leaders and members care enough about each other as persons to achieve a consensus about the principles of fairness, respect, and equality.

Some organizations point to their published codes of ethics to illustrate their moral commitment. An empirical study of the corporate ethical practices of the Fortune 1000 in the mid-1990's examined several different types of formal ethical activity including:

- ethics-oriented policy statements
- formal commitment of management to ethics
- free standing ethics offices
- ethics and compliance telephone reporting and advice systems
- involvement of top management and department heads in ethics activities
- use of ethics training and other ethics awareness activities
- investigatory functions
- evolution of ethics program activities

Results showed a high degree of corporate adoption of ethics policies, but a wide variability in the extent to which these policies were implemented by various supporting structures and managerial activities. The majority of firms had committed themselves to the low cost symbolic side of ethics management (Weaver et al., 1999).

Ethics is usually not of a major concern in an organization until either an individual or individuals, or the organization itself, violates boundaries of behavior that create "a moral or legal problem." A breach of ethics causes "a problem" when it becomes public knowledge, when a grievance or lawsuit is filed, or there is sufficient disruption among organizational members to impact the organization's morale and productiveness that brings the breach to the attention of appropriate persons. It is generally assumed that an organization is ethical until it is found to be otherwise. Yet, everyone knows that there are breaches of ethics in and by organizations daily, most of which are not reported. Therefore, an ethical organization is often known by what it is not, that is, it lacks a reputation for known violations of ethical principles and standards. Organizations have different tolerance levels for ethics failure depending on how the failure is regarded in the organizational community, e.g. reactions may range from a petition, to looking the other way.

THE ORGANIZATION AS AN ETHICAL COMMUNITY

An organization is composed of individuals who have their own ethical standards. When they become members of an organization they must abide by another set of ethics, namely, those of the organization. There may be differences between the attitudes and behavior of some individuals and those of the organization, but while engaged in organizational activities, it is the organization's ethical principles that prevail. When individuals join organizations they accept the standards of the group, although individual members sometimes may differ strongly with the ethical views and practices of other individuals in the organization. It is not uncommon for organizational members to believe that it is their duty to oversee the ethical behavior of others. Frequently these overseers are disappointed by what they see and file grievances or complaints, or become whistleblowers.

Communities have five major characteristics that help to build a foundation for ethical standards and behavior. First, when individuals join a community they become *socialized* into its culture. Hartman (1996) says that a good community encourages the good life. It does so by promoting rules, practices, and social contracts, but it also encourages abiding by principles that are fair and impartial. Such principles are those that members can agree upon and use to justify acts to each other. When members join an organization they "buy into" its culture of ethics; existing members help in the socialization of new members including its ethical practices and expectations. Second, communities provide *social support.* Members have a concern for, and respect, each other so they provide a social network and sometimes a safety net when members are in need. Socially supportive behavior helps to bolster morale, reinforce common values and beliefs, and provide a sense of security "that we are all in this together." Third, communities provide for the *economic welfare* of members. Organizations are communities which bring together the skills, knowledge and expertise of persons to contribute to a common goal. The organization could not be effective without the sharing of diverse talents. There are "ground rules" regarding compensation, advancement, how people will use their time, and individual and collective benefits in economic endeavors. A fourth characteristic of community is *social control.* There is probably no greater pressure than that from peers and colleagues. Approval is sought and valued by those we associate with and work for. Communities provide formal and informal means of social control to keep a group cohesive and working toward common goals. Social control helps define the boundaries of acceptable and unacceptable behavior. Fifth, communities provide *social participation.* Social participation is key to survival. It provides opportunities for friendships, sharing, learning, and connectedness. Through community participation individuals learn and practice civic virtues and become enmeshed in networks involving mutual obligations. It is through social participation that we learn what others believe and value.

An organization can be regarded as a community because it focuses on shared behavior directed toward a common goal, it establishes boundaries for responsibility and acceptable and unacceptable behavior, it provides the opportunity to strengthen social bonds, and it provides mechanisms for protection, cooperation, competition, and communication. An organization can be regarded as an ethical community in that it can be only as good as the best abilities and qualities of its members. Hartman (1996) would say we are better off in a community that preserves the commons—to pull one's weight and to take only one's share—then there is a reason to be moral. "Morality is about what sort of community causes ordinary people to believe, to prefer, to feel, and to act so that they are better off in the whole."[3]

There are organizations that are models of ethical communities. For example, WalMart recently announced that employees who have been called for full-time active duty during America's Operation 'Enduring Freedom', and who earn less than their wages were while working at WalMart, will be paid the difference. In addition, their benefits will be continued while on military duty. Organizations that build an ethical community on fairness and equity will generate trust among members as well as reinforce other virtues such as loyalty, that contribute to a healthy organization. (See Figure 9.1)

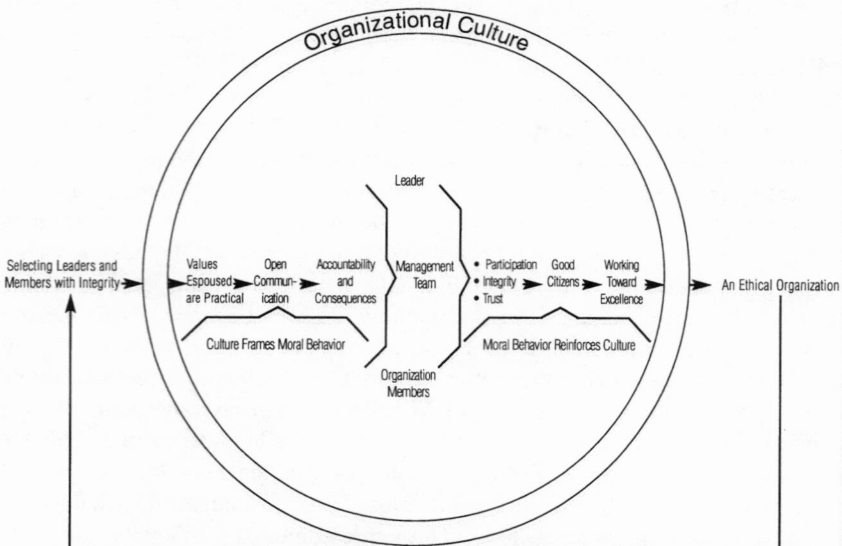

Figure 9.1. Concept of an Ethical Organization.

A CULTURE OF ETHICS

Chen and his associates (1997) point out that the ability to see and respond ethically may be related more to attributes of organizational culture than to attributes of individual employees. Efforts to increase ethical standards and decrease pressure to behave unethically should be apparent in an organization's culture. There are five important aspects to building a culture of ethics.

First, Chen proposes that members of organizations need to recognize that ethical issues exist. This involves more than creating awareness. Mautz and Sharaf (1961) noted, long ago, that being ethnically sensitive rivaled the importance of being technically proficient. Integrity has been a pronouncement of many organizations over the years, but in this age of accountability, when ethical achievements can be measured, it is incumbent upon organizations to make declarations about what ethics mean to them (Calhoun et al., 1999).

Some organizations may not consider some issues to be of an ethical nature, while others may find it difficult to be objective in assessing whether or not an issue is a moral one. Some organizations may not be explicit about what constitutes moral and immoral behavior. When ethical standards and behavior are not made explicit, individuals use their own standards. The two things that encourage grievances or lawsuits are ambivalent or unclear ethical standards and inconsistencies in resolving or arbitrating them. In some organizations, like Johnson and Johnson, organizational values are explicitly taught, employees are compelled to discuss them, and they are supported with incentives as well as examples (Hartman, 1996).

Making organizational values explicit is especially important where members are from different cultures (Kanungo & Mendonca, 1996). Often a newcomer to a multicultural organization will be assigned to someone to orient them to the organization, and possibly become their mentor. This usually works well, but the author witnessed one such pairing where an organizational member of an ethnic group volunteered to be a "mentor" and used this opportunity to criticize leaders of the organization and gave inaccurate information about his colleagues that led the newcomer's eventual filing of a grievance at the encouragement of the "mentor." The newcomer, naive to the organization's values, was used by the "mentor" to get back at the organization for what the "mentor" considered unethical behavior toward him in the past. Culture affects the determination of what is or isn't ethical as well as the evaluation of the consequences of unethical behavior, i.e., whether the punishment is too lenient or too severe.

Second, organizational members should have a voice in framing their organization's ethical standards and procedures for dealing with violations. If organizations are ethical communities they need to have many sets of eyes and ears to protect ethical boundaries. Indeed, the rank and file members of organizations are the first-to-know and to assess ethical violations. If the organization functions as a community, minor violations are usually dealt with informally by members. It is in organizations that do not function as communities where minor ethical violations are debated and gossiped about, which then become larger issues and reach the offices of Human Resources, Affirmative Action and organizational leaders. Usually members in low trusting, loosely-knit organizations, become obsessed with monitoring each other's behavior. Ironically, in the author's experience, the members of low trusting organizations have a great deal of difficulty in agreeing on the nature and consequences of violations of ethics. It is not uncommon in such organizations to see a member repeatedly file a grievance against the same person or persons because their desire for vengeance is unfulfilled or they are dissatisfied with the outcome of previous grievances they have filed.

Third, it is important for organizational members to be given honest explanations, while protecting individual rights and privacy, when punishments for ethical violations are given. Often organizational members' ears are trained to listen for any inequities or inconsistencies in how similar situations are resolved for different individuals. It may not be possible to reveal all aspects of a case that have influenced its outcome, hence there will always be some unhappy people irrespective of the information they are given.

Open communication is essential in maintaining an ethical community. The importance of a climate supportive of open communication and sharing is consistent with Hosmer's (1994) argument for "right", "just" and "fair" treatment of employees. He notes that all members must agree that decision processes are "right", "just" and "fair." Agreeing on principles used in such decisions requires communication. Organizations that have a climate of sharing and an attention to human relations and employee interests are more likely to have open communications among employees. While there may be some disagreement among members on what outcome is considered "right", "just" and "fair," as long as the majority agree that the decision process has considered the rights and interests of all, there should be a high degree of trust.

Ruppel and Harrington (2000) found a strong relationship between communication and ethical work climate. Employee communication was enhanced when the organization had rules, procedures and mechanisms for sharing information between groups. The authors concluded that management sets the tone for open communication that, in turn, influences trust (Butler & Cantrell, 1994).

Fourth, to maintain an ethical organization requires more than adopting a formal code of ethics, but, in addition, communicating it and reinforcing it with supportive organizational values. In an interesting study of relationships between corporate and professional codes of ethics and employee attitudes and behaviors it was found that members of organizations with formal codes of ethics were less aware of wrongdoing than were members in organizations without formal codes of ethics (Somers, 2001). The author concluded that professional codes of ethics have little or no relationship to employee awareness of wrongdoing in organizations, nor does the existence of a code of ethics have any influence on members propensity to report observed wrongdoing. Members of organizations that had codes of ethics were significantly less aware of wrongdoing than were members of organizations without codes of ethics. Somers suggested that professional codes of ethics play a less important role in influencing employee behavior because codes are not part of the organizational environment. Personal experience and behavior speak louder about human values than framed commitments on walls, or statements made in brochures and in annual reports.

Fifth, ethical organizations have leaders and leadership teams that work to model, reaffirm, and hold members accountable for their ethics. In ethical organizations leaders are *given* trust by their followers. Trust is part of the background or culture of an ethical organization (Solomon, 1998). Unfortunately there is a great deal of public cynicism about leaders' following through on what they say they will do. Kouzes and Posner (1993) reviewed the outcomes of polls conducted by several national sources, which affirmed that leaders had a poor track record of "earning" trust. Ciulla emphasized "ultimately … there is no such thing as *deserving* trust … but whether or not trust can be *earned*, it can be wisely or foolishly *given*. Thus, it is those who would follow, not those who would lead, who are the ultimate power in any leadership relationship."[4]

This points out the importance in carefully choosing leaders and members of organizations. The late Roberto Goizueta, former CEO of Coca Cola said, "You hope you don't hire anybody who is stupid, but if you do, pray that they don't have a lot of energy."[5] New leaders and members of organizations do not earn trust, they are *given* trust by existing members. Trust is awarded by the members of an organization after the leader passes informal tests of integrity. The "tests of trust" begin when new leaders and members are interviewed and screened. The recruitment process has many agendas, but the major one is to assess a candidate's integrity (Bruhn, 1996). One human relations director commented "search committees select the individuals that they deserve." Organizations seem to attract leaders who match their respective organizational culture, that is, ethical organizations attract ethical leaders while organizations that focus less on personal qualities seem to attract leaders who are weak in these characteristics.

The ethical climates of organizations can be measured.[6] The Ethical Climate Questionnaire distinguishes between three climates, maximizing one's own self-interests, maximizing joint interests, and adherence to universal principles. The questionnaire was designed to tap respondent's perceptions of how the members of an organization typically make decisions concerning various events, practices, and procedures requiring ethical criteria. This questionnaire needs to be tested in a greater number and variety of organizations, but it is a tool that can help organizations gain insights into how their organization's ethical climate is perceived by its members.

HOW ORGANIZATIONS AND INDIVIDUAL MEMBERS BECOME UNETHICAL

Brien (1998) states that the cause of ethical failure in organizations can often be traced to their organizational culture and the failure on the part of the leadership to actively promote ethical ideals and practices. This is true for all types of organizations, including professions. For example, McCabe and Trevino (1997) report from a study of nine state universities, that the context of the classroom can have an impact on student dishonesty. Cheaters have described their classes as less personalized, less satisfying, and more task-oriented than non-cheaters (Pulvers & Diekhoff, 1999).

One way organizations and individuals can become unethical is the failure of leaders to specify, clarify, reinforce and model ethical behavior. Many leaders take ethics for granted and assume members will do the right thing. However, ethics is a personal, human endeavor, that must be discussed, nourished, and continually brought to the attention of the total organization. In a task-oriented business-as-usual organization ethics will only be as important as they are jointly upheld by the leader and members. When leaders fail to establish prior boundaries of behavior in their organization they often find that they are forced to set them after a major ethical breach has occurred, resulting in members perceiving the boundaries to be capricious and arbitrary.

Organizations can become unethical by the outright neglect of ethics by its leader. The CEO of a large corporation arrived at work every day at 7:00 a.m., walked up the back stairs to his office, closed the door, kept the TV on to watch his stock holdings, worked at his desk, and left for golf at 3:30 p.m. He made no effort to communicate with employees except by memo. When the company's stock fell by one half during the recession of 2001, the Manager of the Office of Human Resources asked the CEO if he wanted to have a forum for employees to explain the company's financial situation. The CEO replied, "That's not necessary. They will find out about it." The CEO has continued in his job as the company's stock and profits continue to fall. When I asked the Human Resources Director how the Board of Directors could permit this, he replied, "The CEO has the Board in his back pocket." In this example the CEO never showed any concern for ethics in his organization. As a result, the ethical climate of the organization was what every member wanted it to be. Ethics in such situations are likely to become a topic of concern to the CEO when there is a major violation, usually of a legal nature, that requires the direct intervention of the CEO.

If an organization, its leaders, and individual members, want to be trusted they must be seen to act ethically. That is, actions must be in accord with the norms of the organizational culture. But, all organizations do not have the same ethical rigor. Darley (1996) discusses how organizations socialize individuals into evil-doing. There is wiggle room in the practice of ethics. Organizations and individuals in them often define what is moral by what is legal. The following example illustrates this point.

> A brother and sister each had accounts in a large U.S. brokerage firm, referred to here as Firm A. The sister had been unhappy with the performance of her account and her broker's advice, so she responded to a letter, sent as part of a marketing campaign by a broker in investment firm B, offering to review her account. The sister asked her brother to accompany her on this visit. The broker raised questions about some of the sister's annuities and discussed features she had not been advised of before. At the conclusion of the session the broker asked the brother if he wished a similar review. He agreed, although he stated that he was happy with his current broker. The broker assured the brother there was no obligation to change brokers but said he needed to obtain contract numbers for the annuities to check into possible options. The brother provided this information, assuring the broker again, in the presence of the sister, that he did not want to change brokers or firms. The broker said again, that there was no obligation to do so.
>
> The broker in Firm B spoke with two internal wholesalers for the Long Life Insurance Co. about features on the brother's annuities, providing them with contract numbers but assuring them that the client did not wish to, nor had he authorized, a change in brokers. The wholesalers marketed their products to both Firms A and B.
>
> About two weeks later the brother's broker in Firm A called him to ask about a change of agent of record form that had come across his desk. Since this was a surprise to the broker he wanted to know if his client was dissatisfied and wanted to change brokers. The client (brother) called the broker in Firm B who had contacted the internal wholesalers about this matter and the broker denied that he had initiated a change of agent of record form. The client believed that his confidentiality had been breached. The client was dumbfounded, having given no verbal or written permission to change brokers. The distressed client requested that the Long Life Insurance Co. release his annuities without penalty so that they could be transferred to the High Quality Insurance Co. The client also retained a lawyer claiming that his confidentiality was breached by the two wholesalers of Long Life Insurance Co. The chief legal counsel for Long Life Insurance Co. denied the request to transfer the annuities without penalty affirming the client's confidentiality was not breached. She wrote, "Agents are notified about inquiries to their customers' accounts as a general practice here at Long Life. This is done routinely to insure that our clients receive good service. If a client (or his authorized representative) for instance, inquires about certain contract features, we want our agents to be able to discuss these issues promptly and accurately. If a client is interested in a contract feature his contract does not currently have, perhaps there is a way of addressing this to their satisfaction with their existing contract or exploring other Long Life options with them."
>
> The client's lawyer was unsuccessful in getting Long Life to reconsider their position. It took a phone call from the Senior Vice President and Branch Manager of Firm B to the President of Long Life Insurance Co., to get the client's annuities released to the High Quality Insurance Co., without penalty.

An organization's practices can be within the law, but it can still act in immoral ways. According to the attorney for the Long Life Insurance Co., the two wholesalers did nothing illegal, they were only providing good service to a client of

Long Life. What is important in this example is that the representatives of Long Life Insurance Co. learned the boundaries of morality of the company's culture, and as long as they acted legally they didn't worry about what behavior was or wasn't moral. The representatives never admitted that they did anything wrong. The Vice President of Long Life Insurance Co. called the broker who had initially contacted the wholesale agents and offered to send him on a paid golfing vacation to compensate for the "misunderstanding." The broker declined and the two wholesalers were banned by the Senior Vice-President and Branch Manager in Firm B from doing business at this brokerage firm. The client was never contacted directly. No admission of wrongdoing was ever made by Long Life. What is distressing, as Philip Howard (1994) has pointed out in his book, *The Death of Common Sense*, is that we have become a society of "whatever works is good." Organizations and individuals in them become unethical when the buck never stops or decisions are made without ever consulting the heart.[7]

A third way organizations and individuals can become unethical is if there are no consequences for unethical behavior. Some organizations and individuals push the boundaries of unethical behavior to see how far they can go without being caught. In this case members "use" the organization for their own purposes with minimal personal investment or cost.

A fourth way organizations and individuals can become unethical is a business as usual approach—"This is the way we have always operated and it has worked for us—no one has questioned it before." This is the type of organization where there is a casual attitude toward any formal social controls, legal or ethical. For example, an employee of a state educational institution mailed over one hundred personal Christmas cards to be metered through the institution's post office. When the manager of the postal station returned the cards to the employee, the employee seemed surprised. He had apparently done this before but had not been caught. (He had, however, been "taken to task" by his supervisor for using the office Xerox and telephone on weekends for personal business.) Interestingly enough, upon informal questioning of other employees about this practice, some admitted to doing the same thing, but staggering their mailings so that they would not draw the attention of the postal manager, or mailing the cards on the manager's day off when temporary employees in the post office might be reluctant to confront the sender about this practice (Bruhn et al., 2002).

A fifth way organizations can become unethical is when they become obsessed with profitability. In the aftermath of the terrorism attacks on New York City and Washington, and the resulting decline in the economy, a CEO of a large business sent a memo to all employees telling them that the way to demonstrate their loyalty and support for their country, and help revitalize the economy, was by more aggressively selling the company's products. When profitability can be advocated as a way to compensate for loss and grief following a national tragedy, think what other events or actions can be subjugated to profitability.

WHY UNETHICAL LEADERS PERSIST

Unethical leaders persist in organizations because the Boards to whom they report decide the tradeoffs to changing leaders would be more harmful than helpful to the organization at a particular point in its lifecycle. How the tradeoffs are weighed depends on the Boards' evaluation of the leader's performance of which morality is only a part. The enormous success of a leader in fund raising, sales and public support may compensate for personal behavior such as romantic encounters or occasional overimbibing. The administrative admittance of a relative of a Board member to an academic program, for example, will certainly cause that Board member to overlook minor personal failings of the CEO. The morally questionable behavior of a CEO, who is a member of a "protected group" may be disregarded when confronting the CEO is likely to result in a grievance or lawsuit which would embarrass the organization. Unethical leaders are often successful (and powerful); some seem to "get by", others are even retained with accolades. It depends on how unethical behavior is defined and judged as to whether or not it is a problem.

What is key here is what members of the organization and others outside the organization (who may interact with the leader more frequently than Board members) see and hear what the Board does not know. It is impossible for an organization to be trusting and healthy when a leader is viewed as unethical. If Boards commend, reward, and retain such leaders the message to others in the organization is that the leader's behavior is what is expected and will be rewarded publicly. Some Boards may regard integrity and loyalty to be interchangeable. Politics is often more powerful than ethics in the lives of leaders and organizations.

FINDING INTEGRITY, CREATING TRUST

There are two major steps in creating ethical, trusting, and healthy organizations. The first step is to find leaders who have integrity to head organizations. Jack Welch was asked at a business school forum how he could be a good Catholic and a businessman at the same time. He answered, "By maintaining integrity. Establishing it and never wavering from it. People may not have agreed with me on every issue ... but they always knew they were getting it straight and honest ... It set the tone for the organization."[8]

Too often recruiting a leader is all credentials, a preoccupation with the resumé (Peters, 1994). Usually leaders are recruited because of what they have done, not what they will do. Often selecting a leader is a political process, or looking for an image, rather than a strategy (Bruhn, 1996c). Resumés are constructed, and references selected, to present an autobiographical sketch of accomplishments and successes. These sources tell little about the nature of the *interaction* of the leader and the organization he/she currently is affiliated with; how the leader copes with change, handles the "people side" of leading an organization, and how the leader deals with failure. References are solicited from people who know the candidate from a certain time period; referees describe personal traits of the candidate vis-à-vis interactions they had during limited times, circumstances and with certain people. Today, referees are reluctant to commit their opinions in writing about a candidate's values and beliefs, psychological make-up and stability, and the degree of "fit" between a candidate and the prospective organization. Candidates solicit letters from those who will present them in the best light. Often these referees do not know the culture of the organization the candidate proposes to join to make judgments about the candidate's suitability and match. Basically organizations do a poor job in selecting leaders; they do not utilize strategies that will result in selecting a person of integrity.

Authors have suggested that as a society we need to educate leaders to be sensitive to ethics, uphold ethical standards and institutionalize them by formulating contracts structured around ethics to ensure that employee-employer dealings are more moral (Sims, 1994). Yet, integrity cannot be obtained by training, or mandated; it must be learned. Every leader models ethics silently or verbally in every action and inaction.

I propose that the selection of leaders needs to be ethical if we are to select leaders of integrity and offer several suggestions to enhance the selection of moral leaders.

- Every finalist for a leadership position in an organization should be visited by two to three members of the search committee at the organization they are currently affiliated with. It should be no secret that the candidate is a finalist so no one should be uncomfortable with this process. The visitors will conduct interviews with at least six of the candidate's superiors and associates and a few representatives from the community, probing opinions about the candidate's leadership style, projects and activities that the candidate has initiated, how the candidate approached these projects and activities, the candidate's general reputation in the organization, and why the interviewers think the candidate should remain where he is, or what particular strengths the candidate would bring to the new organization.
- Every finalist for a leadership position in an organization should spend at least two hours in a face to face meeting with the search committee or leadership team from the organization he/she wishes to join, during which time the candidate would be presented with real problems in the organization and asked to discuss their strategies for handling them.
- Every finalist should be evaluated separately on their human relations skills, their ability to relate to people, and their experience in dealing with the human side of organizations.

- Every finalist for a leadership position in an organization should spend at least two hours in a face to face meeting with 15 to 20 rank and file members of the organization to discuss human relations issues in the organization. This should not be a session to discuss the grievances of individual members, but rather to elicit the candidate's approaches to these issues, values and beliefs, and problem-solving styles.

The search and selection process is a two way street. Leaders select organizations, too. Most prospective applicants know little about the culture of the organization they wish to join. A reading of public relations material sent by the organization and two or three on-site visits will not provide an adequate assessment of the organization's culture. Usually applicants are interested in new positions to: (1) get out of their current position; (2) get a position of higher salary and title; (3) take on a similar position in a larger organization with new challenges; (4) take on a similar position in a less demanding environment; or (5) take a position to leave a geographical area for personal or family reasons. Often leaders do not ask the right questions in order to learn about an organization's culture. Once "on board" leaders learn quite rapidly the realities of the organization they just joined. It may be a healthy or an unhealthy organization. It would be to a prospective candidate's advantage to know in advance of making a decision to join an organization what the challenges are.

I suggest ten questions that, if asked by prospective leaders could yield valuable insights into the organization's culture. I have found these questions helpful in learning more about an organization's culture in interviews for leadership positions. There are obviously many more questions which could be added, but the ten offered here provide the start of interesting dialogues (Table 9.1). These questions can be asked of individuals during individual interviews or in groups. Comparisons of responses often reveals the strengths and weaknesses that any CEO will have to deal with.

The reader might respond by saying "hire a professional search firm" to conduct the search and they will do all these things for you, or that it would be too time-intensive for organizations to do these things with finalists each time there was a leadership vacancy. No approach to selecting leaders is perfect even with the expense and expertise of search firms. Search firms rely strongly on reputational references from key sources and individuals that they know, or who have been candidates the firm has successfully placed. Considering the retention of leaders of organizations worldwide, the track record of integrity and staying power is less than exceptional. How can we create trust in organizations if we do not spend the time and energy to select leaders who can be trusted?

If searches for leaders of organizations were less political and social and more honest and realistic, and if prospective leaders asked the right questions to better understand an organization's culture, there should be fewer surprises for

Table 9.1. Questions for Prospective Leaders to Ask During the Organizational Search Process

1. How would you rate the current morale in your organization?
2. What is the most successful activity, program or endeavor that this organization has undertaken? Why was it so successful?
3. What is the least successful activity, program or endeavor that this organization has undertaken? Why was it unsuccessful?
4. What are some adjectives that you would use to describe your organization?
5. How would you describe the leadership style of your current CEO or President?
6. What are the major goals of your organization in the next 3 to 5 years?
7. How would you describe the decision-making process in your organization? Who has a voice and in what matters? Are there topics or issues in which the members of the organization have no voice?
8. Do you have an organizational chart? Describe how well it is followed? When was the last time it was modified?
9. Would you say people have authority along with responsibility in their jobs in your organization?
10. What were the major reasons you joined this organization?

both parties. Seemingly there would be fewer regrets and disappointments, and possibly fewer grievances, lawsuits, and terminations due to "poor fits" between leaders and organizations—after all, organizations and leaders choose each other.

Leaders and organizations make mistakes, sometimes they are bad choices for each other. Leaders and organizations become scapegoats for each other when a "match" has been unsuccessful. Leaders find other positions and organizations once again look for another hero/heroine CEO. This often becomes an unhealthy cycle and organizational members become cynical about any leader. Organizations that have had a succession of unsuccessful leaders will have built up so much distrust that any leader would be overwhelmed about where to start in rebuilding trust.

We tend to treat organizations like individuals with bad habits. Its usually only after a catastrophic event that an individual will change unhealthy habits. It is similar with organizations. We think we know an organization well enough to be an honest critic of its strengths and weaknesses and choose appropriate goals, and leaders to help reach those goals. Sometimes organizations are not discriminating about choosing its leaders. Leaders, in turn, need to put egos aside and turn down opportunities to lead organizations that are not good matches for them. In my opinion, organizations spend so much time in rehabilitating the effects of past mistakes that they are unable to generate a forward momentum. Finding and replacing leaders with integrity, who can trust and be trusted, establishing an ethical culture, and re-setting goals seems to be an endless cycle for some organizations. We can have healthy organizations that are good communities. There are no secrets to the creation of healthy organizations. There is, however, a formula for success:

$$\frac{\text{Integrity} \times \text{Trust}^2}{\text{Ethical Culture}} = \text{A Healthy Organization}$$

SUMMARY

One interviewee defined an ethical organization as “the result of a building process, something that is built upon practice.” Moral persons are necessary to have good organizations and good organizations help to make people moral. Another CEO characterized an ethical organization as “one in which decisions are made on trust.” A third organizational leader said, “In an ethical organization you can assume everyone will do the right thing.” In ethical organizations there is an unspoken understanding between people of reliability and a sense of security.

How do organizations become ethical? There are several key elements. Participation has been shown to promote better decisions and create more effective and higher performance in organizational members. An ethical organization, by insuring participation, creates good citizens. Good citizenship means exhibiting what has been called “the good soldier syndrome”, characterized by altruism, helping, conscientiousness, neighborliness, sportsmanship, and civic virtue; good citizens go beyond the minimum required. Another characteristic of an ethical organization is that it strives to become better; it competes with itself. Ethical organizations become so by subscribing to “we” instead of “I.” They work together for the benefit of all people in the organization. Finally, the leader of an ethical organization leaves an ethical culture for his/her successor. Codes of ethics, ethics workshops, and ethics contracts, are all ways to help reenforce organizational standards and values, but these efforts in and of themselves do not make an organization ethical.

An ethical organization is a community into which members are socialized, receive social support from each other, benefit economically from collective efforts, learn from each other through social participation, and are valued by peers who help keep the community focused and cohesive. Organizations that build an ethical community on fairness and equity will generate trust among members as well as reinforce other virtues such as loyalty, which contribute to a healthy organization.

On the other hand, when organizations hire leaders that lack integrity, and who cannot trust or be trusted, and when the organization sees that its only response is to change leaders, without examining it’s own culture, the organization is likely to perpetuate its cultural practices and attract leaders who also practice them. Integrity is often assumed to be a common characteristic in all leaders.

Similarly, organizations have complacently relegated their concern about ethics to those behaviors that are illegal; behaviors that are legal, but immoral, are left to whistleblowers.

Many unethical leaders keep their jobs in organizations because of expediency; removing them might result in greater negative effects for the organization than retaining them. Unethical leaders are often successful and powerful. It depends on how unethical behavior is defined in an organization as to whether or not it is a problem.

There are two major steps in creating ethical, trusting, and healthy organizations. The first step is to find leaders who have integrity. Too often recruiting a leader is all credentials. Usually leaders are recruited because of what they have done, not what they will do. Often selecting a leader is a political process or looking for an image, rather than a strategy. We need to do a better job in screening for and selecting leaders for all types of organizations. Several suggestions are offered such as evaluating leader-finalists separately on their human relations skills, sending a team to interview the current colleagues of finalists, and giving finalists real problems to work through in interview situations.

The track record in selecting and retaining leaders of integrity in organizations could be better. Prospective leaders should be careful about the organization's culture they choose to lead. Organizations, in turn, need to take ethics seriously. As was said previously, an ethical organization is one based on practice. Good organizations help make the people in them moral and it takes moral people to make a good organization. There are no secrets to creating better organizations and matching them with leaders of integrity. There is a formula for success, we need to put it into practice.

Notes

CHAPTER 1: THE DECLINE OF TRUST

1. Singer, P. (1995). *How are we to live?* p. 35. Amherst, NY: Prometheus Books.
2. Gibb, J.R. (1978). *Trust: A new view of personal and organizational development*, p. 13. Los Angeles, CA: The Guild of Tutors Press.
3. See Lipsett, S.M., & Schneider, W.C. (1983). *The confidence gap: Business, labor, and government in the public mind*. New York: The Free Press; Couto, R.A., & Guthrie, C.S. (1999). *Making democracy work better: Mediating structures, social capital, and the democratic prospect*. Chapel Hill, NC: University of North Carolina Press.
4. Mitchell, T.R., & Scott, W.G. (1990). America's problems and needed reforms: Confronting the ethic of personal advantage. *Academy of Management Executive, 4(3)*, 23–35.
5. See Wellman, K. (1999). *Networks in the global village: Life in contemporary communities*, Boulder, CO: Westview Press. These authors studied "Netville," a suburb of Toronto, one of the world's first residential developments to be equipped with a broadband local network. They report that the Internet can encourage the resurgence of the civic involvement that has been argued to be in decline in the Western world. These findings challenge researchers who have argued that, as people spend more time online, they become isolated in the home and reduce their social contacts.
6. See Putnam, R.D., Leonard, R., & Nanetti, R.Y. (1993). *Making democracy work: Civic traditions in modern Italy*. Princeton, NJ: Princeton University Press. To measure people's involvement in public life, Putnam developed an index of the strength of civic community based on things like the percentage of the population voting, newspaper readership, and sporting activities per head of population. The correlation between this index and his measure of government performance was 0.92, suggesting that over three-fourths of the differences in performance could be accounted for by differences in the strength of the community.
7. Handy, C. (1994). *The age of paradox*, p. 261. Cambridge, MA: Harvard Business School.
8. Fukuyama, F. (1995). *Trust*, p. 311. New York: The Free Press.
9. Adams, G.B., & Balfour, D.L. (1998). *Unmasking administrative evil*. Thousand Oaks, CA: Sage. These authors point out that as a society we lament acts of administrative evil while dismissing them as temporary and isolated observations or deviations from proper administrative behavior. Individualism, they stress, is a barrier to our understanding of group and organizational dynamics, and administrative evil.
10. Myers, D.G. (2000). *The American paradox: Spiritual hunger in an age of plenty*, p. 177, New Haven, CT: Yale University Press, points out that, while extreme individualism begets self-indulgence, extreme collectivism begets intolerance. Each way of life offers benefits, for a price.
11. Fukuyama, F. op. cit, p. 57.

12. Horowitz, D., & Jarvick, L. (1995). *Public broadcasting and the public trust*. Los Angeles, CA: Center for the Study of Popular Culture.
13. Bok, S. (1978). *Lying: Moral choice in public and private life*, p. 31. New York: Pantheon Books.
14. See Jellinek, M. (1976). Erosion of patient trust in large medical centers, *Hastings Center Reports, 6(3)*, 16–19; Rogers, D.E. (1994). On trust: A building block for healing doctor/patient interactions. *The Pharos, 57(2)*, 2–6; Cassel, C.K. (1996). The patient-physician covenant: An affirmation of Asklepios. *Connecticut Medicine, 60(5)*, 291–293; Rothman, D.J. (2000). Medical professionalism—focusing on the real issues. *New England Journal of Medicine 342(17)*, 1284–1286; Schneider, C.E. (1998). *The practice of autonomy: Patients, doctors, and medical decisions*. New York: Oxford University Press.
15. Garrett, L. (2000). *Betrayal of trust: The collapse of global public health*, pp. 557–558. New York: Hyperion.
16. Garrett, op. cit., p. 585.
17. Goldfarb, J.C. (1991). *The cynical society. The culture of politics and the politics of culture in American life*. Chicago, IL: University of Chicago Press; Braithwaite, V., & Levi, M. (Eds.), (1998). *Trust and governance*. Vol. 1 in the Russell Sage Foundation Series on Trust. New York: Russell Sage Foundation.
18. Wilson, S. (2000). In business, greed often displaces ethics. (2000 August, 24), *Arizona Republic*, p. A2.
19. Reuters Wire Service (2001), Legal fees criticized in tobacco settlement(2001, March 21), *The New York Times*, Section A, p. 21, col. 1.
20. Barringer, F. (1992) Affiliates fear bitter fight by ex-head of United Way (1992, April 5), *The New York Times*, Section 1, Part 1, p. 18, col. 1.
21. See Stevenson, H.W., & Stigler, J.W. (1994). *The learning gap. Why our schools are failing and what we can learn from Japanese and Chinese education*. New York: Touchstone Books; Hirsch, E.D. (1999). *The schools we need: And why we don't have them*. New York: Doubleday.
22. Fairweather, J.S. (1996). *Faculty work and public trust: Restoring the value of teaching and public service in American academic life*. New York: Allyn & Bacon; Alfred, R.L., & Weissman, J. (1987). *Higher education and the public trust: Improving stature in colleges and universities*. Ashe-Eric Higher Education Research Report No. 6. College Station, TX: Association for the Study of Higher Education.
23. See Kors, A.C., & Silvergate, H.A. (1998). *The shadow university: The betrayal of liberty on America's campuses*. New York: The Free Press.
24. See also Hudson, J. (2001). Bad pastors: Clergy misconduct in modern America. *The Christian Century, 118(5)*, 59.
25. Putnam, *Bowling alone*, op. cit., Appendix 1, pp. 415–424.
26. See *Youth violence: A report of the Surgeon General* (2001). Superintendent of Documents: Washington, D.C. U.S. Government Printing Office.
27. *The Tao at work: On leading and following* (1994) p. 133. San Francisco, CA: Jossey-Bass.
28. As quoted in Howard, *The death of common sense*, p. 184.

CHAPTER 2: TRUST IN PERSONS

1. Riker, W.H. (1974). The nature of trust. In J.T. Tedeschi (Ed.), Perspectives on social power. p. 75. Chicago, IL: Aldine.
2. Gabarro, J.J. (1978). The development of trust, influence, and expectations. In A.G. Athos and J.J. Gabarro (Eds.), *Interpersonal behavior: Communication and understanding in relationships*, pp. 290–303. Englewood Cliffs, NJ: Prentice-Hall.
3. For a discussion of how trust works in a non-Western culture see Yamamoto, Y. (1990). A morality based on trust: Some reflections on Japanese morality. *Philosophy East and West, 40*, 451–469.

4. Robert Fulghum (1989) relates this ambiguity about trust in *All I really need to know I learned in kindergarten. Uncommon thoughts on common things*. New York: Villard Books, when Fulghum's neighbor says he is a professional gambler involved in organized crime, but the truth is that he is an insurance agent with a healthy disrespect for his business and extends that skepticism in his philosophy of life. Three of many sayings hanging on his office wall are: "Always trust your fellow man and always cut the cards;" "Always trust God and always build your house on high ground;" "Place your bet somewhere between turning-the-other-cheek and enough is enough already."
5. A quoted in Coleman, P.T. (2000). Power and conflict. In M. Deutsch & P.T. Coleman (Eds.), *The handbook of conflict resolution: Theory and practice* p. 123. San Francisco, CA: Jossey-Bass.
6. Research has indicated that hostility is associated with mistrust of others. See Smith, T.W., & Frohm, K.D. (1985). What's so unhealthy about hostility? Construct validity and psychosocial correlates of the Cook and Medley Ho Scale. *Health Psychology, 4*, 503–520.
7. Braithwaite, J. (1998). Institutionalizing distrust, enculturating trust. In V. Braithwaite & M. Levi (Eds.), *Trust and governance*, Vol. 1. Russell Sage Foundation Series on Trust, pp. 343–375. New York: Russell Sage Foundation. The author points out that institutionalizing distrust is a powerful weapon in fighting the abuse of trust.
8. Interview with Pam Gaber, Executive Director, Gabriel's Angels, Phoenix, Arizona, May 21, 2001.

CHAPTER 3: TRUST IN ORGANIZATIONS

1. Carnevale, D.G. (1995). *Trustworthy government: Leadership and management strategies for building trust and high performance*, p.4. Francisco, CA: Jossey-Bass.
2. Trust is studied cross-culturally in Brazil and the United States. See G.F. Farris, E.E. Senner, & D.A. Butterfield (1973). Trust, culture, and organizational behavior. *Industrial Relations, 12*, 144–157.
3. As quoted in Fox, A. (1974). *Beyond contract: Power and trust relations*. London: Faber & Faber.
4. See Butler, J.K. (1999). Trust expectations, information sharing, climate of trust, and negotiation effectiveness and efficiency. *Group and Organization Management, 24(2)*, 217–238 for a discussion of the economic value of trust.
5. Covey, S.R. (1999). High-trust cultures. *Executive Excellence, 16(9)*, 3–4.
6. See Senge, P. (1999). *The dance of change: The challenges to sustaining momentum in learning organizations*. New York: Currency Doubleday for a discussion of the dynamics of "walking the talk."
7. Alderfer discusses the effects of the extremes of impermeable and permeable boundaries. See Alderfer, C.P. (1976). Boundary relations and organizational diagnoses. In H. Meltzer, F.R. Wickert (Eds.), *Humanizing organizational behavior*, pp. 109–133. Springfield, IL: Charles C. Thomas. Also see Finkelstein, M.S. (1999). Good boundaries make good neighbors: Boundary management—tearing down the walls and fostering organizational change. *Sociological Practice: A Journal of Clinical and Applied Sociology, 1(3)*, 193–208; and, Bruhn, J.G. & Lewis, R. (1992). Boundary fighting: Territorial conflicts in health organizations. *Health Care Supervisor, 10(4)*, 56–65.
8. Sharing information alone, without the expectation of trust, does not help in developing a climate of trust. See Butler, J.K. (1999). Trust expectations, information sharing, climate of trust, and negotiation effectiveness and efficiency. *Group and Organization Management, 24(2)*, 217–238.
9. See Bennis, W. (1999). The end of leadership: Exemplary leadership is impossible without full inclusion, initiatives, and cooperation of followers. *Organizational Dynamics, Summer*, 71–79.
10. For an interesting study of the conditions for cognition-based and affect-based trust among managers and professionals see McAllister, D.J. (1995). Affect-and cognition-based trust as foundations for interpersonal cooperation in organizations. *Academy of Management Journal, 38(1)*, 24–59.

11. Hostility has been found to moderate the relationship between job enrichment and health care costs. However, employees who have more control in their jobs have fewer health problems, even when they demonstrate hostility. Dwyer, D.J., & Fox, M.L. (2000). The moderating role of hostility in the relationship between enriched jobs and health. *Academy of Management Journal, 43(6)*, 1086–1096. Also see Karasek, R., & Theorell, T. (1990). *Healthy work: Stress, productivity, and the reconstruction of working life*. New York: Basic Books. These authors review evidence showing how high demand/low control jobs affect employee's productivity and health. Also see Ouchi, W.G., & Johnson, J.B. (1978). Types of organizational control and their relationship to emotional well being. *Administrative Science Quarterly, 23*, 293–315. This paper illustrates the central point that the manner in which people at work are linked to each other can be a source of moral integration in their lives and in their society.
12. Also see Schein, E.H. (1983). The role of the founder in creating organizational culture. *Organizational Dynamics, Summer*, 13–28.

CHAPTER 4: TRUST AND THE LIFECYCLE OF ORGANIZATIONS

1. Anonymous author.
2. There is an interesting debate on whether organizations should be considered moral persons for the purpose of analyzing their social responsibilities. The moral person approach has been proposed by French, P.A. (1979). The corporation as a moral person. *American Philosophical Quarterly, 16*, 207–215 and Ozar, D.T. (1979). The moral responsibility of corporations In T. Donaldson & P.H. Werhane, (Eds.), *Ethical issues in business*, pp. 294–300. Englewood Cliffs, N.J.: Prentice-Hall. Also see Keeley, M. (1981). Organizations as non-persons. *Journal of Value Inquiry, 15*, 149–155.
3. One of the issues in ascribing lifecycles to organizations is that, unlike individuals, they may "stay" in a particular stage of a lifecycle for various lengths of time. For example an organization conceivably could "stay" at the midlife stage if it was an organization that changed little and was minimally affected by external change (this would almost have to be a closed system). Depending on the organization one would expect it to move from midlife to maturity, be re-organized, merged, or cease existence. It would be almost impossible to exist in one stage indefinitely.
4. As quoted in Rosen, R.H. & Berger, L. (1991). *The healthy company,* p. 21. New York: G.P. Putnam's Sons.
5. Ouchi, W.G. *Theory Z*, p. 67.
6. Rosen & Berger, *Ibid*, p. 32.
7. Dauten, D. (2001) Wisest bosses have the smallest key rings. (2001, July 9). *Arizona Republic*, p. D2.
8. Douglas McGregor coined the Terms Theory X and Y as sets of assumptions we hold about people. Theory X managers hold assumptions that people cannot be fully trusted, need to be checked up on, need motivation, or really don't like to work that hard. Theory Y managers, on the other hand, assume that most people will exercise self-control, self-initiative, actively seek responsibility, and have untapped capacity for creativity and ingenuity, Maslow, A.H. (1988). *Maslow on Management*, pp. 69–80.
9. For a different view See Howard, P., Rainie, L. & Jones, S. (2000). Days and Nights on the internet: The impact of a diffusing technology, *American Behavioral Scientist, 45* (Special Issue), pp. 1–21. These authors found, in data collected by the Pew Internet and American Life Project, that it is no longer sensible to speak of the generic Internet user and that education strongly predicts the kinds of activities people pursue, and allows users to build social capital. Also see Uslaner, E.M. (2000). Trust, civic engagement and the internet. (Paper presented for the Joint Sessions of the European Consortium for Political Research, University of Grenoble, April 6–11.) Uslaner using 1998 survey data from the Pew Center for The People and The Press and a 2000 survey by

the Pew Internet and American Life Project found no evidence to claim that people who have stronger social networks in the real world avoid the Web. There is little support that the Net is a haven for people who don't trust others, nor is there any evidence that people who spend time on-line are less likely to trust others. Also see Guernsey, L. (2001). Cyberspace isn't so lonely after all (2001, July 26). *New York Times*, pp. D1, D5.

10. For another viewpoint that the internet can encourage the resurgence of civic involvement see Note 5, Chapter 1.

CHAPTER 5: HOW TRUST AND DISTRUST WORK IN ORGANIZATIONS

1. Interview with a religious leader, March 6, 2000.
2. Interview with the president of a national trade union, April 29, 2001.
3. Interview with a superintendent of schools, February 21, 2001.
4. Welch, J.F., General Electric Company, 1991 Annual Report, p. 2.
5. Interview with a professor, January 15, 2001.
6. Interview with a high-ranking military commander, July 25, 2000.
7. Interview with a senior vice president of major brokerage firm, November 9, 2000.
8. Interview with the president and CEO of a major health care system, January 8, 2001.
9. Interview with a dean of a law school, February 8, 2000.
10. Interview with a president of a national insurance company, January 29, 2001.
11. Interview with the president and CEO of large health care system, January 30, 2001.
12. Interview with the executive director of large Chamber of Commerce, January 10, 2001.
13. Interview with the executive director of large non-profit hospice, November 11, 2000.
14. Interview with a professor, January 15, 2001.
15. Interview with the mayor of a moderate-sized city, March 21, 2001.
16. Interview with the city manager of a moderate-sized city, January 24, 2001.
17. Johnson, S. (1998). *Who moved my cheese?* New York: G.P. Putnam's Sons.
18. Interview with the dean of a major school in a university, May 9, 2001.
19. Interview with the president of international garment manufacturing company, July 7, 2000.
20. Interview with the president and CEO of a major national professional organization, April 29, 2001.
21. Interview with the CEO of a laser technology manufacturing and service company, June 27, 2000.
22. Interview with a university executive, February 20, 2000.
23. Interview with a superintendent of schools, February 21, 2001.
24. Interview with an account executive, February 24, 2000.
25. Interview with a superintendent of schools, February 21, 2001.
26. Interview with a military commander, July 25, 2000.
27. Interview with the CEO of a major health care corporation, January 30, 2001.
28. Morgan, G. (1997). *Images of organization*, 2nd ed., pp. 246–247. Thousand Oaks, CA: Sage.
29. Interview with a university president, February 24, 2000.
30. Interview with a human resources executive, March 2, 2001.
31. Interview with the president of national professional trade association, April 29, 2001.
32. Interview with the CEO of a family business, July 26, 2000.

CHAPTER 6: CHALLENGES TO TRUST DURING CHANGE AND CRISES

1. Welsh, John F. Jr. (1991) *General Electric Company 1991 Annual Report*, p. 3.. Fairfield, CT.
2. *General Electric Company 1991 Annual Report*, p. 5. Fairfield, CT.

3. The question of the moral obligation of organizations to involve employees and others in planned change is discussed in Zajac, G., & Bruhn, J.G. (1999). The moral context of participation in planned organizational change and learning. *Administration & Society, 30(6)*, 706–733.
4. For an interesting discussion of how boundaries discourage organizational change see Finkelstein, M.S. (1999). Good boundaries make good neighbors: Boundary management – tearing down the walls and fostering organizational change. *Sociological Practice: A Journal of Clinical and Applied Sociology, 1*(3), 193–208.
5. See Stacey, R.D. (1992). *Managing the unknowable: Strategic boundaries between order and chaos in organizations*. San Francisco, CA: Jossey-Bass.
6. Smart, T. (1997), No. 2's No. 1 Problem: The ritual of corporate succession is shifting as CEO turnover rates accelerate (1997, November 9). *The Washington Post*, p. H1.
7. Meece, M. (2000). Does staff turnover help a company? (2000, December 3) *The New York Times*, p. 10.
8. Interview with CEO of a travel agency (family business), July 25, 2000.
9. Interview with the CEO of data processing and consulting firm, July 27, 2000.
10. Interview with a university vice president, March 27, 2001.
11. Interview with a superintendent of schools, February 21, 2001.
12. Bearak, B. (2001), Lost in America: Jobs, trust: When boardroom math shuttered a West Virginia plant (2001, November 26). *Los Angeles Times*, A-1.
13. Tahmincioglu, E. (2001), Vigilance in the face of layoff rage (2001, August 1). *The New York Times*, C1, C6.
14. Schein, E.H. (1992). *Organizational culture and leadership*, 2nd. ed. pp. 4–5, San Francisco, CA: Jossey-Bass.
15. Interview with the CEO of a health care corporation, January 8, 2001.
16. As quoted in Rosen, R.H., & Berger, op. cit., p. 107.
17. Pearlstein, S. (1994), Large U.S. companies continue downsizing unlike recession-era cuts, goal is efficiency (1994, September 27). *The Washington Post*, C1.
18. See Petzall, B.J., & Parker, G.E. (2000). Another side to downsizing: Survivors' behavior and self-affirmation, *Journal of Business & Psychology, 14(4)*, 593
19. Davis, M. (1998), Pennzoil, Quaker State to form motor oil giant (1998, April 16). *Houston Chronicle*, p.1.
20. As quoted in Rosen, R.H., & Berger, L. op. cit. p. 100.
21. As quoted in Rosen, R.H., & Berger, L. op. cit. p. 109.
22. Donald Campbell used a fish scale model to illustrate a comprehensive, integrated multiscience as an answer to the ethnocentrism of disciplines in academia, See D.T. Campbell (1969) Ethnocentrism of disciplines and the fish-scale model of omniscience. In M. Sherif, & C. Sherif (Eds.) *Interdisciplinary relationships in the social sciences*, pp. 328–348, Chicago, IL: Aldine.
23. Bridges, W. (1991). Managing transitions: *Making the most of change*. p. 3. Reading, MA: Addison-Wesley.
24. See Hartmann, E. (1991). *Boundaries in the mind: A new psychology of personality*. New York, Basic Books, for an excellent discussion of personality and boundaries.
25. As quoted in Baum, D. (2000). *Lightning in a bottle: Proven lessons for leading change, p. 196.* Chicago, IL: Dearborn.
26. As quoted in Rosen, R.H., & Berger, L. op. cit., p. 2.

CHAPTER 7: THE CULTURE THAT WOULDN'T BUDGE

1. Farson, R. (1996). *Management of the absurd: Paradoxes in leadership*, p. 85. New York: Simon & Schuster.

2. Levinson has developed a comprehensive outline for consultants to organizations for conducting a case study including historical, structural and process data utilizing structured and written questionnaires. See Levinson, H. (1991). Diagnosing organizations systematically. In M.F.R. Kets de Vries & Associates (Eds.) *Organizations on the Couch* pp. 45–68. San Francisco, CA: Jossey-Bass; and Levinson, H. (1972). *Organizational diagnosis*, pp. 519–538. Cambridge, MA: Harvard University Press, see especially Appendix A.

CHAPTER 8: THE HEALTH OF ORGANIZATIONS

1. Maslow, A.H., op. cit., p. 94.
2. Maslow, A.H., op. cit. p. 67.
3. Kimberly, J.R., Miles, R.H. & Associates (1980). *The organizational lifecycle: Issues in the creation, transformation, and decline of organizations*. San Francisco, CA: Jossey-Bass.
4. Welch, J.F. with Byrne, J.A. (2001). *Jack: Straight from the gut* pp. 106–107. New York: Warner Books.
5. Rosen, R.H., & Berger, L. op. cit., pp. 1–2.
6. Rosen, R.H. & Berger, L. op. cit., p. 9.
7. As quoted in Rosen, R.H., & Berger L., op. cit. p. 1.
8. Bennis, W. (1990). *Why leaders can't lead*. San Francisco, CA: Jossey-Bass.
9. World Health Organization (1958). *The first ten years of the World Health Organization*. Geneva, Switzerland: World Health Organization.
10. Clark, J.V. (1969). A healthy organization. In W.G. Bennis (Ed.). *The planning of change*, 2nd ed. New York: Holt, Rinehart and Winston.
11. Kets de Vries, M.F.R. (1989). *Prisoners of leadership*. New York: John Wiley.
12. Schaef, A.W., & Fassel, D. (1988). *The addictive organizaiton*. San Francisco, CA: Harper & Row.
13. Garfield, C. (1986). *Peak performers*. New York: Avon.
14. De Pree, M. (1989). *Leadership is an art*. p. 116. New York: Dell.

CHAPTER 9: THE ETHICAL ORGANIZATION

1. Carnevale, D.G. (1995). *Trustworthy government*, op. cit., p. 13.
2. Sinclair, A. (1993). Approaches to organizational culture and ethics. *Journal of Business Ethics*, 12, 63–73; and Ford, R.C., & Richardson, W.D. (1994) Ethical decision making: A review of the empirical literature. *Journal of Business Ethics*, 43, 205–211.
3. Hartman, E. (1996). *Organizational ethics and the good life*, p. 185. New York: Oxford University Press.
4. Ciulla, J.B. (1998). *Ethics, the heart of leadership*, p. 104. Westport, CT: Quorum Books.
5. Huey, J. (1997). In search of Roberto's secret formula. *Fortune, 136(12)*, 230–234.
6. Cullen, J.B., Victor, B., & Bronson, J.W. (1993). The ethical climate questionnaire: An assessment of it's development and validity. *Psychological Reports, 73*, 667–674.
7. See Johnson, S. (1992). *"Yes" or "No": The guide to better decisions*. New York: Harper Collins.
8. Welch, J.F. op. cit., p. 381.

Bibliography

Adizes, I. (1979). Organizational passages—diagnosing and treating lifecycle problems of organizations. *Organizational Dynamics, Summer*, 3–25.

Albrecht, K., & Albrecht, S. (1987). *The creative corporation*. Homewood, IL: Dow Jones-Irwin.

Anderson, L.M., & Bateman, T.S. (1997). Cynicism in the workplace: Some causes and effects. *Journal of Organizational Behavior, 18(5)*, 449–469.

Annison, M.H., & Wilford, D.S. (1998). *Trust matters: New directions in health care leadership*. San Francisco, CA: Jossey-Bass.

Appelbaum, S.H., Close, T.G., & Klasa, S. (1999). Downsizing: An examination of some successes and more failures. *Management Decision, 37(5)*, 424–436.

Argyris, C., & Schön, D.A. (1996). *Organizational learning II: Theory, method and practice*. Reading, MA: Addison-Wesley.

Arsenian, J., & Arsenian J.M. (1948). Tough and easy cultures: A conceptual analysis. *Psychiatry, 11*, 377–385.

Atwater, L.E. (1988). The relative importance of situational and individual variables in predicting leader behavior: The surprising impact of subordinate trust. *Group and Organization Studies, 13(3)*, 290–310.

Backer, T.E., & Porterfield, J. (1998). Change at work: Why it hurts and what employers can do about it. In S. Klarreich, (Ed.), *Handbook of organizational health psychology: Programs to make the workplace healthier* (pp. 203–217). Madison, CT: Psychosocial Press.

Baier, A. (1986). Trust and antitrust, *Ethics, 96*, 231–260.

Barnes, L.B. (1981). Managing the paradox of organizational trust. *Harvard Business Review, 59*, 107–116.

Barber, B. (1983). *The Logic and limits of trust*. New Brunswick, NJ: Rutgers University Press.

Bartolomé, F. (1989). Nobody trusts the boss completely—now what? *Harvard Business Review, 67*, 135–142.

Baum, D. (2000). *Lightning in a bottle: Proven lessons for leading change*. Chicago, IL: Dearborn.

Baum, H.S. (1991). How bureaucracy discourages responsibility. In M.F.R. Ket de Vries & Associates. (Eds.) *Organizations on the couch: Clinical perspectives on organizational behavior and change* (pp. 264–285). San Francisco, CA: Jossey-Bass.

Beasley, J.D. (1991). *The betrayal of health*. New York: Times Books.

Becker, T.E. (1998). Integrity in organizations: Beyond honesty and conscientiousness. *Academy of Management Review, 23(1)*, 154–161.

Beckhard, R. (1997). The healthy organization: A profile. In F. Hesselbein, M. Goldsmith, & R. Beckhard, (Eds.). *The organization of the future* (pp.325–328). San Francisco, CA: Jossey-Bass.

Bellah, R.N., Madsen, R., Sullivan, W.M., Swidler, A., & Tipton, S.M. (1985). *Habits of the Heart: Individualism and commitment in American life*. Berkeley, CA: University of California Press.

Bennis, W. (1984). The 4 competencies of leadership. *Training & Development Journal, 38(8)*, 14–19.
Bennis, W. (1989). *On becoming a leader*. Reading, MA: Addison-Wesley.
Bennis, W. (1993). *An invented life: Reflections on leadership and change*. Reading, MA: Addison-Wesley.
Bennis, W.G., Schein, E.H., Berlew, D.E., & Steele, F.I. (Eds.). (1964). *Interpersonal dynamics: Essays and readings on human interaction* (pp. 564–582). Homewood, IL: Dorsey.
Berube, M. (1996). Public perceptions of universities and faculty. *Academe, 82(4)*, 10–17.
Bies, R.J.,& Tripp, T.M. (1996). Beyond distrust: "Getting even" and the need for revenge. In R.M. Kramer (Ed.) *Trust in organizations: Frontiers in theory and Research*, (pp. 246–260) Thousand Oaks, CA: Sage.
Bigley, G.A., & Pearce, J.L. (1998). Straining for shared meaning in organization science: Problems of trust and distrust. *Academy of Management Review, 23(3)*, 405–421.
Binney, G., & Williams, C. (1995). *Leaning into the future: Changing the way people change organizations*. London: Nicholas Brealey.
Blau, P.M. (1964). *Exchange and power in social life*. New York: Wiley.
Bok, S. (1978). *Lying: Moral choice in public and private life*. New York: Pantheon Books.
Bolman, L.G., & Deal, T.E. (1991). *Reforming organizations*. San Francisco, CA: Jossey-Bass.
Bolman, L.G., & Deal, T.E. (1995). *Leading with soul: An uncommon journey of spirit*. San Francisco, CA: Jossey-Bass.
Bolino, M.C. (1999). Citizenship and impression management: Good soldiers or good actors. *Academy of Management Review, 24(1)*, 82–98.
Boss, R.W. (1977). Trust and managerial problem solving revisited. *Group and Organization Studies, 3(3)*, 331–342.
Bowlby, J. (1953). Some pathological processes set in train by early mother-child separation. *Journal of Mental Science, 99*, 265–272.
Brien, A. (1998). Professional ethics and the culture of trust. *Journal of Business Ethics, 17*, 391–409.
Brossard, M.A. (1996) Americans losing trust in each other and institutions (1996, January 28 & 29). *Washington Post*. p. A1.
Bruhn, J.G. (1993). Administrators who cannot let go: The super manager syndrome. *Health Care Supervisor, 11(3)*, 35–42.
Bruhn, J.G. (1996a). Management by intimidation: "Cooling out" perceived competitors. *Health Care Supervisor, 14(4)*, 29–34.
Bruhn, J.G. (1996b). Creating an organizational climate for multiculturalism. *Health Care Supervisor, 14(4)*, 11–18.
Bruhn, J.G. (1996c). Finding heroes and heroines: Fads, fantasies, and foibles of search and screen committees. *Health Care Supervisor, 15(1)*, 16–23.
Bruhn, J.G. (1997). The organization as a person: Analogues for intervention. *Clinical Sociology Review, 15*, 51–70.
Bruhn, J.G. (1998). Mixing apples and oranges: Sociological issues in the process of an academic merger. *Clinical Sociology Review, 16*, 1–21.
Bruhn, J.G. (2001a). Equal partners: Doctors and patients explore the limits of autonomy. *Journal of the Oklahoma State Medical Association, 94(2)*, 46–54.
Bruhn, J.G. (2001b). Being good and doing good: The culture of professionalism in the health professions. *Health Care Manager, 19(4)*, 47–58.
Bruhn, J.G. (2001c). Managing tough and easy organizational cultures. *Health Care Manager, 20 (2)*, 1–10.
Bruhn, J.G. (2001d). Learning from the politics of a merger: When being merged is not a choice. *Health Care Manager, 19(3)*, 29–41.
Bruhn, J.G., & Chesney, A.P. (1994). Diagnosing the health of organizations. *Health Care Supervisor, 13(2)* , 21–33.

Bruhn, J.G., & Chesney, A.P. (1995). Organizational moles: Information control and the acquisition of power and status. *Health Care Supervisor, 14(1)*, 24–31.

Bruhn, J.G., Zajac, G., & Al-Kazemi, A.A. (2001). Ethical perspectives on employee participation in planned organizational change: A survey of two state public welfare agencies. *Public Performance and Management Review, 25*, 208–228.

Bruhn, J.G., Zajac, G., Al-Kazemi, A.A., & Prescott, L.D. (2002). Moral positions and academic conduct: Parameters of tolerance for ethics failure. *Journal of Higher Education* (in press).

Butler, J.K., & Cantrell, R.S. (1994). Communication factors and trust: An exploratory study. *Psychological Reports, 741*, 33–34.

Calhoun, C.H., Olivero, M.E., & Wolitzer, P. (1999). *Ethics and the CPA: Building trust and value-added services*. New York: John Wiley.

Cangemi, J.P., Rice, J., & Kowalski, C.J. (1989). The development, decline and renewal of trust in an organization: Some observations. *Organization Development Journal, 7(4)*, 46–53.

Carnevale, D.G., & Wechsler, B. (1992). Trust in the public sector: Individual and organizational determinants. *Administration & Society, 23(4)*, 471–494.

Carnevale, D.G. (1995). *Trustworthy government: Leadership and management strategies for building trust and high performance*. San Francisco, CA: Jossey-Bass.

Carter, S.L. (1996). *Integrity*. New York: Basic Books.

Carosso, V.P., & Sobel, R. (1975). (Eds.). *The New York Stock Exchange*. New York: Arno Press.

Caudron, S. (1996). Rebuilding employee trust. *Training & Development, August*, 18–21.

Chen, Al Y.S., Sawyers, R.B., & Williams, P.F. (1997). Reinforcing ethical decision making through corporate culture. *Journal of Business Ethics, 16*, 855–865.

Clancy, J.J. (1996). The old dispensation: Loyalty in business. (Doctoral dissertation, Washington University, 1996). *Dissertation Abstracts International*, Vol. 57-06A, NAAI 9633436, p. 2537.

Clews, H. (1887). *Twenty eight years in Wall Street*. New York: J.S. Olgilvie Publishing Co.

Coleman, J.S. (1988). Social capital in the creation of human capital *American Journal of Sociology, 94*, Supplement, 595–5120.

Collins, J.C., & Porras, J.I. (1994). *Built to last: Successful habits of visionary companies*. New York: Harper Business.

Conviser, R.H. (1973). Toward a theory of interpersonal trust. *Pacific Sociological Review, 16(3)*, 377–399.

Corazzini, J.G. (1977). Trust as a complex multi-dimensional construct. *Psychological Reports, 40*, 75–80.

Costigan, R.D., Itler, S.S., & Berman, J.J. (1998). A multi-dimensional study of trust in organizations. *Journal of Management Issues, 10(3)*, 303–317.

Courtney, S.L. (1998). *Impact of trust on employee perceptions of organizational and leader effectiveness*. (Doctoral dissertation, Arizona State University, 1998). *Dissertation Abstracts International*, Vol. 59-01A, No. AAI 9821684, p. 313.

Covey, S.R. (1990). *Principle-centered leadership*. New York: Summit Books.

Covey, S.R. (1999). High-trust cultures. *Executive Excellence, 1(9)*, 3–4.

Covey, S.R. (1999). Making time for gorillas. *Harvard Business Review, 77(6)*, 185.

Cufaud, J. (1999). Creating organizational trust. *Association Management, 51(7)*, 25–34.

Dasgupta, P. (1988). Trust as a commodity. In D. Gambetta, (Ed.) *Trust: making and breaking cooperative relations* (pp. 49–72). New York: Blackwell.

Darley, J.M. (1996). How organizations socialize individuals into evildoing. In D.M. Messick, & A.E. Tenbrunsel, (Eds.) *Codes of conduct: Behavioral research into business ethics* (pp. 13–43). New York: Russell Sage Foundation.

Davis, J.A., & Smith, T.W. (2000). General Social Survey, National Opinion Research Center, Chicago, IL: University of Chicago.

Deal, T.E., & Jenkins, W.A. (1994). *Managing the hidden organization*. New York: Warner Books.

Deal, T.E., & Kennedy, A.A. (1999). *The new corporate cultures: Revitalizing the workplace after downsizing, mergers, and re-engineering*. Reading, PA: Perseus Books.

Dean, J.W., Jr., Brandes, P., & Dharwadkar, R. (1998). Organizational cynicism. *Academy of Management Review, 23(2)*, 341–352.

Deetz, S.A., Tracy, S.J., & Simpson, J.L. (2000). *Leading organizations through transition*, Thousand Oaks, CA: Sage.

Delattre, E.J. (1988). *Education and the public trust: The imperatives for common purposes*. Washington, D.C.: Ethics and Public Policy Center.

DeMott, J.S. (1986) Finger pointing: Wall Street's scandal (1986, July 14). *Time*, p. 46.

De Pree, M. (1989). *Leadership is an art*. New York: Dell.

Deutsch, M. (1964). Cooperation and trust: Some theoretical notes. In W.G. Bennis, E. Schein, D. Berlew, & F. Steele, (Eds.). *Interpersonal dynamics: Essays and readings on human interaction* (pp. 564–582). Homewood, IL: Dorsey.

Driscoll, J.W. (1978). Trust and participation in organizational decision making as predictors of satisfaction. *Academy of Management Journal, 21(1)*, 44–56.

Drucker, P.F. (1995). *Managing in a time of great change*. New York: Truman Talley Books/Dutton.

Drucker, P.F. (1999). *Management challenges for the 21st* century. New York: Harper Business.

Dyer, W.G. (1986). *Cultural change in family firms: Anticipating and managing family transitions*. San Francisco, CA: Jossey-Bass.

Earle, T.C., & Cvetkovich, G.T. (1995). *Social trust: Toward a cosmopolitan society*. Westport, CT: Praeger.

Elangovan, A.R., & Shapiro, D.L. (1998). Betrayal of trust in organizations. *Academy of Management Review, 23(3)*, 547–566.

Elias, C. (1971). *Fleecing the lambs*. Greenwich, CT., Fawcett Crest.

Elsbach, K.D., & Elofson, G. (2000). How the packaging of decision explanations affects perceptions of trustworthiness. *Academy of Management Journal, 43(1)*, 80–89.

Engelhardt, H.T., & Rie, M.A. (1988). Morality for the medical-industrial complex: A code of ethics for the mass marketing of health. *New England Journal of Medicine, 319(16)*, 1086–1089.

Erickson, E.H. (1963). *Childhood and society*, 2nd ed. New York: W.W. Norton.

Fairholm, G.W. (1994). *Leadership and the culture of trust*. Westport, CT: Praeger.

Farson, R. (1996). *Management of the absurd: Paradoxes in leadership*. New York: Simon & Schuster.

Fein, M.L. (1999).*The limits to idealism: When good intentions go bad*. New York: Kluwer Academic/ Plenum Publishers.

Flores, F., & Solomon, R.C. (1998). Creating trust. *Business Ethics Quarterly,8(2)*, 205–232.

Fritzche, D.J., & Becker, H. (1984). Linking management behavior to ethical philosophy. *Academy of Management Journal, 27*, 166–175.

Fox, A. (1974). *Beyond contract: Work, power and trust relations*. London: Faber and Faber.

Freeman, V.G., Rathore, S.S., Weinfurt, K.P., Schulman, K.A., & Sulmasy, D.P. (1999). Lying for patients: Physician deception of third-party payers, *Archives of Internal Medicine, 159(1)*, 2263–2270.

Friedson, E. (1990). The centrality of professionalism to health care. *Jurimetrics Journal, 30(4)*, 431–445.

Frost, T., Stimpson, D.V., & Maughan, Michol R.C. (1978). Some correlates of trust. *The Journal of Psychology, 99*, 103–108.

Fukuyama, F. (1995). *Trust*. New York: Free Press.

Gabarro, J.J. (1978). The development of trust, influence, and expectations. In A.G. Athos and J.J. Gabarro (Eds.), *Interpersonal behavior: Communication and understanding in relationships* (pp. 290–303). Engelwood Cliffs, NJ: Prentice-Hall.

Gambetta, D. (Ed.) (1988). *Trust: Making and breaking cooperative relations*. New York: Basil Blackwell.

Gamson, W. (1968). *Power and discontent*. Homewood, IL: Dorsey Press.

Garrett, L. (2000). *Betrayal of trust: The collapse of global public health*. New York: Hyperion.

Garvin, D.A. (1993). Building a learning organization. In D.A. Kolb, J.S. Osland, & I.M. Rubin, (Eds.), *The organizational reader*, 6th ed. (pp. 96–124). Englewood Cliffs, NJ: Prentice Hall.

Geisst, C.R. (1997). *Wall Street: A history*. New York: Oxford University Press.

General Electric Co. (1991). *1991 Annual Report*. Fairfield, CT.

Gephart, M.A., Marsick, V.J., Van Buren, M.E., & Spiro, M.S. (1996). Learning organizations come alive. *Training & Development, December*, 35–45.

Gibb, J.R. (1978). *Trust: A new view of personal and organizational development*. Los Angeles, CA: The Guild of Tutors Press.

Gilkey, R. (1991). The psychodynamics of upheaval: Intervening in merger and acquisition transitions. In M.F.R. Kets de Vries and Associates, (Eds.), *Organizations on the couch: Clinical perspectives on organizational behavior and change* (pp. 331–360). San Francisco, CA: Jossey-Bass.

Glenn, E.N. (2000). Creating a caring society. *Contemporary Sociology, 29(1)*, 84–94.

Godwin, R.K. (1976). Trusting behavior and social modernization. *Studies in Comparative International Development, 11*, 44–62.

Goffman, I. (1952). On cooling the mark out: Some aspects of adaptation to failure. *Psychiatry, 15(4)*, 451–463.

Golay, M., & Rollyson, C. (1996). *Where America stands 1996*. New York: John Wiley.

Govier, T. (1997). *Social trust and human communities*. Montreal: McGill-Queen University Press.

Graham, J.W. (1991). An essay on organizational citizenship behavior. *Employee Responsibilities and Rights Journal, 4(4)*, 249–270.

Gratton, C. (1973). Some aspects of the lived experience of interpersonal trust. *Humanitas, 9*, 273–296.

Grenier, L.E. (1972). Evolution and revolution as organizations grow. *Harvard Business Review, 50*, 37–46.

Hall, J.A. (1992). Trust in Tocqueville. *Policy Organization and Society, Winter*. 16–24.

Handy, C. (1994). *The age of paradox*. Boston, MA: Harvard Business School Press.

Handy, C. (1995). Trust and the virtual organization. *Harvard Business Review, 73 (May/June)*, 40–50.

Handy, C. (1995). *Gods of management: The changing work of organizations*. New York: Oxford University Press.

Hardin, R. (1991). Trusting persons, trusting institutions. In R.J. Zeckhauser (Ed.) *Strategy and choice* (pp. 185–209). Cambridge, MA: The MIT Press.

Hardin, R. (1993). The street-level epistemology of trust. *Politics and Society, 21(4)*, 505–529.

Hart, K.M., Capps, H.R., Cangemi, J.P., & Caillouet, L.M. (1986). Exploring organizational trust and its multiple dimensions: A case study of General Motors. *Organization Development Journal, 4*, 31–39.

Hartman, C. (1969). The key jingler. *Community Mental Health Journal, 5(3)*, 199–205.

Hartman, E. (1996). *Organizational ethics and the good life*. New York: Oxford University Press.

Held, V. (1968). On the meaning of trust. *Ethics, 78*, 156–159.

Henslin, J.M. (1972). What makes for trust? In J.M. Henslin (Ed.), *Down to earth sociology*, New York: The Free Press.

Hertzberg, L. (1988). On the attitude of trust. *Inquiry, 31*, 307–322.

Hirschhorn, L. (1988). *The workplace within: Psychodynamics of organizational life*. Cambridge, MA: The MIT Press.

Hirschhorn, L. (1991). *Managing in the new team environment: Skills, tools, and methods*. Reading, MA: Addison-Wesley.

Holzner, B. (1973). Sociological reflections on trust. *Humanitas, 9*, 333–345.

Hosmer, L.T. (1994). Why be moral? A different rationale for managers. *Business Ethics Quarterly, 4(2)*, 191–204.

Howard, P.K. (1994). *The death of common sense: How law is suffocating America*. New York: Warner Books.

Howard, P.K. (2001). *The lost art of drawing the line: How fairness went too far*. New York: Random House.

Howell, J.P. (1990) Substitutes for leadership: Effective alternatives to ineffective leadership. *Organizational Dynamics, 19(1)*, 21–38.

Hudson, J. (1998). Dollars and clergy misconduct. *The Christian Century, 115*(25), 856.

Hymowitz, C. (2001) Psychotherapists enter the workplace to aid dysfunctional staffs (2001, November 27). *The New York Times*, p. B1.

Into, E.C. (1969). Some possible childbearing antecedents of interpersonal trust (Master's Thesis, University of Connecticut, 1969).

Isaacs, W. (1999). *Dialogue and the art of thinking together*. New York: Currency.

Isenberg, D.J. (1984). How senior managers think. *Harvard Business Review, 62(6)*, 80–90.

Jarvenpaa, S.L., Knoll, K., & Leidner, D.E. (1998). Is anybody out there? Antecedents of trust in global virtual teams. *Journal of Management Information Systems, 14(4)*, 29–64.

Jarvenpaa, S.L., & Leidner, D.E. (1999). Communication and trust in global virtual teams. *Organization Science, 10(6)*, 791–815.

Judis, J.B. (2000). *The paradox of American democracy*. New York: Pantheon Books.

Kagan, R.C. (1991). Adversarial legalism and American government. *Journal of Policy Analysis and Management, 10*, 369–378.

Kanter, D.L., & Mirvis, P.H. (1989). *The cynical Americans*. San Francisco, CA: Jossey-Bass.

Kanungo, R.N., & Mendonca, M. (1996). *Ethical dimensions of leadership*. Thousand Oaks, CA: Sage.

Katz, H.A., & Rotter, J.B. (1969). Interpersonal trust scores of college students and their parents. *Child Development, 40*, 657–661.

Karen, R. (2001). *The forgiving self: The road from resentment to connection*. New York: Doubleday.

Kearns, D.T., & Harvey, J. (2000). *A legacy of learning: Your stake in standards and new kinds of public schools*. Washington, DC: Brookings Institution.

Kegan, D.L.,& Rubenstein, A.H. (1973). Trust, effectiveness, and organizational development: A field study in R&D. *Journal of Applied Behavioral Science, 9(4)*, 498–513.

Kelley, R,E., (1992). *The power of followership*. New York: Doubleday.

Kets de Vries, M.F.R. (1991). Introduction: Exploding the myth that organizations and executives are rational. In M.F.R. Kets de Vries & Associates (Eds.), *Organizations on the couch: Clinical perspectives on organizational behavior and change* (pp. 1–21). San Francisco, CA: Jossey-Bass.

Kets de Vries, M.F.R., & Miller, D. (1991). Leadership styles and organizational cultures: The shaping of neurotic organizations. In M.F.R. Kets de Vries & Associates, (Eds.), *Organizations on the Couch: Clinical perspectives on organizational behavior and change* (pp. 243–263). San Francisco, CA: Jossey Bass.

Kets de Vries, M.F.R. (1993). The dynamics of family controlled firms: The good and the bad news. *Organizational Dynamics, 21(3)*: 59–71.

Kets de Vries, M.F.R., & Balazs, K. (1999). Transforming the mind-set of the organization. *Administration & Society, 30(6)*, 640–675.

Kinsella, N.A. (1973). Some psychological dimensions of the trusting attitude. *Humanitas, 9*, 253–271.

Klarreich, S. (1998). Resiliency: The skills needed to move forward in a changing environment. In Klarreich, S. (Ed.), *Handbook of organizational health psychology: Programs to make the workplace healthier* (pp. 219–238). Madison, CT: Psychosocial Press.

Koepp, S. (1987) Serving his client all too well: Wall Street's spreading scandal fells a prominent trader. (1987, March 30) *Time*, p. 52.

Kohlberg, L. (1981). *The philosophy of moral development*. New York: Harper & Row.

Koller, M. (1988). Risk as a determinant of trust. *Basic and Applied Social Psychology, 9(4)*, 265–276.

Konovsky, M.A., & Pugh, S.D. (1994). Citizenship behavior and social exchange. *Academy of Management Journal, 37(3)*, 656–669.

Kotter, J.P. (1988). *The leadership factor*. New York: The Free Press.

Kotter, J.P., & Heskett, J.L. (1992). *Corporate culture and performance*. New York: Free Press.

Kotter, J.P. (1995). Leading change: Why transformation efforts fail. *Harvard Business Review, 83(2)*, 59–67.

Kouzes, J.M., & Posner, B.Z. (1993). *Credibility*. San Francisco, CA: Jossey-Bass.

Kouzes, J.M., & Posner, B.Z. (1995). *The leadership challenge*, 2nd ed., San Francisco, CA: Jossey-Bass.

Kurzynski, M.J. (1998). The virtue of forgiveness as a human resource management strategy. *Journal of Business Ethics, 17*, 77–85

La Chapelle, L.K. (1997). *The role of trust in leadership and continuity of family-owned businesses*. (Doctoral dissertation, Union Institute Graduate School 1997). *Dissertation Abstracts International*, Vol. 58-06B, No. AAI 9736715, p. 3349.

Leana, C.R., & Van Buren, H.J. (1999). Organizational social capital and employment practices. *Academy of Management Review, 24(3)*, 538–555.

Levinson, H. (1972). Easing the pain of personal loss. *Harvard Business Review, 50*, 80–88.

Lewicki, R.J. & Wiethoff, C. (2000). Trust, trust development, and trust repair. In M. Deutsch & P.T. Coleman, (Eds.), *The handbook of conflict resolution: Theory and practice* (pp. 86–107), San Francisco, CA: Jossey-Bass.

Lewis, J. (1985). *Excellent organizations: How to develop and manage them using Theory Z*. New York: J.L. Wilkerson Co.

Lewis, J.D., & Weigert, A. (1985). Trust as a social reality. *Social Forces, 63 (4)*, 967–985.

Locke, E.A. (1997). Individualism: The only cure for organizational racism. *The Industrial-Organizational Psychologist, 34(4)*, 128–129.

Locke, J.L. (1998). *The de-voicing of society, why we don't talk to each other anymore*. New York: Simon & Schuster.

Loomis, C.P., & Loomis, Z.K. (1973). Social and interpersonal trust—it's loss by dysfunction. *Humanitas, 9*, 317–331.

Luhmann, N. (1979). *Trust and power*. New York: John Wiley.

Lynch, J.J. (2000). *A cry unheard: New insights into the medical consequences of loneliness*. Baltimore, MD: Bancroft Press.

Lynn, A.B. (1999). *In search of honor: Lessons from workers on how to build trust*. Belle Vernon, PA: Bajon House Publishing.

Lyth, I.M. (1991). Changing organizations and individuals: Psychoanalytic insights for improving organizational health. In M.F.R. Kets de Vries and Associates (Eds.), *Organizations on the couch* (pp. 361–378). San Francisco, CA: Jossey-Bass.

Mahoney, M.A. (2000). *Saving the soul of medicine*. San Francisco, CA: Robert D. Reed Publishers.

Martin, J. (1992). *Cultures in organizations: Three perspectives*. New York: Oxford University Press.

Maslow, A.H. (1998). *Maslow on management*. New York: John Wiley & Sons.

Mautz, R.K., & Sharaf, H.A. (1961). *The philosophy of auditing*. Sarasota, FL: The American Accounting Association.

Mayer, M. (1955). *Wall Street: Men and money*. New York: Harper Brothers.

Mayer, R.C., Davis, J.H.,& Schoorman, F.D. (1995). An integrative model of organizational trust. *Academy of Management Review, 20(3)*, 7-9-734.

McArthur, H., & Moore, F.D. (1997). The two cultures and the health care revolution. *Journal of the American Medical Association, 277(12)*, 985–989.

McCabe, D.L., & Trevino, L.K. (1997). Individual and contextual influences on academic dishonesty: A multicampus investigation. *Research in Higher Education, 38(3)*, 379–396.

McLain, D.L., & Hackman, K. (1999). Trust, risk, and decision-making in organizational change. *Public Affairs Quarterly, Summer*, 152–176.

Mechanic, D. (1996). Changing medical organization and the erosion of trust. *Milbank Quarterly, 74(2)*, 171–189.

Milk, L. (1994). 2000. Here we come. *Washingtonian Magazine, (1994, June) 29(9)*, 12.

Miller, G. (2001). Why is trust necessary in organizations? The moral hazard of profit maximization. In K.S. Cook, (Ed.). *Trust in society*, Vol. II in the Russell Sage Foundation Series on Trust (pp. 307–331). New York: Russell Sage Foundation.

Misztal, B.A. (1996). *Trust in modern societies*. Cambridge, UK: Polity Press.

Morgan, G.W. (1973). On trusting. *Humanitas, 9*: 237–251.

Morgan, G. (1997). *Images of organization*, 2nd ed., Thousand Oaks, CA: Sage.

Morris, J.H., & Moberg, D.J. (1994). Work organizations as contexts for trust and betrayal. In R. Sarbin, R.M. Carney & C. Eoyang (Eds.). *Citizen espionage: Studies in trust and betrayal*, (pp. 163–187). Westport, CT: Praeger.

Nadler, D.A., & Tushman, M. (1995). A congruence model for diagnosing organizational behavior. In D.A. Kolb, J.S. Osland, & Rubin, J.M. (Eds), *The organizational behavior reader*, 6th ed., (pp. 562–578). Englewood Cliffs, NJ: Prentice Hall.

Naroll, R. (1983). *The moral order*. Beverly Hills, CA: Sage.

National Commission on Civic Renewal (1998), *The Index of National Civic Health*, University of Maryland, Baltimore, Institute for Philosophy and Public Policy, College Park, Maryland.

Nee, V., & Sanders, J. (2001). Trust in ethnic ties: Social capital and immigrants. In K.S. Cook (Ed.) *Trust in society*, Vol. II, Russell Sage Foundation Series on Trust (pp. 374–392). New York: Russell Sage Foundation.

Neustadt, R.E. (1997). The politics of mistrust. In J.S. Nye, Jr., P.D. Zelikow & D.C. King (Eds.), *Why people don't trust government* (pp. 179–201). Cambridge, MA: Harvard University Press.

Noorderhaven, N. (1994). Opportunism and trust in transaction cost economics (Paper presented for the Conference TCE and Beyond, Erasmus University, Rotterdam, The Netherlands, June).

Nye, J.S. (1997). Introduction: The decline of confidence in government. In Nye, J.S., Jr., P.D. Zelikow, & D.C. King, (Eds.), *Why people don't trust government* (pp. 1–18). Cambridge, MA: Harvard University Press.

Nyhan, R.C. (2000). Changing the paradigm: Trust and its role in public sector organizations. *American Review of Public Administration, 30(1)*, 87–109.

Okin, S.M. (1989). *Justice, gender, and the family*. New York: Basic Books.

Oncken, W., & Wass, D.L. (1974). Management time: Who's got the monkey? *Harvard Business Review, 52(6)*: 75–80.

Ordway, N.K., Leonard, M.F., & Ingles, T. (1969). Interpersonal factors in failure to thrive. *Southern Medical Bulletin, 57*, 23–28.

O'Reilly, C.A., & Chatman, J.A. (1996). Culture as social control: Corporations, cults, and commitment. *Research in Organizational Behavior, 18*, 157–200.

Organ, D.W. (1988). *Organizational citizenship behavior: The good soldier syndrome*. Lexington, MA: D.C. Heath.

Ouchi, W.G. (1980). A framework for understanding organizational failure. In J.R. Kimberly, R.H. Miles & Associates (Eds.), *The organizational lifecycle: Issues in the creation, transformation and decline of organizations*. (pp. 395–429). San Francisco, CA: Jossey-Bass.

Peck, J.S., & Brown, F.H. (1991). Families in the divorce and post-divorce process. In F.H. Brown, (Eds.). *Reweaving the family tapestry* (pp. 191–218): New York: W.W. Norton.

Peters, T. (1994). *The pursuit of WOW!* New York: Vintage.

Phillips, R.A., & Margolis, J.D. (1999). Toward an ethics of organizations. *Business Ethics Quarterly, 9(4)*, 619–638.

Podsakoff, P.M., Ahearne, M., & MacKenzie, S.B. (1997). Organizational citizenship behavior and the quantity and quality of work group performance. *Journal of Applied Psychology, 82(2)*, 262– 270.

Podsakoff, P.M., MacKenzie, S.B., Moorman, R.H., & Fetter, R. (1990). Transformational leader behaviors and their effects on followers' trust in leader, satisfaction, and organizational citizenship behaviors. *Leadership Quarterly, 1(2)*, 107–142.

Popper, M., & Lipshitz, R. (2000). Organizational learning: Mechanisms, culture and feasibility. *Management Learning, 31(2)*: 181–196.

Pulvers, K., & Dielzhoff, G.M. (1999). The relationship between academic dishonesty and college classroom environment. *Research in Higher Education, 40(4)*, 487–498.

Purdy, J. (1999). *For common things*. New York: Vintage Books.

Putnam, R.D. (2000). *Bowling alone: The collapse and revival of American community*. New York: Simon & Schuster.

Quinn, R.E., & Cameron, K. (1983). Organizational lifecycles and shifting criteria of effectiveness: Some preliminary evidence. *Management Science, 29(1)*: 33–51.

Rahn, W.M., & Transue, J.E. (1998). Social trust and value change: The decline of social capital in American Youth, 1976–1995. *Political Psychology, 19(3)*, 545–565.

Raskas, D.F. (1998). *Familiarity breeds trust as well as contempt; What about familiarity? An examination of familial involvement and trust in family firms*. (Doctoral dissertation, Columbia University 1998). *Dissertation Abstracts International*, Vol. 59-11A, No. AAI 9910656, p. 4217.

Reichers, A., & Schneider, B. (1990). Climate and culture: An evolution of constructs. In B. Schneider (Ed.). *Organizational climate and culture* (pp. 5–39). San Francisco, CA: Jossey-Bass.

Reina, D.S., & Reina, M.L. (1999). *Trust and betrayal in the workplace*. San Francisco, CA: Berrett-Koehler Publishers, Inc.

Richards, L.J. (1998). Hiring multicultural vagabonds. *Workforce, 3(6)*, 28–30.

Riker, W.H. (1974). The nature of trust. In J.T. Tedeschi (Ed.), *Perspectives on social power* (pp. 63–81). Chicago, IL: Aldine.

Ring, P.S. (1996). Fragile and resilient trust and their roles in economic exchange. *Business & Society, 35(2)*, 148–175.

Rodwin, M. (1993). *Medicine, money and morals: Physician's conflicts of interest*. New York, NY: Oxford University Press.

Rogers, C.R. (1961). *On becoming a person*. Boston: Houghton Mifflin.

Rosen, R.H., & Berger, L. (1991). *The healthy company*. New York: G.P. Putnam's Sons.

Rotter, J.B. (1971). Generalized expectancies for interpersonal trust. *American Psychologist, 26*, 443–452.

Rotter, J.B. (1980) Interpersonal trust, trustworthiness, and gullibility. *American Psychologist, 35(1)*, 1–7.

Rousseau, D.M., Sitkin, S.B., Burt, R.S., & Camerer, C. (1998). Not so different after all: A cross-discipline view of trust. *Academy of Management Review, 23(3)*, 393–404.

Rowan, R. (1989). Listen for those warning bells. In W.H. Agor, (Ed.), *Intuition in Organizations* (pp. 195–204). Thousand Oaks, CA: Sage.

Ruppel, C.P., & Harrington, S.J. (2000). The relationship of communication, ethical work climate, and trust to commitment and innovation. *Journal of Business Ethics, 25*, 313–328.

Sanders, B. (1991). The human side of e-mail. *Computerworld. 25*(*13*),: 49.

Sanders, W.B. (1994). *Gangbangs and drive-bys*. New York: Aldine DeGruyter.

Schein, E.H. (1981). Coming to a new awareness of organizational culture. *Sloan Management Review, Winter*, 3–16.

Schein, E.H. (1992). *Organizational culture and leadership*. 2nd ed., San Francisco, CA: Jossey-Bass.

Schindler, P.L., & Thomas, C.C. (1993). The structure of interpersonal trust in the workplace. *Psychological Reports, 73*, 563–573.

Schneiderman, G. (1999). An advisor's guide to forgiveness and the family. *Trusts and Estates, 13(8)*, 30–33.

Scott, C.L. (1980). Interpersonal trust: A comparison of attitudinal and situational factors. *Human Relations, 33(11)*, 805–812.

Scott, W.R., Ruef, M., Mendel, P.J., & Caronna, C.A. (2000). *Institutional change and healthcare organizations: From professional dominance to managed care*. Chicago, IL: University of Chicago Press.

Seligman, A.B. (1997). *The problem of trust*. Princeton, NJ: Princeton University Press.

Seligman, A.B. (2000). Trust, confidence, and the problem of civility. In L.S. Rouner (Ed.). *Civility* (pp. 65–77), Notre Dame, IN: University of Notre Dame Press.

Shaw, R.B. (1989). *Trust and distrust in organizations: An intergroup analysis*. (Doctoral dissertation, Yale University, 1989). *Dissertation Abstracts International*, Vo. 50-11B, Vol. AAI 9010678, p. 5361.

Shaw, R.B. (1997). *Trust in the balance: Building successful organizations on results, integrity, and concern*. San Francisco, CA: Jossey-Bass.

Shupe, A., Stacey, W.A., & Darnell, S.E. (Eds.) (2001). *Bad pastors: Misconduct in modern America*. New York: New York University Press.

Simon, L.S. (1994). *Trust in leadership: Its dimensions and mediating role*. (Doctoral dissertation, Kansas State University, 1994). *Dissertation Abstracts International*, Vol. 56-01B, Vol. AAI 9517487, p. 556.

Sims, R.R. (1994). *Ethics and organizational decision making: A call for renewal*. Westport, CT: Quorum Books.

Singer, P. (1995). *How are we to live?* Amherst, NY: Prometheus Books.

Smith, C.A., Organ, D.W., & Near, J.P. (1983). Organizational citizenship behavior: Its nature and antecedents. *Journal of Applied Psychology, 68(4)*, 653–663.

Smith, J. (1997). Does familiarity breed success? *Management Review, 86(9)*, 7.

Smith J.G., Mitchell, T.R., & Summer, C.E. (1985). Top level management priorities in different stages of the organizational life cycle. *Academy of Management Journal, 26(4)*, 799–820.

Solomon, R.C. (1998). Ethical leadership, emotions, and trust: Beyond "charisma". In J.B. Ciulla, (Ed.), *Ethics, the heart of leadership* (pp. 87–107). Westport, CT: Quorum Books.

Southon, G., & Braithwaite, J. (1998). The end of professionalism? *Social Science and Medicine, 46(1)*, 23–28.

Somers, M.J. (2001). Ethical codes of conduct and organizational context: A study of the relationship between codes of conduct, employee behavior and organizational values. *Journal of Business Ethics, 30*, 184–195.

Spitz, R.A. (1950). Anxiety in infancy: A study of its manifestations in the first year of life. *International Journal of Psychoanalysis, 31*, 138.

Spreitzer, G.M., & Mishra, A.K. (1999). Giving up control without losing control: Trust and its substitutes' effects on managers' involving employees in decision making.*Group and Organizational Management, 24(2)*, 155–187.

Stacey, R.D. (1992). *Managing the unknowable: Strategic boundaries between order and chaos in organizations*. San Francisco, CA: Jossey-Bass.

Stewart, T.A. (1996). Why value statements don't work. *Fortune, 133(11)*, 137–138.

Strebel, P. (1996). Why do employees resist change? *Harvard Business Review, 74(3)*, 86–92.

Sullivan, W.M. (1995). *Work and integrity: The crisis and promise of professionalism in America*. New York: Harper Business.

Sztompka, P. (1999). *Trust: A sociological theory*. Cambridge, UK: Cambridge University Press.

Thornton, E., & Timmons, H. (2001) Suing the street over bum advice. (2001, March 5) *Business Week*, p. 102.

Tichy, N.M. (1980). Problem cycles in organizations and the management of change. In J.R. Kimberly, R.H. Miles & Associates (Eds.), *The organizational lifecycle: Issues in the creation, transformation, and decline of organizations* (pp. 164–183). San Francisco, CA: Jossey-Bass.

Tyler, T.R. (2001). Why do people rely on others? Social identity and the social aspects of trust. In K.S. Cook, (Ed.), *Trust in society* (pp. 285–306), New York: Russell Sage Foundation.

Urban, G.L., Sultan, F., & Qualls, W.J. (2000). Placing trust at the center of your internet strategy. *Sloan Management Review, 42(1)*, 39–48.

Veenker, J. (1999). How to heal a broken church. *Christianity Today, 43(9)*, 21.

Ward, J.L. (1987). *Keeping the family business healthy*. San Francisco, CA: Jossey-Bass.

Webb, W.M., & Worchel, P. (Eds.) (1986). *The social psychology of intergroup relations*, 2nd ed., Chicago, IL: Nelson-Hall.

Weber, L.R., & Carter, A.I. (1997). On reconstructing trust: Time, intention, and forgiveness. *Clinical Sociology Review, 15*, 24–39.

Weber, L.R., & Carter, A.I. (1998). On constructing trust: Temporality, self-disclosure, and perspective-taking. *International Journal of Sociology and Social Policy, 18(1)*, 7–26.

Weber, T.E. (2000) To build virtual trust, web sites develop 'reputation managers.' (2000, July 17) *Wall Street Journal*, p. B1.

Weaver, G.R., Trevino, L.K., & Cochran, P.L. (1999). Corporate ethics practices in the mid-1990's: An empirical study of the Fortune 1000. *Journal of Business Ethics, 18*, 283–294.

Weisberg, J. (1996). *In defense of government*. New York: Scribner.

Whiteley, A. (1995). *Managing change: A core values approach*. South Melbourne, Australia: Macmillan Education Australia.

Whitener, E.M., Brodt, S.E., Korsgaard, M.A., & Werner, J.M. (1998). Managers as initiators of trust: An exchange relationship framework for understanding managerial trustworthy behavior. *Academy of Management Review, 23(3)*, 513–530.

Whitney, J.O. (1996). *The economics of trust*. New York: McGraw Hill.

Whittington, J.L. (1997). *An integrative model of transformational leadership and follower behavior*. (Doctoral dissertation, University of Texas at Arlington, 1997). Vol. 58-08A, No. AAI 9804688, p. 3216.

Wilkins, A., & Ouchi, W. (1983). Efficient cultures: Exploring the relationship between culture and organizational performance. *Administrative Science Quarterly, 28*, 468–481.

Williams, B. (1985). *Ethics and the limits of philosophy*. Cambridge, MA: Harvard University Press.

Wilson, J.Q. (1993). *The moral sense*. New York: Free Press.

Wise, R. (1990). Last year's strongest IPOs never lost their luster, *Electronic Business, 16(3)*, 36–38.

Wolfe, A. (1998). *One nation after all: What Americans really think about God, country, family, racism, welfare, immigration, homosexuality, work, the right, the left, and each other*. New York: Viking.

Wolfe, A. (2001). *Moral freedom: The search for virtue in a world of choice*. New York: W.W. Norton & Co.

Worchel, P. (1979). Trust and distrust. In W.G. Austin, & S. Worchel (Eds.). *The social psychology of intergroup relations* (pp. 174–187). Monterey, CA: Brooks/Cole.

Worchel, P., & Austin, W.G. (1986). Trust and distrust. In W.M. Webb & P. Worchel, (Eds.). *The social psychology of intergroup relations*, 2nd ed. (pp. 213–228), Chicago: Nelson-Hall.

Wuthnow, R. (1994). *Sharing the journey: Support groups and America's new quest for community*. New York: Free Press.

Wuthnow, R. (1998). *Loose connections: Joining together in America's fragmented communities*. Cambridge, MA: Harvard University Press.

Wuthnow, R. (1999). The role of trust in civic renewal. In R.K. Fullinwider (Ed.), *Civil society, democracy and civic renewal*. (pp. 209–230), Lanham, MD: Rowman & Littlefield, Inc.

Yamagishi, T. (2001). Trust as a form of social intelligence. In K.S. Cook, (Ed.), *Trust in society*. Vol II in the Russell Sage Foundation Series on Trust (pp. 123–147). New York: Russell Sage Foundation.

Zand, D.E. (1972). Trust and managerial problem solving. *Administrative Science Quarterly, 17(2)*, 229–239.

Zand, D.E. (1997). *The leadership triad: Knowledge, trust and power*. New York: Oxford University Press.

Zajac, G., & Bruhn, J.G. (1999). The moral context of participation in planned organizational change and learning. *Administration & Society, 30(6)*, 706–733.

Zucker, L.G. (1986). Production of trust: Institutional sources of economic structure, 1840–1920. *Research in Organizational Behavior, 8*, 53–111.

Appendix A Characteristics of Respondents

The 60 respondents for this study were CEO's or former CEO's of public and private, and profit and not-for-profit organizations. They resided in ten different states; 15 were female and 45 were male; and 10 were Asian, Hispanic, or African-American; 50 were Anglo-American.

The average length of time in the position of CEO was 10.5 years (range from 1 year to 29 years). The average budget of the organization was $119 M (range from $3 M to $.5 B). The largest organization had 11,000 members and the smallest organization had 30 members. Fourteen of the 60 respondents were CEO's of family businesses. The oldest organization was 106 years old and the youngest was 10 years old.

Forty-eight respondents were interviewed in face-to-face situations, 12 were interviewed by telephone. About half of the CEO's were known to the author, and half were referred by interviewees.

REFUSALS

Only five CEO's who were contacted for an interview declined, although not directly. The usual method was that their administrative assistants did not return calls to set up an appointment or said that the CEO had a "full plate". As in any study relying on information from interviews with very busy people there can be a host of unknown reasons to decline an interview, including not wanting to discuss the topic of trust in one's organization. However, the CEO's who were interviewed were candid about their organization's history regarding trust and present challenges facing them and their organization.

OBSERVATIONS ON METHODOLOGY

One of the difficulties in carrying out a study such as this is to gain access to a sample of CEO's and former CEO's. There can be some randomness built into a sample, but in order to gain access to a CEO an interviewer either needs to know the CEO personally, know someone in the organization who can help arrange an interview, or ask another interviewee if he is willing to make a personal referral to another CEO. These methods of entry worked well in the present study. Interviews were scheduled well in advance so the CEOs were able to give freely of their time. Interviews lasted 30 to 60 minutes. In a few cases where special rapport was established between the author and the interviewee, follow-up interviews were conducted.

One of the limitations of this study is that information was obtained only from the leader of the organization. The leader's interpretation and analysis of events in the organization and the leader's perceptions and expectations regarding trust were what the interviewer heard. Ideally, trust in organizations could be more fully understood if it were possible to interview samples of constituents at all levels in an organization from the Board of Trustees or Directors to the workers, and clients or customers of the organization. Furthermore, being able to observe behavior in an organization provides a different view from what people tell you. Of course, such studies take a great deal of time, money, a team of observers, and the willingness of organizations to let themselves be put under scrutiny.

Another limitation of this study, indeed of all social and behavioral science investigations which depend upon the views and opinions of cooperative respondents, is the individual being questioned wants to put on a good face. CEO's don't like to admit that they have a distrusting organization. Indeed, a CEO may be the problem or part of a problem in an organization unknown to the interviewer.

Some CEO's were very well read in literature on organizational dynamics and management and leadership. They could "talk the talk", but the interviewer had no way to confirm how the talk was put into action.

Overall, the interviewer felt that the CEO's interviewed were honest and willing to talk about the strengths and weaknesses of their organization and themselves as leaders. Not all of the organizations they led were healthy or trustful and most admitted that and were eager to learn techniques for improving their organizations.

Trust will remain a well-known and talked about virtue in organizational life, difficult to study and to quantify, and almost impossible to generalize about. Trust has common features but many faces. It is actually easier to study distrust as there are always the disenfranchised eager to talk about it and if problems are pervasive they are usually obvious enough for effects to be known outside the organization. The challenge to social and behavioral scientists, and management and organizational specialists, is learn more about how to create healthy organizations rather than try to "fix" broken organizations. Culture is difficult to change. Indeed, we often ask or expect leaders to transform cultures, and the CEO often becomes a victim in this attempt.

Appendix B Interview Schedules

CEO INTERVIEW

Name of Person ________ Date ________

I am studying trust in organizations. I would like to ask you a few questions about how you see trust, and your experience with it, in the organization you are currently working in.

First, some information about your organization:

How long has it existed? ____

How many employees does it currently have? ____ Has it been downsized?

If so, when? Effects of downsizing?

How long have you been CEO? ____

Approximate annual budget? ____ Is this the largest budget?
Has the budget been cut? When? Effects?

Now, in turning to trust…

1. How would you define trust? What does it mean to you?

2. How do you know when you have an organization that trusts? Signs of trust?

3. What is your organization's history regarding trust? Has it been a trusting or distrusting organization over the years? How has the leadership affected trust in your organization?

4. Has there been a particular time of mistrust in your organization?

   What were the symptoms? What did you do?

5. Are there situations or times in an organization's life when trust is more important than other times? Describe.

6. Is there an organization, other than your own, that you know is an excellent example of how trust works?

   How (in what way) does trust work in this example?

7. How do you personally maintain trust in an organization that must be continually challenged by social change?

8. When you first became CEO what was your reading on trust in your organization? What were some of the first things you did as CEO?

9. How healthy do you consider your organization now? Rate on a scale of 1 to 10? Has it been healthier in the past? If so, what happened?

10. What are the major characteristics of a leader who trusts? What factors determine whether employees trust a CEO?

11. Of all of the organizations you have worked for (been employed by), is the current organization more trustful or less trustful? Why? In what ways?

12. What would you say is the biggest challenge facing you as CEO in the next two years?

13. When you leave your current position, what is the major legacy you want to leave?

14. Finally, what would be a few words of advice you might give your successor?

FORMER CEO'S

Name of Person ________ Date ________

I am studying trust in organizations. I would like to ask you a few questions about how you see trust and experienced it when you were a CEO.

First, some information about the organization you left (or retired from) as CEO?

How many employees were there? ____

How long were you CEO? ____

Now about trust ...

1. How do you define trust?

2. How does an organization become a trusting organization?

3. It is said that the leader sets the stage or tone for trust, what did you do as CEO to create trust in your organization?

4. How does distrust come about, what creates distrust? Did you experience a period or periods of distrust as CEO? Explain.

5. In your opinion, what is an excellent example of a trusting or healthy organization? Has it always been so? Why is it healthy?

6. Oftentimes when things go wrong in an organization, the Governing Board wants to change leaders, what are your views about that? Is changing leaders always the best way to turn an organization around?

7. How much of trust, in your view, is politics?

8. Are there policies, procedures, etc. in organizations that help to create distrust? Discuss. Examples.

9. What are the major lessons you learned as a CEO?

Index